SOUTH ATLANTIC URBAN STUDIES   VOLUME 1

SOUTH

ATLANTIC

URBAN STUDIES

Volume 1

Jack R. Censer, *Editor*

N. Steven Steinert, *Editor*

Amy M. McCandless, *Assistant Editor*

Published for the
College of Charleston
by the
UNIVERSITY OF SOUTH CAROLINA PRESS

SAUS is an interdisciplinary periodical
published annually by the University
of South Carolina Press. Its contents
include papers presented at conferences,
seminars, and symposia sponsored by
the College of Charleston's Urban
Studies Program as well as individual
manuscripts dealing with various
aspects of urban concern.

Manuscripts and editorial
correspondence should be sent to:

> Editor
> SOUTH ATLANTIC URBAN
> STUDIES
> Urban Studies Center
> College of Charleston
> Charleston SC 29401

All manuscripts should be submitted in
triplicate and conform to the style
prescribed by the latest edition of
A Manual of Style, published by the
University of Chicago Press.

Standing orders for *SAUS* may be placed
with the University of South Carolina
Press, Columbia SC 29208.

SAUS disclaims responsibility for statements,
either of fact or opinion, made by contributors.

CONTENTS

INTRODUCTION

South Atlantic Urban Studies, an annual publication of the College of Charleston Urban Studies Program, hopes to provide a forum for academics, researchers, and practitioners from the many disciplines involved in urban studies. To encourage debate and to ensure a diversity of topics and opinions, each volume will include invited essays on pertinent urban issues as well as articles and book reviews of a more formal nature.

This volume contains seven essays dealing with various facets of urban life. The first selection by Michael Lewis initiates a debate on urban conflict and compromise by suggesting the need for a "Reform of Urban Reform." He contends that reforms are often only practical when they do not offend substantial members of the community. Such practical reforms are eminently unrealistic because they prevent any real change. Ronald Parris gives support to Lewis' thesis. In his discussion of policy goals in housing strategies and urban planning, Parris concludes that interracial housing has not resulted in racial equality because minority culture and concerns are sublimated to majority mores and interests.

Practitioners are guardedly more positive about the coming decades. Robert Maffin and George Sternlieb agree that reformers have been held back by the desire of those in power to maintain the status quo, but they are more optimistic about future reform. With increasing shortages of resources and continuing decline in prosperity, Americans will be forced to abandon their policies of consumption and production in favor of preservation and rehabilitation. The poor, already living in crowded and decrepit areas, will be the direct beneficiaries of these changes. Arthur Ziegler's survey of preservation in Pittsburgh substantiates Maffin's and Sternlieb's predictions. Ziegler also demonstrates that the less privileged classes do not have to watch passively while their communities are planned for them. By enlisting the aid of local residents in the rehabilitation of their community, Pittsburgh's Mexican War Streets Program was able to preserve not only buildings but, more important, the essential human character of the neighborhood.

Indeed, the findings of two historians suggest that the poor have often been able to control or at least affect their own destinies. Robert Forster's study of Paris during the Reign of Terror reveals that the common man can and does play a part in bringing about social and political reform. The ability of the oppressed to change or at least influence their environment is evident in Joel Williamson's essay on "The Oneness of Southern Life." Even in the antebellum period there was a continuous symbiosis between black and white culture which Williamson believes can serve as a model for the future. Perhaps, Parris and Lewis are too involved in the present; on the other hand, today's problems may be greater than ever before.

Additional areas of urban concern, both theoretical and practical, are considered in the formal articles. Although these contributions are primarily in the disciplines of political science, history, and sociology, subsequent volumes plan to include articles in the fields of law, architecture, planning, and economics. The final portion of the volume is devoted to a book review section which examines publications of interest to urban specialists.

The editors wish to thank the editorial and advisory boards for their assistance in the selection and preparation of the manuscripts. Donald Bain, Kenneth Griffith, Robert Mundell, and Linda Pearson gave critical appraisal of individual papers. Claretha Fennick of the College of Charleston Urban Studies Program also provided needed assistance.

We are most grateful to the College of Charleston for providing funds for publication and allowing the use of Urban Studies Center facilities. Our appreciation also extends to Helen Needham of the Urban Studies Center, who not only patiently typed and retyped manuscripts, but rendered numerous other services necessary for the completion of the volume.

PART I

ESSAYS

THE REFORM OF URBAN REFORM*

Michael Lewis

A number of years ago I was invited by an association of school administrators to speak at a conference. In the course of the phone conversation during which the invitation was extended, my caller said something like, "Well Professor Lewis, we need someone to keynote the conference who can be provocative and stimulating—you know, someone who can focus our attention in a realistic way on practical solutions for the problems confronted by urban school systems." At the time, I did not make much of the assumed association between realism and practicality. It fell easily on the ear, a routine phrase often heard but rarely assimilated. When, however, I began to prepare my remarks, the issue lurking in my caller's statement started to trouble me, and it has continued to trouble me. I questioned then and continue to question now whether it is really justifiable to assume that practicality and realism about our problems and their possible resolution are in fact synonymous—whether those reforms offered in the name of down-to-earth practicality are in fact realistic reforms in that they are likely to remedy the problems that they are presumably intended to solve.

* Invited article for the inaugural edition of *South Atlantic Urban Studies*.

My doubt about the association between practicality and realism arises from the fact that what often appear to have been very practical solutions to some of our most significant urban problems have turned out to be appalling failures—and as failures they can hardly be acclaimed as realistic. Has urban renewal, for example, presumed by many to be an eminently practical solution to the problem of urban blight (it upgrades land values by upgrading land use characteristics and is therefore quite attractive to a community's business interests) been a realistic solution if in community after community it has merely shifted the locus of blight from one area to another in its failure to generate adequate housing and services for those the bulldozer has displaced?[1] Has the welfare system—practical (although some would question the use of such a term) in extremis with its emphasis on providing minimum funding for the destitute together with psychological and social services presumably intended to improve their ability to cope—been a realistic approach to the alleviation of poverty? Where is the realism in an approach which, on the one hand, does not provide the poor with a standard of living adequate to their needs, while on the other hand, stigmatizes them by insisting that, at best, their destitution is a function of a personal incapacity to cope and, at worst, that it is a function of their moral infirmity?[2] There is at least one thing about which both the recipients and those fortunate enough not to need welfare assistance can and do agree upon—both groups find little to cheer about when it comes to the matter of the effectiveness of welfare! Realism? On the contrary, it is much easier to make a case for the assertion that the welfare system has been and continues to be devoid of realism, both in its limited capacity for economic upgrading and in its depiction of the poor as incompetent and/or unworthy.

Did the job corps, the federal government's practical program for upgrading the employment opportunities of the poor by providing a network of skill development programs throughout the United States realize its ostensible goals?[3] Can we regard the job corps as a realistic program if, as in so many instances, its graduates, armed with new found skills, found little opportunity to make use of them either because economic retrenchment reduced the number of reasonably remunerative jobs in community after community or because employers and unions still discriminated against them on grounds extraneous to the skill requirements of those jobs which were available?

Perhaps no reform programs in recent years have appeared to be as practical as those, like Head Start, which fall under the rubric of compensatory education. Assuming that educational success is central to economic achievement and noting that in community after community there were groups of children, most frequently the children of the poor and the non-whites, who were invariably underrepresented among the academically successful, educators during the 1960s concluded that it was necessary to establish programs which would compensate for the intellectual deficiencies which they presumed were at the root of the problems these children were having in the public schools. The logic underlying such efforts was straightforward enough: Compensate for intellectual deficiencies early and the children of the poor will succeed in the schools. Accomplishing this, they will be qualified for opportunities which have been inaccessible to their parents and their older siblings. With an ability to make the most of such opportunities, they will climb out of their disadvantaged circumstances and the cycle of poverty will be broken. Compensatory education, in this view, is not merely the key to a more rewarding school career, but more important it is the key to social and economic mobility.[4] There is no doubt as to the practicality of the compensatory programs—their rationale fit our conventional conception of the educational function very well, and in comparison to other school programs involving ethnic minorities and the poor (cross-bussing, for example), the social costs which the non-disadvantaged within the community would have to bear appeared to be negligible. But for all its practicality, compensatory education has been an unrealistic strategy for improving the chances of educational success for the so-called disadvantaged child.

Evaluations of compensatory education, such as the Westinghouse Study of Head Start,[5] indicate that while the children in such programs show initial gains, these gains appear to be dissipated as they proceed through the first few years of elementary school. And when we consider the myriad social, political, and economic predicates for the maintenance of poverty it must seem foolhardy to all save those who are ignorant of these factors to assume that the persistence of poverty could be significantly mitigated by even a highly successful compensatory pedagogy. Compensatory education has indeed been a practical reform in our school systems; but if the realism of a reform is to be assessed in terms of the measure of success it has in achieving its ostensible purpose, then we must conclude that, whatever its practicality, compensatory education is an exceedingly unrealistic reform strategy.

This roster of practical reforms which turned out to be unrealistic could be extended: I could, for example, point to the ill-fated establishment of biracial commissions in many southern communities during the 1950s and early 1960s as a mechanism for promoting interracial amity; to the development of human relation programs in community school systems which never really appear to have much impact upon the character of human relations; to efficiency-oriented charter reforms and government reorganization plans which do not appear to have much impact upon the quality of service provided by municipal governments; to revenue sharing which, although apparently instituted to stimulate local flexibility in community problem solving, appears to have created confusion; to Chamber of Commerce plans for the economic revitalization of moribund local economies, launched with considerable fanfare but having very little positive impact—and so on and on and on!

The point is simply that the assumed positive association between practicality and realism is subject to considerable doubt. We would do well to rethink our commitment to presumed practicality when, with the best of intentions, we embark upon those efforts which hopefully will render our communities more humanly serviceable.

I would like to give some impetus to the reevaluation of this commitment by holding it up to the light of sociological analysis. It seems to me that what we mean when we speak of a reform program as being practical is not that it is necessarily realistic from the point of view of goal attainment—or actual reformation—but rather that it is a feasible program, a program that whatever its potential impact, can be put into operation in a given community at a given point in time. At first surmise it would appear that feasibility is a major step in the direction of realism or functional realization of the goals of the reform effort. After all, it would hardly appear to be realistic to commit ourselves to programs which cannot be put into effect. The most brilliant plan to ease the traffic problems of New York City is hardly realistic if it so offends local interests and so strains local resources that it cannot be made operational. No antipoverty program can be deemed realistic if the non-poor in a given community find it to be inequitable to the point where they take political and legal action to prevent its actual operation.

A closer look at the meaning of feasibility, however, reveals it to be something less than an option chosen in the pursuit of realistic or effective reform. In fact, it can and often does mean the opposite: the choice of an option which forecloses on the possibility of engaging in effective and, therefore, realistic reform.

In order to assume that feasibility portends realistic reform one has to assume that the problem in need of solution or remediation exists apart from the existing status quo in the community. If feasibility means choosing an option that will be acceptable in the existing social context of a community, the choice of such an option can only be effective or realistic when the problem it is intended to remedy is not a product of that context. If the problem in question is inextricably wed to the existing economic, social, and political life of the community, if its very existence is an implication of behaviors which serve the apparent self-interests of significant elements in the community, then the choice of a program which can be put into operation because it is acceptable to these significant elements is unlikely to be an effective or realistic choice. If, as in such cases, the effectiveness of a reform effort depends on the extent to which the behaviors that sustain the problem can be modified, and if these very behaviors serve the interests of politically significant elements in the community, then it is difficult to imagine these elements accepting reforms which have a high probability for positive effect. Such reform efforts are seen as "unfeasible" and "impractical" and they are therefore rarely the options which are chosen. The practical or feasible options—those which are chosen— are those which do not offend the interests of the significant elements. Given the causal importance of these interests, these practical-feasible efforts are unlikely to have much reformative impact upon the problem in question.

Unfortunately, it would appear that this theoretical logic is more than minimally represented in empirical experience; that all too frequently the problems which are in need of remediation in our communities must be understood as the products of existing social context, of behaviors on the part of significant elements within the community —behaviors which serve their narrowly defined self-interests—and that consequently the practical-feasible solutions to these problems are all too often unrealistic because they have little potential for positive effect.

In too many communities the existence of dilapidated slum housing has been and is a function of discriminatory housing practices which are tied to a conception of the housing market that worries about—in the manner of a self-fulfilling prophecy—the impact of so-called undesirable elements on property values. Such practices also mean a financial windfall for those who can rent inadequate accommodations to people who, because they have been frozen out of the general housing market, must take what they can get. Consequently, urban renewal and slum clearance have been practical-feasible but not very realistic.

In too many communities poverty has been and is a function of the need to keep the poor with us. Sometimes this need is economic, as when we benefit from the availability of a surplus of labor ready to take on out of desperation the most onerous and least remunerative of labors; or when we benefit by limiting, as a result of exclusionary practices, the labor supply available for remunerative vocations and in doing so we keep compensation in such job categories relatively high. Sometimes the need is psychological, as when in the emptiness of our lives we assure ourselves that "we're doing all right" by casting our gaze downward upon those who are clearly not making it and who in conventional terms are obviously unsuccessful. Consequently our poverty reforms—welfare, job corps, compensatory education—all of them practical and feasible are nonetheless ineffective and unrealistic when judged in terms of their results.

In too many communities many of us benefit from the very inadequacies in the provision of services which we so loudly decry: in the neglect of publicly supported health care services whose scarcity and almost total relegation to the private sector keep their cost inordinately high; in the neglect of adequately subsidized quality legal services available to all, which also makes them high priced commodities in the private sector; in the inattentiveness to adequate land-use planning and control which allows our communities to be defaced by the sprawl of jerry-built, speculative housing construction.

Put simply and perhaps somewhat starkly, it seems to me that our problems are not extrinsic and alien to the interests many of us wish to protect at one time or another. Thus, although in the abstract we may recognize them to be problems in need of remediation, when we get down to concrete cases where our interests appear to be threatened we shy away from effective and, therefore, realistic reform. Instead, in the name of practicality we choose the feasible option, the option which is acceptable precisely because it does not threaten our interests. Unfortunately, it is also the option which at the level of the commonweal, the common interest, does not solve the problem before us.

If what I have argued is valid, then we are indeed in a difficult position, a position which makes it foolhardy to be optimistic about maximizing the human serviceability of our urban future. For if the practical-feasible is unrealistic by virtue of built in ineffectiveness, it is also true that theoretically realistic reforms are unlikely to be tried because they threaten significant community interests. If this is so— their theoretical realism notwithstanding—they too are, in actuality, unrealistic. Thus, sociologically speaking, we are in the position of venturing the ineffective to little positive end, while ignoring what theoretically might be effective to no positive end. The future in such a circumstance hardly seems promising.

What is it then that we should do? What course is there left open to us? It seems to me that the reform of urban reform necessitates an honest reckoning with our illusions. It may well be that the impractical but realistic approaches will go untried in the near future, but we must stop deluding ourselves about the supposed realism of those practical (feasible) programs we do try. Even if we do not embrace realistic reform efforts now, the fact that we have become disenchanted—that we have divested ourselves of the illusion that when we are being practical we are being realistic—will hasten the day when we will try to do what needs to be done. Everyday that we persist in our illusions about practicality, we delay the necessary reckoning which portends the best hope for realistic reform. The only course open to us is disenchantment based upon what might be termed analytic pessimism.

At this point I should like to offer an example of the kind of analytically based/critical disenchantment I have been speaking of—the kind of analytic pessimism upon which future reform efforts must stand.

We have at present two valued models of feasible problem solving and they may be described as follows: As a result of our technological successes we have come to value what may be termed the engineering model of problem solving. The engineer is a highly trained specialist who, within a narrowly defined field of attention, is expected to arrange available elements in innovative combinations in order to actualize an intention or goal at a level of cost which can be borne by those who will presumably benefit from these innovations. The engineer is a creator of mechanisms, a designer of systems whose efficiency or success is measured by the ratio of reliable outputs to the cost of operation. The engineering model of problem solving operates on the assumption of intense specialization of training and competence spread over a great many problem areas. Thus, while the engineer is often a highly creative individual his professional creativity is also highly specific. His work is focused on a single problem or set of problems while his colleagues are specialized in other areas.

As I have noted, the engineering model is a product of our obvious success in the realm of creating new technologies. But it has been applied in the social sphere as well. Perhaps because of its visible success in the area of technological problem solving it has been adopted by those who regularly attend to policy planning in such areas as education, welfare, housing, and general urban affairs.

The action counterpart of the engineering model and the second of our highly valued practical-feasible problem-solving approaches is the therapeutic model. The therapeutic model stands on the assumption that on the one hand there are those people who are possessed of a certain problematic condition and on the other hand there are trained professionals who possess the skills necessary to rid the troubled of their particular affliction. Medicine is the prototype of this approach.

The therapeutic model has been adopted in many problem areas besides medicine. It is the preferred action style in social work and education where it is assumed that the problems to be solved—the difficulties which threaten to immobilize the individual as well as the learning problems of the child—are products of conditions which are personal and which therefore must be treated by properly certified experts who, like the physician, can administer appropriate "cures."

Whether we are speaking about the engineering model or the therapeutic model, this fact emerges clearly: The basic social arrangements which characterize American social life and urban life, in particular, remain unquestioned. The social engineer will tinker with the system, will generate what appear to be new mechanisms to get the system to work better, but in the narrowness of his (her) focus he (she) rarely thinks to question the efficacy of the system itself. He (she) has what might be described as a trained incapacity to analyze the system as a whole and, therefore, he (she) is unable to develop plans for broadly based social reconstruction. The social therapist is most comfortable when he (she) can assume that the difficulties he (she) addresses are localized in a given individual or identifiable group of individuals. He (she) too is trained to ignore the possibility that the social ills he (she) confronts have their source in social arrangements which confound our notions of maximum human serviceability.

These approaches, it should be noted, are precisely those which have been used in the genesis of the practical "solutions" which, as we have seen, turn out to be highly unrealistic, e.g., urban renewal, welfare, and the job corps. Thus, these disturbing questions: If urban Americans are distressed and discontented with their lot and if the professionalized approach to reform does not appear to be very productive, why is it that this approach continues to command support? Why is it that professionalized reform is yet the dominant pattern of response to the issues which trouble the lives of those whose personal destinies are played out on the urban scene?

While it is probably true that most of those involved in pursuing the engineering and therapeutic models of social problem solving are sincere in their belief that these models will bring about positive change, it is also paradoxically true that the popular support which these approaches continue to command derives from the fact that they are unlikely to be very successful. In contemporary urban America we are frequently confronted with conflicts between our values (equal opportunity and equal justice) and our narrow interests (keep the blacks out of our union and out of our neighborhood); between our desire to improve the humn serviceability of our communities (bring peace to the streets to make the city a good community in which to live and grow) and our perceived interest in pursuing a course which impedes such improvement (we do not wish to have our taxes raised and we do not wish to change the electoral structure to ensure equitable representation). It may be suggested that these conflicts are themselves a major facet of our discontent with urban life. We want things to get better. We cannot escape the importance of such normative ideals as equal opportunity and social justice; but we often find ourselves behaving in ways which, while personally useful or profitable, also violate our ideals and contribute to the troubling nature of the way "things are." To the extent that we are conscious of the conflict between our ideals and our behaviors, between our desire for reform and our investment in those very conditions which inhibit it, we are likely to be troubled by the contradictions within ourselves, and this sense of moral dilemma is profoundly disquieting.

Given this circumstance, the continued support of professionalized social reform can be understood as a function of the need to reduce the dissonance and consequent discomfort arising from the sense that we are not doing what we ought to be doing about those conditions which render the cities less than habitable for many and minimize their serviceability for almost everybody. Endorsing the professionalized approach accomplishes several things. First, by asserting that the problematic conditions of the urban communities can only be solved by the application of professional expertise, we divorce these problems from our own sphere of personal responsibility. In effect we tell ourselves that problems, while affecting us, cannot be solved through our own efforts for we simply do not have the expertise to deal with them. Second, by supporting or endorsing the efforts of the professional reformers we convince ourselves that within the limits imposed by our own lack of expertise we are in fact doing something about urban problems. We may not be able to take direct action, but our commitment to the efforts of the professionals indicates (at least to ourselves) that we are doing that which is within our power to do to improve the quality of urban life. Finally, we support the endeavors of these individuals because their efforts rarely if ever put us in the unhappy position of having to relinquish the personal gains we derive from the persistence of a problem-generating condition (for the professionalized approach is largely insensitive to this dimension). In its style of largely abstracted planning and direct therapy with those who have a problem, the professionalized approaches allow us to deny that our personal interests have anything to do with the persistence of the problems which trouble the urban experience.

In sum, continued support of the professional approach to reform and remediation is support for the absence of success, which nevertheless removes or reduces the discomfort which arises out of an awareness of the conflict between our values and hopes for better communities and the behaviors which serve our narrow self-interests. By continued support of the professionalized approach we delude ourselves into believing that there is little we can do about the problems which trouble the urban experience, except to support the notion that these problems should be left to the ministerings of those who are professionally trained to deal with them. We convince ourselves that the problems in need of solution, the conditions in need of change, have little or nothing to do with the manner in which we pursue our interests. By such support we are able to deny the conflict between what we ought to do—or ought not do—and how we actually behave. We sustain in our communities and in our society a condition which may be termed progressive-status-quoism whereby change and progress are apparent but the status quo is real.[6]

It is not that we do this consciously. We do not sit down and deliberately attempt to delude ourselves. We do not ask, "How may I relieve this moral tension which troubles me?" Doing so would defeat the purpose of progressive-status-quoism. If we were conscious of what we were doing, we could no longer delude ourselves: to under-

stand the process is to render it ineffective. It is simply that history
has provided us with a way out (the existence of the engineering and
the therapeutic models of problem solving) and in our collective need
to avoid the contradictory implications of our behaviors juxtaposed
against our values and intentions, we have consciously invested these
approaches with a potency which has no basis in fact.

The consequences of continuing on this present course will, in my
view, only exacerbate already trying conditions in American cities and
will render the urban experience increasingly troublesome. The mutual
estrangement between the "haves" and the "have nots" in American
communities will increase, and as a consequence of this, life in many
of our cities will become even more threatening than it is presently. On
poverty related issues, in particular, the following scenario does not
seem beyond the limits of reasonable prediction: The disinherited,
those for whom the professionalized practical reform programs are
often intended, do not seem to benefit very much from such efforts.
The indicators of their disadvantage remain. They are poor, their
children drop out of school, they have a high incidence of family
disruption, the crime rate in their neighborhoods continues to rise
steadily. The solid citizens of the community, having supported the
professional reform efforts, interpret these indicators as meaning that
the disinherited have not responded to sincere attempts in their behalf.
(Given their endorsement of professionalized reform, the solid citizens
are hardly likely to interpret these indicators to mean that such efforts
are ill-conceived and inappropriate.) They blame the victims for the
continuing conditions of their victimization. The disinherited, for their
part, lose patience with the social workers, educational specialists, and
program planners in their midst. They begin to respond positively to
the militants who stand for a radical reconstruction of American life.
This increased militancy on the part of the disinherited serves only to
reinforce the opinion of the solid citizens that the disinherited are dis-
reputable. Judging the disinherited to be almost totally without merit,
the solid citizens withdraw much of their support for the professionalized efforts intended ostensibly for such people. Instead they increase
their clamor for greater control measures, for more police protection,

for a hard line. The disinherited, in turn, see in this "call to arms" an expression of the solid citizens' implacable hostility to their just aspirations and as such become more militant. Our communities are polarized to the point where rapprochement is all but impossible, where the solid citizens as well as the disinherited become parties to a state which can accurately be described as bordering on internal war.

For those, appalled by such a prospect, who react by saying that it cannot happen here, may I suggest that they look more carefully at circumstances now existing in their communities. Not only can this unfortunate scenario come to pass, in many communities it has begun to unfold.

Thus, I am led to conclude that professionalized social reform and remediation is not only inadequate to the task of maximizing human serviceability in American cities but that it is contributing to a marked increment in the troubled quality of urban life. It would seem to me, therefore, that it is time to disgard these approaches and begin the search for a more realistic if impractical politics of redistributive reform.

You may ask whether, given an analytic justification for pessimism, it is morally justified. Does not pessimism itself result in the kind of inattentiveness which only serves to perpetuate social arrangements in need of change? Is there not a final irony in the fact that if the optimistic illusion—the association of practicality with realism— forestalls basic change, the pessimistic frame of mind immobilizes those very people who perceive the need for basic change, thus insuring the maintenance of the status quo for some time to come?

It is true that analytic pessimism may work against the realization of basic change. It can immobilize, but it can only immobilize those who will be immobilized. It is possible to resist the atrophy of the drive to bring about meaningful change which is often associated with pessimism. The association is not a necessary one. While no one should be optimistic about a reconstruction of the parameters of our existence, the pessimistic rejection of anything short of this must be seen as a step in the right direction as must be our pessimistic reading of what it will take to effect such a reconstruction. The optimistic illusion of practicality will not serve us in our quest for meaningful change, whereas disenchantment born of analytic pessimism may paradoxically be our best hope.

NOTES

[1] Lawrence M. Friedman, *Government and Slum Housing: A Century of Frustration* (Chicago: Rand McNally and Co., 1968), Ch. IV. Also see Jane Jacobs, *The Death and Life of Great American Cities* (New York: Vintage Books, 1961).

[2] William Ryan, *Blaming the Victim* (New York: Vintage Books, 1971). Also see: Frances Fox Piven and Richard A. Cloward, *Regulating the Poor: The Functions of Public Welfare* (New York: Pantheon Books, 1971) and Michael Lewis, *Urban America: Institutions and Experience* (New York: John Wiley and Sons, 1973). Ch. 6.

[3] For an assessment of Job Corps and other OEO programs see: Ben B. Seligman, *Permanent Poverty: An American Syndrome* (New York: Quadrangle Books, 1968).

[4] Bernard Farber and Michael Lewis, "Compensatory Education and Social Justice" in *The Peabody Journal of Education,* Vol. XLIX (January 1972), pp. 85–96.

[5] Westinghouse Learning Corporation, *The Impact of Head Start: An Evaluation of the Effects of Head Start on Children's Cognitive Development,* June, 1969.

[6] This formulation was originally developed in Bernard Farber, David Harvey, and Michael Lewis, *Community Kinship and Competence,* Vol. III of Research and Development Program on Preschool Disadvantaged Children OE6–10–235. U.S. Department of Health, Education and Welfare, Office of Education, 1969, pp. 211–14.

BIBLIOGRAPHY

Farber, Bernard, Harvey, David, and Lewis, Michael, *Community Kinship and Competence,* Vol. III of Research and Development Program on Preschool Disadvantaged Children OE6–10–235. U.S. Department of Health, Education and Welfare, Office of Education, 1969, pp. 211–214.

Farber, Bernard, and Lewis, Michael, "Compensatory Education and Social Justice," in *The Peabody Journal of Education,* Vol. XLIX (January 1972), pp. 85–96.

Friedman, Lawrence M., *Government and Slum Housing: A Century of Frustration.* Chicago: Rand McNally & Co., 1968, Ch. IV.

Jacobs, Jane, *The Death and Life of Great American Cities.* New York: Vintage Books, 1961.

Lewis, Michael, *Urban America: Institutions & Experience.* New York: John Wiley & Sons, 1973.

Piven, Frances Fox, and Cloward, Richard A., *Regulating the Poor: The Functions of Public Welfare.* New York: Pantheon Books, 1971.

Ryan, William, *Blaming the Victim.* New York: Vintage Books, 1971.

Seligman, Ben B., *Permanent Poverty: An American Syndrome.* New York: Quandrangle Books, 1968, gives an assessment of Job Corps and other OEO programs.

Westinghouse Learning Corporation, *The Impact of Head Start: An Evaluation of the Effects of Head Start on Children's Cognitive Development,* June, 1969.

THE BLACK COMMUNITY

AND HOUSING STRATEGY*

Ronald G. Parris

In 1965, James Q. Wilson wrote an article called "Urban Renewal Does Not Always Renew," in which he argued that there was no urban problem in the United States, except perhaps the problem of "urban aesthetics."[1] Housing in the cities, according to Wilson, was not so much a problem of housing as it was of race, poverty, and culture. This definition of housing problems and urban problems has been used to support the opponents of urban renewal. And there is some merit to the conception of urban problems as essentially problems of poverty, race, and culture, which become manifest in the more visible problems of housing and urban blight.

At a more general level, I would argue that urban problems, including housing problems, are socio-structural in nature and must be understood in terms of the basic structure of American society—in terms of how goods, services, opportunities and choices are distributed within and among the population. Two questions are of concern here: (1) What is the particular nature of that structure in the United States?

* This is a revised version of a paper presented to the Conference on Neighborhood Preservation and Rehabilitation, Charleston, S.C., February 14–15, 1975.

(2) What is the specific connection between that structure and urban problems that confront us?

CASTE AND CLASS

The title "The Black Community and Housing Strategy" does not mean to imply that blacks form a single homogeneous community in a cultural sense and that there is one appropriate set of strategies that can be used to solve their housing problems. Blacks in central cities, although generally poor, unemployed, and underemployed (i.e., generally deprived) are, in fact, diverse in other characteristics and attitudes. It might well be useful to take such variation into account in the formulation and implementation of public policy.

Yet, it must be recognized that blacks as blacks represent an appropriate target population toward which particular policies are to be directed. In this respect, I regard the black population as constituting a boundary maintaining social system, which is in itself internally differentiated. In the more general sense, I am talking about the structure of American society. This structure is viewed by some sociologists as a color-caste system, a system consisting of two major castes, white and black, and internally stratified along class lines.

Such a view of the structure of American society can be an appropriate starting point for designing urban programs. This view of the social structure is not meant to obfuscate the more general class inequalities of production relations in American society, but points clearly to the significance that color has played in the process of class exploitation. The policy implications of this view of the social structure are important. It makes a difference, for example, whether housing and other urban strategies are to be directed toward fundamentally changing the structure of housing choices in the total environment or merely toward increasing the future choices of low-income blacks, relative to the past and the present, within the existing housing framework. It is a difference between revolution and reform in the production and distribution of housing as a resource. A fundamental change in housing distribution and choice would require a fundamental transformation of existing production relations and a different set of strategies than simply seeking to improve the housing of the black poor, through an assumed process of the "choice filter," or even through neighborhood preservation or rehabilitation.

The fact is that urban renewal, as articulated in relocation, rehabilitation, or conservation strategies, represents, however well intentioned, little more than a palliative short-run effort at housing reform and is not generally directed at fundamentally changing the general structure of housing choices. It is not even reasonable to expect that basic structural change could be affected by present housing strategies alone.

Present housing strategies seem to result, if not so actually designed, in the perpetuation of class and caste relations between blacks and whites—in the maintenance of two unequal societies. Let us consider what constitutes a caste structure. Besides rules that restrict social mobility across caste lines and the prohibition of intercaste marriages, the essential feature of a caste structure is a definitive restriction of social contact between members of different castes. Such contact is considered polluting and an elaborate set of rituals exists for prohibiting such contact or maintaining social distance.

Adequate understanding of residential segregation in American society must necessarily take these features of caste into account. Housing segregation and dislocation represent the outcome of behavior of real estate agents, finance and banking interests, public officials, and individual homeowners in conforming to the ritual expectations of caste relations.

FAILURE OF INTERRACIAL INTEGRATION

This is a social fact that explains the failure of various housing strategies to achieve stable interracial integration. Whites do not want blacks next door, because they view them as ritually polluting, as members of a stigmatized category. This attitude is then rationalized in a variety of ways. For example, the presence of blacks is viewed as having the effect of depressing property values and deteriorating the neighborhood.

This attitude and its accompanying rationalizations are never completely absent even among those whites who remain or choose to live in integrated neighborhoods. They generally remain only insofar as blacks do not become a majority in the block or neighborhood.[2] Anthony Downs describes this as the "law of cultural dominance," which is an euphemism for race prejudice. He explains the general absence of stable racial integration in housing and public schools in terms of this law and argues that a vast majority of whites of all income groups would be willing to send their children to integrated schools or live in integrated neighborhoods, "as long as they were sure that the white group concerned would remain in the majority" in the facility or area.

These whites have to be sure, according to this argument, that the social, cultural, and economic milieu and values of their own group dominate their own residential and educational environments. They will accept integration only to the extent that such integration is of a kind that is value reinforcing. As Downs sees it, the expansion of non-white residential areas has led to "massive transition from white to non-white occupancy mainly because there has been no mechanism that could assure the whites in any given areas that they would remain in the majority after non-whites once began entering."[3] To ensure stable integration, it is therefore proposed that some guarantee should be made to the white majority that it will remain the dominant majority.[4] According to this perspective, this guarantee should be made by assigning quotas, restricting the number of non-whites in a given area or facility, a "balancing device" that should form an explicit part of public policy legislation. These "benign quotas"[5] would represent for a given neighborhood its tolerance level or "tipping point" for interracial living.

CONFOUNDING OF INTEGRATION AND EQUALITY

I propose that such a policy confounds the criteria for evaluating the success or failure of housing strategies (and urban policy). There is a conceptual confusion between integration and equality as policy goals. The degree of residential integration is not the sole criterion by

which housing policies should be judged. Some consideration should
be given to the actual degree of equality that such policies generate.
Increased equality would presumably be reflected in greater housing
choices (including ability to pay) and a greater movement toward the
norm of house ownership as well as increased levels of satisfaction
among those who were formerly ill-housed either in an absolute or
relative sense. In the longer run and within the context of fundamental
economic changes for the urban poor, the latter achievement might
well be attainable outside an explicit policy of interracial housing and
the level of equality might therefore diverge from that of racial integration. There might well be, too, valid political and cultural reasons
for blacks in central cities to pursue strategies of increased housing
equality outside the context of housing integration.

True, in specific institutional areas (e.g., public accommodation),
the promotion of integration has often served hitherto as the chief
mechanism for black advancement. But I share the view expressed by
Frances Piven and Richard Cloward that efforts to improve deterio-
rated housing and inferior schools for blacks might have been more
successful, had these efforts not been so closely linked with integration
and thus provoked massive resistance.[6]

There is, I believe, an urgent need for housing experts and other
urban reformers to maintain the conceptual clarity between integration and equality. Further, the scope of the concept of equality should
be carefully defined. In an abstract sense, the concepts of equality/
inequality refer to the nature of the distribution of some value within
some population. That value may be wealth, occupation, power, prestige, social choice (the subjective choice of alternatives), or the distribution of access or opportunity (recruitment). Where planners and
policy makers do not confuse integration with equality, they restrict
the latter to only one of its operational values—the distribution of opportunity or access, with the expressed goal of providing "equal opportunity." The American Institute of Planners recently adopted, for
example, what they called an "equal opportunity element" as an integral part and baseline for evaluation of planning at the municipal,
state, and federal levels. This is an attempt to deal explicitly with the
problem of equality in planning theory and practice and more ex-

plicitly ties together the social and physical aspects of planning. My reservation is, however, in the restricted definition of equality to the distribution of opportunity and to its elaboration in the general but unfounded assumption that "equal opportunity" is attainable in class-stratified society. The concept of equal opportunity is, in fact, inherently contradictory.

The baseline for evaluating urban planning, policies, or strategies should be in terms of the general concept of equality in all its various dimensions—a more egalitarian distribution of wealth, occupation, power, prestige, subjective choices, and opportunities or access. It must not be assumed that changes in the distribution of opportunities are both necessary and sufficient to lead to fundamental changes in the other dimensions, though this is a fundamental assumption of laissez-faire liberalism.

It is in terms of the broader definition of equality, and not merely in terms of integration, that urban strategies, including housing strategies, could be evaluated. We may ask to what extent, if any, have these strategies improved both in an absolute and relative sense the economic position or political power of blacks. To what extent have they increased their range of social choice and to what extent have they changed recruitment in their favor?

ABSOLUTE AND RELATIVE POVERTY

The answers to such questions of improvement are not encouraging. Present urban policies and housing strategies are not designed to bring about such change on behalf of the urban poor. The problem partly lies in how poverty is conceptualized. The official statistical definition of poverty in terms of certain minimums is, in fact, a conservative definition of poverty, for although the numerical value of the poverty line is annually adjusted in terms of the cost of living index, the quantity of goods and services represented by it remains fixed. Which is to say that poverty is defined only in an absolute sense, in terms of the level of resources necessary to provide the basic necessities of food, clothing, and shelter. An alternative way of defining poverty is in relative terms. In a relative sense, persons are poor or deprived, if they do not possess the life chances or are unable to participate in the activities, customs, or lifestyles that are typical of the community or society in which they find themselves.

IS WATTS A SLUM?

I therefore take strong objection to George Sternlieb's[7] assertion that Watts is not a slum. Perhaps it is not a slum in the same degree as is the South ward of Newark, but in terms of the life chances of its residents, Watts reveals features of poverty, deprivation, and neglect characteristic of slums; i.e., there are sharp contrasts with the life chances of the residents of the surrounding communities. This relative comparison is the appropriate approach for assessing community poverty or well-being. In the case of Watts, we have had a riot that expresses the validity of such relative comparisons. The emphasis on relative poverty or deprivation highlights the general problem of social inequality and suggests that relative poverty cannot be eliminated, except under conditions of economic equality, since the poverty line rises as life conditions improve within the context of social inequality.

The appropriate criteria for judging social and societal change for evaluating urban strategies is therefore in terms of the degree of equality that results. This view has significant implications for how urban, regional, or even national progress or development is defined. As Robert Maffin indicated, the ethic of more production and more growth and more consumption in the postwar period needs to be reexamined.[8]

PROGRESS AND DEVELOPMENT AS EQUALITY

I have proposed elsewhere that development is not simply economic growth, but is rather physical, social, and economic change by which inequalities are reduced between and within such units as racial or class groups, neighborhoods, communities, regions, and nations.[9] At the urban level, the measure of progress is how much inequality is reduced between and within classes and racial groups as a result of strategies designed to bring about urban change. At the national level, there is no developed society today, but societies that are developing or stagnating along various dimensions. In the final analysis, development is to be measured not merely in terms of the level of production and growth, but in terms of the character of production relations—in terms of the distribution of valued goods and the reduction of inequalities between and within national and regional groups. Further, at the urban level, the criteria of success are not how much economic growth, business expansion, physical redevelopment, or how many houses are rehabilitated, but how much inequality is reduced as a result of what, if any, growth or rehabilitation has occurred. The differentiation between change, growth, and progress in the 1973 Preliminary Development Plan of the City of Charleston is, in this respect, a step in the right direction. Progress involves improvement, and improvement must be measured in terms of community values. From the point of view of the black community, one of these values should be equality in the fundamental sense of a more equitable distribution of economic and political resources and choices and not merely in terms of opportunity or access.

HOUSING STRATEGIES

The basic housing strategies of clearance and redevelopment, on the one hand, and rehabilitation and conservation, on the other, must be viewed in light of the above discussion as limited attempts to deal with problems of urban blight or "urban aesthetics," rather than fundamental attempts to redistribute housing and urban resources. The structures left behind by the relocated families might either be rehabilitated or bulldozed for new land use, new structures, and new interests. Those who stand to benefit from such efforts are not so much the urban poor, but the real estate, banking, and political interests in the urban environment. Within the context of rehabilitation, a new income group that includes displaced white suburbanites fleeing the high costs of some suburban services and the suburban way of life is often the chief beneficiary of the rehabilitated structures. The Community Development Act of 1974 gives legitimacy to the ascendancy of such class interests by explicitly conjoining the elimination of urban blight and housing rehabilitation with the goal of encouraging middle-income groups back to the cities. In effect, the black poor in the central cities are to be displaced by the white middle class ostensibly for the purposes of eliminating urban blight and improving the financial status of cities.

TYPES OF URBAN FUTURES

Urban relocation, redevelopment, rehabilitation, and "community development" are therefore strategies that are partly used to control and preempt the presence of blacks in central cities. The scenarios for preempting black control of cities were being outlined by urban planners even in the reform conscious 1960s.[10]

One of the most comprehensive attempts to define alternative futures for urban America was that of Anthony Downs. Downs defined five specific types of futures for the city.[11] These were based on sets of choices involving the degree of geographical concentration or dispersal of blacks in the population, the character of racial relationships (segregation or integration), and the level of enrichment (the degree of equality).

Futures of enrichment might take the form of "enrichment only," where the most disadvantaged citizens are helped and the quality of life in the city and its contiguous areas are upgraded, but under conditions of residential segregation and geographical concentration of blacks. Enrichment that involves the elimination of racial segregation would create a socially, economically, and racially "integrated core" or community through strategies of large-scale urban renewal programs, including scattered site public housing, middle-income housing and high quality public services. Explicit in his evaluation of this urban outcome is the recognition of the political goal of preempting black dominance in the city by avoiding a high percentage of low-income residents (mainly blacks) at the center and attracting whites and middle-income residents from its periphery, so shifting the thrust of the integration process from the suburbs to the central cities.

Other forms of urban enrichment, according to Downs, could involve the geographical dispersal of blacks that might result either in enrichment within the context of racial segregation ("segregated dispersal") or in enrichment under conditions of racial integration after such dispersal ("integrated dispersal"). The fifth image of the future is to continue the strategies of concentration, racial segregation, and nonenrichment.

URBAN POWERLESSNESS

If these constitute the range of alternative futures for the central city, the question to be answered is which of these futures should be pursued? Blacks have hitherto had little or no say in choosing the future of the city or even their status in the long history of their presence in American society. The planning of such urban futures has been done for the urban population rather than with it.

URBAN ACCOUNTABILITY AND
CONFLICTUAL INTERESTS

Blacks on their part have to become organized at a variety of levels, if they are to have some meaningful effect on the formulation, choice, and implementation of such urban decisions. By such organization, public officials, planners, developers, financiers, bankers, and the police could be made accountable to the urban poor in general and blacks in particular—groups toward whom these decision makers generally seem to feel little accountability. Urban blacks must recognize that they could place themselves in a position to make such groups accountable, for it is the urban blacks by whom the functional legitimacy of such professional groups as the police, physicians, social workers, and planners is partly maintained. The organization of urban blacks and their demands for greater accountability could result in class conflict with key groups in the service sector, for just as the police need criminal violations, physicians need ill health, social workers need poverty, and urban planners need urban blight.[12] The black population has to become more conscious of its collective needs and its potential power in the urban environment and the advantages of effective organization.

RACIAL INTERESTS IN THE URBAN FUTURE

Strategies requiring the dispersal of the urban poor and especially blacks from slum or substandard housing in central cities might conceivably result in helping individual members of the poor to the extent that their range of housing choices is extended in the direction of "standard housing," and such greater equality of housing choices is actually reflected in better housing and better neighborhoods. At the baseline, however, these strategies are suggestive of an element of mischievous social engineering to promote more dominant and persuasive political and racial/ethnic interests.

THE CHALLENGE OF EQUALITY AND
THE PUBLIC INTEREST

The interests of the poor as a group, however, are lost in the competitive market place of interests of public officials, realtors, bankers, financiers, and other key institutional players. Because of the strong ethic of individual competition associated with the operation of the "free" market system, government interference on behalf of the poor is viewed as an unwarranted distortion in the struggle for urban survival and progress. But it is the interests of the poor, the interest of blacks, a large proportion of whom are unemployed, underemployed, and generally dominated, that must take primacy over other interests, if a more egalitarian and just society is to be realized. It is not now fashionable to intervene in their behalf. In fact, there are, ironically in this year of bicentennial celebrations and a presidential election, few public spokesmen for the need to continue the unfinished revolution and to uphold the public interests in the face of the excesses and exaggerated pursuit of private interests. It is clear that blacks, in particular, and the poor, in general, must mobilize for their own self determination, if they are not to remain doomed to poverty and deprivation. Obviously more than housing strategies are involved.

NOTES

[1] James Q. Wilson, "Urban Renewal Does Not Always Renew," *Harvard Today*, (January, 1965).

[2] Anthony Downs, "Alternative Futures for the American Ghetto," *Daedalus*, (Fall, 1968) 1343–53; Trudy McFall, "Racially and Economically Integrated Housing: Can It Work? Under What Conditions?" mimeographed (St. Paul, Minnesota: Metropolitan Council, 1974).

[3] Downs, "Alternative Futures."

[4] Ibid; Morton Grodzins, *The Metropolitan Area as a Racial Problem* (Pittsburgh: University of Pittsburgh Press, 1958) 479–501; Oscar Cohen, "The Case for Benign Quotas in Housing," *Phylon*, 21 (1960) 21.

[5] The recommendation of the use of quotas to control the number of blacks living in integrated neighborhoods for purposes of successful racial integration panders to the racial prejudices of whites or what Downs euphemistically calls the "law of cultural dominance." It is an exaggerated commitment to integration for its own sake, which tends to lose sight of integration as an instrument for reducing racial inequalities and is a substitution of means for goals. It is interesting to note that the later use of quotas on behalf of blacks and women for dealing with racial and sexual imbalances with respect to jobs and education has generated fairly widespread and emotional resistance by some of those same liberals who were willing to accept or ignore their use in the late 1960s as a strategy for creating the liberal dream of stable, integrated communities. The recommended use of quotas for purposes of integration, and the rejection of their use for reducing inequalities associated with race and sex points either to conceptual confusion between the concepts of integration and equality or to the mischievous identification of these concepts that renders the attainment of a more egalitarian society more problematic.

[6] Frances Fox Piven and Richard A. Cloward, "The Case Against Urban Desegregation," in *Housing Urban America*, edited by Jon Pynos (Chicago: Aldine, 1973) 97.

[7] George Sternlieb, "Housing, Urban Development and Rehabilitation," *South Atlantic Urban Studies*, Vol. I, 1977.

[8] Robert Maffin, "The Issues, the Parameters and the Options," *South Atlantic Urban Studies*, Vol. I, 1977.

[9] Ronald G. Parris, "Underdevelopment as Inequality: A Description and Application of an Alternative," mimeographed (Nashville: Vanderbilt University, 1974).

[10] Piven and Cloward, "The Case Against Urban Desegregation."

[11] Downs, "Alternative Futures."

[12] Alex Swan, "The Politics of Identification," *Crime and Delinquency* (April 1974) 128.

BIBLIOGRAPHY

Cohen, Oscar, "The Case for Benign Quotas in Housing." *Phylon*, 21 (1960) p. 21.

Community Development Act, 1974.

Downs, Anthony, "Alternative Futures for the American Ghetto." *Daedalus*, Fall. 1968.

Grodzins, Morton, *The Metropolitan Area as a Racial Problem*. Pittsburgh: University of Pittsburgh Press, 1958.

Maffin, Robert, "The Issues, the Parameters and the Options." *South Atlantic Urban Studies*, Vol. I, 1977.

McFall, Trudy, "Racially and Economically Integrated Housing: Can It Work: Under What Conditions?" Mimeographed. St. Paul, Minnesota: Metropolitan Council, 1974.

Parris, Ronald G., "Underdevelopment as Inequality: A Description and Application of an Alternative." Mimeographed. Nashville, Tennessee: Vanderbilt University, 1974.

Piven, Frances Fox, and Cloward, Richard A., "The Case Against Urban Desegregation." In *Housing Urban America*, edited by Jon Pynos. Chicago: Aldine, 1973.

————, "Control of the Cities: How the Negroes will Lose." *The New Republic*, December 1967.

Sternlieb, George, "Housing, Urban Development and Rehabilitation." *South Atlantic Urban Studies*, Vol. I, 1977.

Swan, Alex, "The Politics of Identification." *Crime and Delinquency*, April 1974.

The City of Charleston and the Berkeley-Charleston-Dorchester Regional Planning Council, *Preliminary Development Plan Peninsular Portion of the City of Charleston*, 1973. Charleston, S. C.

Wilson, James, "Urban Renewal Does Not Always Renew." *Harvard Today*, January 1965.

THE ISSUES,

THE PARAMETERS AND THE OPTIONS*

Robert Maffin

Neighborhood preservation and conservation are not for dilettantes and escapists. They are deadly earnest matters. These statements may shock you. I hope so! My purpose is to define the issues, the parameters, and options for neighborhood preservation and conservation. The options are running out.

An overriding issue before us today is the conservation of our resources. This issue has been dramatically thrust upon us by recent international events. As enormous as this nation's economy is, a $30 to $50 billion shift in resource allocation to energy, cannot help but affect the entire economy. A society of approximately 8 percent of the world's population consuming as much as 40 percent of its annual yield must be fundamentally shaken by the demands of the other 90 percent for a larger share of the productive pie. For almost 200 years now we have developed a society and an economy based on production and more production for consumption and more consumption. We are now challenged as a nation to change our consumption of the world's goods and services. We have to rethink which resources we

* Prepared for the Conference on Neighborhood Preservation and Rehabilitation, Charleston, S.C., February 14–15, 1975.

use, how much of them we use, and how we use them, and we are not used to doing that.

Most of us have never been concerned with conservation and have never looked upon the cities and the urban environment as an asset or a resource that deserved to be conserved. If we did not like what we created, we could leave it and build all over again. This was to be expected in a land of abundance and in a pluralistic and mobile society. It is clear now, however, that we must begin to treat what we have already created, already built, as an asset which we must use to the fullest. We would consider it shocking mismanagement in private business if a productive and efficient factory were to be written off and replaced without very careful examination of the costs. Yet, we do just that every day with our cities.

When I say that neighborhood preservation and conservation are deadly earnest matters, not for dilettantes nor escapists, I do not demean the need to dabble nor do I discharge out of hand the often felt need to escape. The problem is that the dilettantish and escapist nature of our urban conservation effort constitutes a major reason for the blight and plight of our cities. We have sought to escape from the cities because we felt no constraint upon our resources or our productive capacity. The dabbling in urban conservation stemmed from the interest and commitment of the few who saw the importance of fine buildings, mature neighborhoods, and historic continuity and by an even fewer who saw the importance of conserving the major assets already accumulated in the cities.

A little urban history may help to illuminate this point. The earliest public concern with our cities was to build whatever streets, sewers, and other facilities that were necessary. In later years standards of health and safety were established so that buildings did not topple and so that air and light might enter. We sought to make sure that gas lines did not burst and that switches worked reliably. Gradually we saw the value of such genteel things as leaving open space for parks and preserving a few buildings with a special history or architecture. In the postwar era we became so bold as to create historic districts and to undertake such programs as urban renewal and urban rehabilitation. We tried to save as much as we could of the existing environment while allowing cities to adjust to change and create new investment opportunities. We even went so far as to begin thinking about modernizing the public housing that had been built over the past forty years, and making low-cost loans to homeowners to rehabilitate their property. While these steps were taken, we were also insuring loans and making grants to extend the sprawl of cities. But we also were penalizing people for maintaining their property by raising their taxes.

This little recitation points to some fundamental attitudes toward conservation. We see that for a long time production rated higher than conservation in our national priorities.

The conservation of our urban investment is now a major and complex issue. First, we must decide what we are going to conserve and why; for whom we are going to conserve and how. Some special reasons for conserving neighborhoods have already been established— important location, historical value, and architectural significance. But conservation is also necessary for the essential vitality, substance, and direction of the economy. Not only is the quality of life involved but also the standard of living. Conservation is no longer an option but a necessity. For the most part, conservation has been the luxury of the affluent or for those who would sacrifice other things for a special style of living or a special place to live. The remaining buildings, houses, and streets were left for those who could not escape—a situation that has compounded the problem. So when the question is asked "for whom conservation," we come face to face with the poor, those left behind in an affluent society.

And how do we accomplish conservation? I am suggesting that it become a major element of public policy and that we stop taxing and building, subsidizing suburban escape, and penalizing those who try to conserve. We can no longer, for example, pursue the dual policies of giving tax credits to individuals for mortgage interest payments and taxes on real property (to the tune of $6 billion a year) while we allow no tax credit for those homeowners who conserve and rehabilitate.

There are many other issues: Are we going to have an urban growth and development policy in this country? Are communities going to have local housing policies? Are we going to provide incentives or impediments for investment in conservation and rehabilitation? Are there going to be subsidies for these purposes? Are we going to insure or assure private investment in building rehabilitation? Are we going to direct our public facility investments to encourage conservation and preservation? These are all issues that events demand we answer now. What are the parameters of neighborhood preservation and conservation? Obviously, it depends in part upon the goals set, the objectives to be achieved.

There are some specific factors that determine the parameters of neighborhood preservation and conservation. First of all, not all of the existing development can or should be saved. Time and use and technology have often altered a city neighborhood or a public building to the point where it is no longer desirable or economic to save it. Most of the housing built in this country was built by craftsman for individuals or small markets. It has limited adaptability to current standards and needs. The cost-effectiveness of rehabilitation is not there. The buildings themselves are located in neighborhoods that are inadequate. The schools may be outmoded—in some cases, even dangerous for occupancy. There is too little open space, no off-street parking. Utility lines, sewer systems, public streets, sidewalks, and street lighting have outlived their usefulness.

But this is not a blanket condemnation of urban conservation for most of the accumulated wealth in this country is in the cities. Many cities still have a useful life, and all of them have areas with historic meaning, social value, and economic utility. Just because mean houses, buildings, and public places cannot be saved efficiently, does not mean you should demolish them. If there is one thing we have learned through urban renewal, it is that the development process is a very delicate and selective one. We must save as much as can be saved, while creating environments for new investment.

Another parameter of preservation and conservation is a negative one. Simply stated, what impact on the national economy, on production, employment, and consumption will a major shift from new production to the conservation of existing investment have? We cannot answer that question. Nobody can tell you how many jobs would be gained or lost, how much material would be saved or spent, what economies in transportation or communication can be achieved, how much of all of these changes the economy could stand. Making a major shift in our economy from consumption to conservation implies changes the consequences of which we cannot now assess. But it is clear we may soon have no other option.

If neighborhood preservation and conservation are to be carried out to the maximum by private action, there are two questions to be answered: (1) What are the alternatives? (2) Can the private investor or owner afford such actions? The answers to these questions of private alternatives can be modified by public decision. Escape can be made more difficult; indeed, economic changes abroad indicate that it will become more difficult in any event. Public commitments to special private efforts at conservation and rehabilitation can be made but not on the timid scale to date. If rehabilitation and conservation are necessary, then we must find ways to rehabilitate housing for poor people. If communities and neighborhoods are going to be saved, we must encourage middle-income investment in them as well. If private investment is to be encouraged, then commensurate public investments in facilities and services must be made.

What, then, are our options? In my opinion we have no option on whether or not to preserve and conserve neighborhoods. We have been gradually moving in that direction for four decades. Events have caught up with us, and action is now a necessity. Major public policy has to be formulated to encourage neighborhood preservation and conservation. Most of the options available deal with for whom and how. We really know that there must be adequate housing for everyone and that the urban environment must serve everyone. We know there are basic tools available to be used—the taxing power, the power to influence the flow and rate of money, the power to allocate public resources, and the power to invest in public facilities and services. All of these tools, employed by every level of government, must be used if neighborhood preservation and conservation are going to be effectively achieved.

On the private side the real question is whether we can construct an economy and society running healthily on the conservation of resources rather than on the unbridled consumption of them. How much of our energy and resources are we prepared to allocate to the con-

servation and rehabilitation of existing assets as against unending
production for consumption?

BIBLIOGRAPHY

Albrandt, Roger S., Jr., and Brophy, Paul C., *Neighborhood Revitali-
zation: Theory and Practice.* Lexington, Massachusetts: D. C.
Heath, 1975.
*Locally-Funded Rehabilitation Programs: What's Being Tried? How
Is It Working?* Reprints from *Journal of Housing,* 1973 to 1975.
Washington, D.C.: National Association of Housing and Rede-
velopment Officials, 1975.
Morris, Peter R., "Federal Strategy for Neighborhood Rehabilitation
and Preservation." *Harvard Journal on Legislation,* V. 11 (April
1974), pp. 509–38.
Real Estate Research Corporation, *Neighborhood Preservation: A
Catalog of Local Programs.* Prepared for the U.S. Department of
Housing and Urban Development. Washington, D.C.: Government
Printing Office, 1975. (Stock number 023–000–00285–0.)
Russo, Ronald A., "Preservation of a Washington Neighborhood
Headed for Success Through a Variety of Approaches." *Journal of
Housing,* v. 31 (October 1974), pp. 408–13.
"The 'State of Affairs' in housing and community development:
NAHRO conversations form first step toward a new Association
policy and program. Panel One: Community/Neighborhood Con-
servation and Housing Rehabilitation." *Journal of Housing,* v. 32
(August–September 1975), pp. 370–76.

HOUSING,

URBAN DEVELOPMENT,

AND REHABILITATION*

George Sternlieb

We have always had a clash in this country between the planner and well-thought-out development and the populace and the tastes of that populace. A regional plan association or any other group of planners looks at the pattern of land development in the United States and says "That's sprawl," while the consumer retorts "Yeah! And I love it! Because what you're calling sprawl is my castle." In this country we seem to have monolithic consumer taste buds; nearly everyone wants a single family dwelling, well separated from everyone else's. There is some diversion, but it is pretty negligible. Even those people who do not have a suburban castle generally tend to think of it as a rather nice objective. Now, there are exceptions: people who have moved back into the central cities and kids who, after tasting the good things that their parents slaved for, have rejected them. One of the patterns in New York City, for example, is the immigrant of three generations ago who was forced by circumstances into a slum of the Lower Eastside and then dedicated himself to making a living so that ultimately he might move out to the suburbs. Three generations later,

* This is a revised version of a paper presented to the Conference on Neighborhood Preservation and Rehabilitation, Charleston, S.C., February 14–15, 1975.

his descendants moved back into a slum on the Lower Eastside just for kicks. There are such people but the center of the pork chop, certainly since the 1930s, has desired room, and all the suburban things that go with it.

Suburbs and the good life have become synonymous for most people. Closely identified with these symbols is capitalism, but there are very few people, if you really push them hard, who revere capitalism for itself. As an ideal, capitalism is no powerhouse, but the consumer loves what it has been able to deliver. In recent decades it has become apparent that capitalism may not be able to provide the principal symbols that advertising, socialization, education, and training have taught us to expect. Americans want a big car not a little car, a couple of cars, a bigger house, and a bigger lot, but the economy may not stand the strain. Such concerns have stimulated some new thinking, particularly in housing. If you look at the last twenty or thirty years of literature in housing, you will see practically a tidal action—rehabilitation, or at least talk about rehabilitation, and numerous proclamations about a shift back to rehabilitation. Despite these announcements, we have concentrated on new construction. We have built lots of new houses; we have made the American middle class the wonder of the ages. It does far better than the affluent in most of Europe. We have not done much, comparatively speaking, for the poor; but in absolute terms, our poor, with some dreadful exceptions, are the affluent poor. As a matter of fact, they are so affluent that we are able to export entry level jobs. We find it cheaper to use a labor force in Formosa than to use the potential labor force of the slums.

But the wealth of the American population is not the only reason that rehabilitation has been neglected. Simply defining rehabilitation is part of the problem. Americans believe that there is little "rehab" work, because they conceive of it only in grand terms, but the reality is that it goes on all the time. The existence of twenty or thirty stores in Charleston for the do-it-yourselfer or for the small contractor in housing is a tribute to that. And there are equivalent chains all over the country. The energy invested in this type of rehabilitation is obvious, if you examine the amount of inadequate housing in both the 1950 census and the 1960 census. For the moment we can employ a very rough measurement of inadequacy, a single variable, "no plumb-ing." That is about the only thing we can count well. "Do you have a toilet? If you do, say yes, if you don't, say no." "Do you have adequate housing?" That is a much tougher question. In any case, if you take the 1950 level of inadequate housing (i.e., those houses without plumbing), subtract all the demolitions, and add all the build-ing permits for the additions of plumbing, you discover that about half of all the improvements that are mirrored in the 1960 census were done illegally. Every homeowner knows that if he files for a building permit he will be reassessed. So illegal improvement goes on all the time.

Although we have had continuous rehabilitation, we have had no large programs, no big "R" rehabilitation. Now Uncle Sam has been saying "there shalt be rehab" periodically for a long time and not delivering too well. The problem, in part, is what I would call the "iron law of the IBM card." Big programs need an effective accounting method. When professional operators of low-class dwelling units figure that they can improve their rent revenues or maybe even fill up some empties by improving the facilities, they call in a local handyman or carpenter and say "Buster, get in there, spend a couple of days, straighten things out, but don't spend more than $200 or $300 a unit." But that level of effort cannot be administered on the federal level. The iron law of the IBM card inhibits it. The IBM card is an idiot mechanism; it only says yes and no. It has no gradients. It cannot say better, worse; it says yes, no. So when the federal government involves itself in rehabilitation, it has difficulty tolerating minor improvements. You cannot say that you straightened out some of the doors, rehung windows that needed it, and generally cleaned the place up. Uniform accounting procedures monitored by computers require that you put in a new roof, a completely new roof. There is no gradient here. You have to say yes, or you have to say no. The rigidity of large programs prohibits owners from spending several hundred dollars on a boiler to get it to work for another five or ten years because that is all it is really worth. You cannot do that. You have to put in a completely new boiler, or, perhaps, repipe the entire building. So in general what we have had under federal guidelines in rehabilitation is an over-

improvement and an overcosting of those improvements conducted
under big "R" rehabilitation. In general, such programs have fallen
down under their own weight, for the neighborhoods would not stand
it and the economics of building would not stand it. It simply did not
make sense. Nonetheless there is a crying need for money for assistance; unfortunately, the federal government has not been very effective in managing to dole out this help.

Another reason for this failure lies in the realities of rehabilitation.
It is basically a retail business. New housing is a wholesale business.
Now I am using these terms in a specialized fashion. A wholesale
business is a cookie cutter. It may cost a lot of money to build and
develop that cookie cutter, but once you have it, you can stamp out a
lot of units. On the other hand, a "retail business" means that each
and every unit, give or take a few, has to be handled separately. Consequently, to administer rehabilitation requires special attention for
each project. The administrative costs under the 312 Program (which
was one of our major efforts, and an effective one for providing rehabilitation in central city areas[1]) came very close to equaling the
actual cost of the reconstruction itself. And as soon as the administrative costs were cut back, there were abuses, and the result was the
scandals of the 235 J Program, its successor program.[2]

Another stumbling block for massive rehabilitation is the difficulty
in formulating policies to apply equally to all locales. Indeed, the
where of building housing has, I think, been drastically oversimplified.
In general, we are still attacking some of our problems of redevelopment as if it were only a question of halting the drift of resources from
the city to the suburb. That is an oversimplification because not all
suburbs are the same. We have old suburbs; we have all black poor
suburbs; we have old industrial suburbs and the like. Each city is
different and requires separate approaches.

Differences among areas leads to another, even more difficult, problem. One of the things that is very obvious in this country is that there
are enormous differences in the places that people live by regions. My
own area is the Northeast, and the Northeast is a declining region. It
is losing population very rapidly now. It is not just a question of
central city, a New York City, for example; states are also depopulat-

ing. If you take New York State as a whole from 1970 to 1973, despite the gap between the fertility and mortality rates, there is a net population drop of better than 200,000. The same thing is true in Pennsylvania and New Jersey. New England provides an intense example of what is happening. Many of the problems we think of as being racial in the big cities, in terms of jobs and the like, are compounded by the fact that the size of the pie for the big Eastern cities is shrinking. If you look where housing is still being built, where jobs are moving, and, where the defense contracts still tend to be going, you can see a broad regional dynamic which cannot be limited or reversed by an individual state. This degeneration poses special problems for rehabilitation. For example, a study of tax delinquency in Pittsburgh, which the Rutgers Center for Urban Policy Research has undertaken, tried to find out why so many housing units in that city (about 15 percent) are now tax delinquent. The investigators concluded that the basic reason was very simple. You have an aging population and you have young people moving out; thus, there is nobody left behind to buy housing. Consequently, in a city that has a stock ready for rehabilitation, there is little population ready to live there.

Nonetheless, we are backing into rehabilitation despite the excesses and failures of past programs. Some economic history should indicate the reasons for this development. There was an interesting study, called *The Zone of Emergence*, done in 1915 by a settlement house worker in Boston. This settlement house dealt with immigrant groups. The author was a classic upperclass YMCA type, bemoaning the problems the settlement house faced. He complained that a new group had moved into the area and that their sanitary habits were beyond belief. They were overcrowding the tenements incredibly, and they tended to have ten, twelve, or fourteen children in a family. He lamented the continuous reports of crime, and he was certain that disease was rampant. This impoverished group of immigrants were Jewish, people now the most affluent group in the town. At the same time our friend from the "Y" pointed out that 85 percent of the occupants of jails in eastern Massachusetts were Irish. Now these groups have moved into the American Main Street. Although they are not represented in the annual St. Cecelia's Ball, there are few who care.[3]

They succeeded, however, in an economy which was moving, which had room for strong backs, not necessarily strong minds, but sweat, manpower, womanpower, exploitable certainly, but there was room for them.

The success of these immigrants had a significant impact on housing. Immigrant groups, earning reasonable salaries, required decent housing, and the federal government intervened to provide it. In examining the governmental sponsorship of housing, we could go through the whole series of federal legislation starting with the simple guarantee that we had in the FHA, which was the most successful single business ever launched. In its better years, the FHA returned net profits to the federal government, based on its insurance business which earned over 100 million dollars per year. In the 1930s, its simple mortgage guarantee was sufficient to generate housing. But by the 1950s, the program had lost its charm and its capacity to deliver. The tastes of the consumer outstripped the capacity of the FHA to lend, causing carrying costs to spiral upward. We had wave, after wave, after wave of legislation designed essentially to reduce interest rates because that is all we knew to do to enable people to purchase houses. We tried to make construction of housing more efficient, but we did not do too well. We also tried to reduce the land costs of housing. We tried to reduce operating costs a little bit, but really did not know how. Local communities did not have the money to help by offering property tax relief. Complicating these efforts was the Environmental Protection Agency, whose programs introduced very consequential cost increments.

We finally came to the rocks with the mortgage programs when we hit indentures that in some cases were as long as 48 years. Forty-eight years from now is the year 2023, and there is some question in my mind whether anybody is going to live in a house in 2023. We drove interest rates down to the 1 percent level, and built a lot of housing. It is very difficult to evaluate the scandals, the short falls, windfalls, the foreclosures versus the numbers of people that were housed. But regardless of these social benefits, the basic message began to come through—these programs were too expensive within the context of American society and the American game as it has been played. Indeed, these programs tended to fly in the face of established property values. By underwriting housing costs, these programs enabled individuals to build more cheaply than their predecessors in a neighborhood. In addition, this federal involvement brought federal guidelines on nondiscrimination and injected the government into controversies on zoning and the problem of placing the poor. The Black Jack, Missouri, case exemplified the problem.[4] HUD, simply trying to enforce its guidelines on housing, was forced to deal with the politically sensitive issue of integrating a community. So given the costs, poor merchandise reports, and the realities of political pressures, the federal government is abdicating from the housing construction business as a more or less direct entrant.

I suggest then that we have a declining role of the federal government in housing. Let me further suggest that this is the case not because there are necessarily bad guys in Washington, but because the guys in Washington tend to reflect, give or take a little bit, the populace, and we no longer have a broad-based housing constituency. There are more people scared of losing what they have than there are those hungry for new housing accommodations. It makes no difference whether the Democrats or the Republicans are in office. The Democrats at least have a better feeling of the forms of symbolic action than the Republicans. The Republicans like to grind the nose of the enemy in the dirt. The other guys pat you on the back and still do nothing.

With the abdication of the federal government, we are left with the housing allowance program, Section 8 of the 1974 housing act. I would suggest that Section 8, if it ever gets funded in any great substantial way at all, will probably last no more than 18 months. In general, it proposes to wrap all of the current housing subsidies into one bundle. These funds would then provide money to enable a poor person to purchase housing equivalent to that of a rich or middle-class person. Dade County, Florida, computed what adequately subsidized rents would be. Then by looking at income levels and the rent-paying capacity of the people who would be serviced by this program, they concluded that a family requiring a 2-bedroom unit would need a subsidy of approximately $4,000 a year. In New York City, the subsidy allowable under the law or under the administrative regulations is $600 a month for a 3-bedroom unit in new construction. That is

$7,200 a year. The economists and the rationalists say "Fellows that's what it costs." They will turn to public housing and prove that if you pull together all the subsidies in the program—the lost taxes, the secondary impacts of government security lending, etc.—it too costs a lot of money. But the difference is that much of it is buried money. Now we have explicit money. And the taxpayer will refuse to bear the burden.

Consequently, despite all the problems with rehabilitation, we are returning to it because it tends not to disturb extant property values. Also, because rehabilitation deals with the results of past zoning, the federal government can avoid the sensitive political issue of zoning. There is, moreover, the belief that *maybe* it can be done cheaper. And it *must* be done cheaper. Rehabilitation has to be done cheaper, not for moral justification, but because of the crushing shortage of resources. We are now rationalizing ourselves into accepting much smaller housing units, and we are going to rationalize our way into party wall construction. When I was a kid, party wall construction was called a row house. Now it is called a townhouse. That change in title is very important. Declining prosperity demands cheaper housing, and rehabilitation is most likely to provide what we need.

Where does that leave us? With the demise of federal programs, rehabilitation has some new luster; and by default, we have invented a new federalism. The states are in business, some of them well, some of them not so well. There are somewhere in the order of thirty states now that have housing finance agencies. Some of them are simply turnstile operations: borrowing tax exempt, giving money to a few favored banks, and hoping that the banks do something that is appropriate with it. Others of them are more involved in the housing business; and to the degree that they are in the housing business, they are a little bit closer to the realities of the market and to the political process than a HUD field office. These new agencies will find rehabilitation a useful strategy. In general, they will probably do a better job than HUD, and I think they are going to grow. In addition to increasing activity on the state level, cities are beginning to respond more vigorously to the dangerous problems that they face. They are realizing that their survival is in jeopardy and that their stock in trade, their capital goods if you will, in this battle for survival include their housing stock. The smartest among them realize that there is no bail out coming from Washington; there will be no new massive housing programs, and they will have to optimize their standing stock. They will have to rehabilitate what they have. There are still lots of romantics who keep waiting for the next national election and the next one after that. They are losers. Those cities with aggressive administrations are getting into housing operations. They have initiated a variety of programs to deal with tax delinquency and to facilitate emergency repair programs. In some cases cities are moving into emergency receivership programs. They are not interested in punishing those who cannot pay their bills or taxes; rather, the city is serving as a life raft to keep the stock in business. This type of intervention is a radical departure from previous intervention which consisted largely of code enforcement that created added expenses for the property owner. There are also the beginnings of some very creative work in tax abatements for specific types of amenities. Some of these tax reductions are being coupled with municipal loan programs. In general, financing programs have a significant future in the right cities.

Does this new federalism and this reemphasis of rehabilitation provide a larger role for the individual? This is probably not the case. All these governmental actions require money, and a larger and larger piece of the disposable income of Americans is going to government to be used as government sees fit. Moreover, this will increase, despite taxpayer revolts. In general, the juggernaut of government will continue, and the consumption of money by government will increase. We are the England of the 1980s. To cite just one reflection of this process, of all the elements of inflation last year the single largest increase for the middle-income family was in actual taxes paid. It was bigger than fuel, bigger than mortgage rates. Now it is not my business to say whether this is or is not "a good" thing. But it is something to note. It means that the capacity for individual action, the capacity to individually finance, even the capacity for charitable operations of one kind or another to finance activity, is on the wane. Private citizens and private organizations have less money and less effective buying power than they once did, and the role of government necessarily increases. Big government, "heavy tax" government, generates its own growth by taxing away the capacity for alternative forms of financing.

The cost of money has destroyed the ability of the government and of the individual to build new houses and has made rehabilitation a more appealing option. This option is likely to grow more desirable, for in the long run the cost of money is not going to decline. As of late the Federal Reserve has been making money a lot more available than Arthur F. Burns seemed to want to do just a very few months ago. Nonetheless, this action to reduce the interest rate will eventually be negated. The biggest single source of money right now, fresh money, is oil money and German money, the latter born of an incredible industrial revival. This money floats wherever it gets paid best. The operating deficits of the country as a whole are enormous and the way to finance those operating deficits is to compete for the "hot" money. But to compete, you have to raise interest rates. When the income derived from lending money to the government is reduced, as it is now, we find that money begins to disappear from the United States. The alternative is to print money, and such action is inevitably inflationary. So I would guess that over the next several months, you will see interest rates decline, but they will rise again. There is little security in the American dollar, and there is little reason for holding it in absolute preference to any other form of currency. At one time we could get away with much lower interest rates than anybody else because we did not need foreign capital and because we could guarantee a secure return on investment. This is no longer the case, so not only will the consumer and the government have less buying power, but this decline may well have a built-in dynamic. This lack of outside capital will force us increasingly to rely on and rehabilitate what we already have.

NOTES

[1] The 312 Program was a program of HUD in which low-income families could borrow to rehabilitate their homes.

[2] In the 235 J Program, individuals could purchase rehabilitated homes with the assistance of nonprofit sponsors.

[3] The St. Cecilia's Ball is an annual party held in Charleston. Tradi-

tionally, only those with upper-class backgrounds and a long residence in the lowcountry area may attend.

⁴ Black Jack, Missouri, is a suburban community that passed an ordinance against public housing.

PRESERVATION, HOUSING,

AND NEIGHBORHOODS IN PITTSBURGH*

Arthur Ziegler

For decades the business world and the federal government looked upon historic preservationists as starry-eyed, intransigent idealists who did not know "how things worked." Only recently has that perception begun to change; preservationists are finally being considered seriously by decision makers at all levels of government and business.

In one sense these businessmen and federal officials were right. It was many years before preservationists became "practical" enough to wield influence, obtain funds, and invade the power structure. In another sense, however, preservationists have always been practical. Without vast financial backing, without power, without reliance on federal assistance, they were forced to pursue all their goals with pure pragmatism—to make scant resources, low budgets, and modest images go as far as possible. And with little help and meager resources they were far more successful in salvaging and enhancing our cities than the amalgamated efforts of business and government.

The failure of federal programs is obvious. In the 1960s the government recognized that much of the housing in this rich country was

* This is a revised version of a paper presented to the conference on Neighborhood Preservation and Rehabilitation, Charleston, S.C., February 14–15, 1975.

a disgrace. Through generous urban renewal subsidies made available by the National Housing Act new units rose on the ashes of the old for middle- and upper-income people. Unfortunately, few can be considered as humane and vitalizing urban ingredients. Through subsidy programs like 221 (d) (3) and 235–6, the government sought the help of the private and nonprofit sectors in building and rehabilitating housing. Today many of these buildings are economic failures and have reverted back to HUD. Through Title I, HUD backed new towns developed by big business as alternatives to old cities; nearly everyone of these new towns today is bankrupt. Through outright grants to public housing authorities, federal programs built accommodations for low- to moderate-income people from the 1940s through the 1970s. Today these bleak ghettos stand—unless, like Pruitt Igo they have fallen to HUD's bulldozers—as mute testimony to architectural dehumanization and bureaucratic disaster.

Pause, however, to look at the results of the housing efforts of those foolish, ignorant, and impecunious preservationists. Savannah's inner city is beautifully restored; Charleston's downtown neighborhoods reflect elegance almost beyond credibility; Georgetown's restored houses sell for three to six times that of houses in the rest of the District of Columbia; Annapolis has regained her delicate beauty and scale; Galveston is coming back fast; while Providence, Newport, Walker's Point, Lafayette Park, and others can be added to the list.

Allow me to relate Pittsburgh's story. Pittsburgh is a business town. Its highest aesthetic aspiration had been to rid itself of the thick pall of smoke which enveloped it. Preservation would be the apogee of practicality. In the eleven years of its existence, Pittsburgh History and Landmarks Foundation (PHLF) has gained a national reputation for the tough pragmatism of its programs. Its most influential effort has been the Mexican War Streets Restoration.

This modest endeavor changed the thinking of preservationists across the nation. Previously, preservationists had thought only of saving buildings with any available means. In the case of districts with architecturally valuable housing, that generally meant inducing well-to-do people to restore and live in them. Neither the opportunity nor the morality of that procedure seemed to fit the situation in Pittsburgh, and so a new set of goals was delineated, ones now shared by many preservation groups across the nation. The Mexican War Street program was designed to preserve not only the buildings but also the essential human character of the neighborhoods. PHLF wanted to make available a range of housing options.

The Mexican War Streets were laid out in 1848. Each street was named to commemorate a battle or general of the then concluding war with Mexico. The neighborhood began as a middle-income residential district for shop owners, mill managers, and the like. By 1966 it was a racially mixed area that was declining rapidly. All of the housing was scheduled for demolition as part of a grand renewal plan.

PHLF launched an experimental program. It acquired property to establish an anchoring presence for preservation and to restore buildings for rental to people of varying income levels. It used local grant funds, bank mortgages, and the then Section 23 housing subsidies of the National Housing Act. Section 23 allowed PHLF to restore dwelling units and then rent them to low-income families under the auspices of the Pittsburgh Housing Authority.

Today the organization owns forty-seven units in this area of which only five rent at market rates. Twelve are undergoing restoration. Thirty are available to low- to moderate-income families. The program has fulfilled other goals as well. More than fifty slumlord-owned houses have been sold to young persons who are taking up residence and are restoring them; more than sixty long-term residents have also restored their homes. Nearly half the houses in the initial pilot area five blocks long and one block deep are now restored or being restored and the program is spreading into the tougher, poorer reaches of the neighborhood. To date, a PHLF expenditure of $325,000 has resulted in over $2,000,000 worth of private work.

Another of Pittsburgh's experimental programs that is beginning to show useful results is taking place in the black ghetto of Manchester. In 1964 PHLF began to seek a way to restore this area of about 300 houses built between 1870 and 1900. They are richly ornamented with elaborate millwork, stained glass, ornamental plaster, and fine mantels. This area, like the Mexican War Streets, was listed for demolition, which would have resulted in the loss of the finest Victorian residential district in the city. The problem was to find a restoration strategy which would not dislocate the residents.

Together with a new and more sensitive Urban Redevelopment Authority (URA) and the residents themselves, an urban renewal technique was developed that found favor with the federal government as well as the neighborhood residents. The steps were relatively simple. First, PHLF was appointed by URA to describe, evaluate, and categorize as A, B, C, or D the architectural character of all of the buildings. With that information in hand, URA then acquired easements on the facades of those buildings listed as A or B and, if financially possible, C structures as well. With the easement right, URA then restores the exterior of each building under the supervision of PHLF at no cost to the owner. Each owner also receives a work write-up for interior improvements so that the house will meet code standards. A three percent, twelve-year loan and a grant are available to enable the owner to carry out that work. In this way a low-income owner can have a fully restored house at a price he can afford. In addition funds are allocated for major public improvements, for selective demolition, and for subsidizing new housing construction. All told, the program has $28 million in funding.

PHLF launched a third community restoration program in the area known as South Side or Birmingham, a five by twenty-nine block area of small houses built between 1860 and 1890. South Side was the traditional home for blue-collar workers of Central European descent. Not poor by any means, these residents had embarked on their own "renewal" program to stave off invasion by the Urban Redevelopment Authority in the early 1960s. Unfortunately, they opted for abusing the architecture by stripping it down and covering it with metal siding and artificial stone. The program enjoyed popularity, but by 1966 Birmingham was rapidly losing its character.

PHLF feared that the neighborhood was destroying the means of its revitalization. Birmingham was losing its image with young people as a good place to live. Its location was good; its population solid; its housing stock generally sound. Nonetheless, the offspring of the old-time residents were leaving for the suburbs.

PHLF officials felt that restoration of the fine Victorian houses of the community would develop a fresh image based upon the unique architecture, the historical streetscape (herring-bone paving, hitching rings, tiny "ways" between yards and houses), and the excellent location near town and along the Monogahela River. Actually only modest restoration investment was required by PHLF; primarily the program was one of "selling" the community on the idea of restoration so that the residents would spend their money restoring instead of covering the buildings. They were told that in some cases restoration was actually cheaper.

A major blemish in the area was the main shopping street. Running through the center and entire length of the area, Carson Street was lined with Victorian buildings in various states of inappropriate remodeling and decay. It contributed to the public view that Birmingham was slipping, if not sliding, downhill.

By enlisting the support of the Chamber of Commerce and the Community Council, PHLF gathered support for a restoration program. PHLF issued a simplified how-to-restore manual and gave it to every family. A series of exhibits on the environmental quality of the area were held and several properties were acquired and restored as models.

The program is now moving along well. Considerable progress has occurred. PHLF expended approximately $135,000. More than $1,000,000 worth of restoration work by longtime residents and businessmen followed. Twelve new shops and boutiques have opened on Carson Street to occupy the vacant stores which blighted the area. The City is now making available through the Community Development Assistance Act three percent loans to residents and business persons to restore their properties; the Chamber of Commerce and PHLF have each pooled $10,000 in a joint fund to be used to fund design studies and to provide staff to encourage people to take advantage of the city funds and spend them wisely.

Another effort of PHLF is its current neighborhood self-study programs funded by the National Endowment for the Arts and a local foundation. This program grew out of PHLF's concern that neighborhoods always have their planning done for them. This is the case even when community groups participate in the process as in Model Cities because professional planners from outside the area lead the way. The self-study program had as its goal learning to what extent a community can assess its own strengths and weaknesses and then direct a staff to delineate solutions to the problems.

Working with the local community organization in three areas, PHLF called a series of town meetings in which people talked about why they liked the area, why they stayed there, and where they thought it was failing. Volunteers and staff then conducted extensive interviews through the community and tabulated the results of the meetings and interviews so that priorities could be established.

The community then assigned the PHLF staff and consultants as needed to lay out the steps required to alleviate the weaknesses. Specific questions were directed to the outsiders: Can business persons obtain a parking lot? How can residents obtain home improvement loans? Participants then planned and built a public exhibit to explain their findings to all the residents and to public officials. A publication about the community's history and needs was distributed.

Each of the three neighborhoods involved is now completing its program which will establish the work for these community organizations for the next several years. It also provides each with the material it needs to submit to the city recommendations for the expenditure of Community Development Assistance (CDA) funds in their neighborhoods. In this latter respect the program was well-timed because the CDA funds will be available for the next several years and can be used to enable the residents to carry out the programs they have developed.

These programs constitute PHLF's major work in inner city neighborhoods. The organization is at work in many other ways as well. It prepares feasibility studies for preserving major individual buildings; it operates three museums; and it carries out broad-scale educational and publicity programs. However, the neighborhoods require the greatest investment of staff time and resources because of the vast numbers of buildings to be saved and because of the complexity of saving them. Although subsidies are often needed, the group does not lament the loss of the federal categorical subsidy programs because they seldom could be made to work. Section 8 Housing, the only remaining categorical subsidy program, offers promise, and PHLF has prepared and submitted to HUD a scattered site program in the Mexican War Streets and Birmingham areas for use under Section 8.

The new CDA act offers potential in Pittsburgh because the city is making available low-interest loans to businessmen and residents for rehabilitation. Because no design or aesthetic standards are part of this program, PHLF has even worked out a design review process with the city so that the aesthetic and environmental character of buildings and areas might be enhanced.

Anyone interested in improving the physical character of the neighborhoods of the nation would do well to remember that civic pride does not occur only where the walls are sound and the roof is tight. The architectural quality of a building and a neighborhood far transcends solid bricks and mortar; it can infuse residents with a sense of commitment to and pride in their area. Only preservation can bring that dimension to the revitalization of life in inner city America.

CHANGING VIEWS

OF THE REIGN OF TERROR

Robert Forster

About a hundred years ago Thomas Carlyle wrote his famous *History of the French Revolution*, and much of his spirit stays with us still. Near the beginning of his section on the Reign of Terror, he wrote, "Yes, Reader, here is the miracle. Out of that putrescent rubbish of Skepticism, Sensualism, Sentimentalism, hollow Machiavellianism, such a Faith has verily risen; flaming in the heart of a People; a whole People, awakened as it were to consciousness of deep misery, believes that it is within reach of a fraternal Heaven-on-Earth."[1] Here in a nutshell was Carlyle's view of the little people of Paris. Carlyle's "people" were not malicious, but full of illusions and vain hopes, victims of a long century of secularism and false enlightenment. Again, in another section, Carlyle wrote, "For a man once committed headlong to republicanism or any other transcendentalism [and fighting and fantasizing amid a Nation of his like] becomes, as it were, enveloped in an [ambient] atmosphere of transcendentalism and delirium."[2] In short, he implied, ideas lead to madness.

Now let us cross the Channel and examine for a moment another popular historian of the French Revolution. With much the same style of Thomas Carlyle, Jules Michelet could also write about the "people," but in a different way. With little of Carlyle's dogged Calvinism or German romanticism, Michelet wrote with the fervor of a mid-nineteenth century French nationalist. Michelet said of the people: "Today the rise and progress of the people are often compared to the invasion of the barbarians. I like the word, and I accept the term. Barbarians! That is to say, full of new, vital, and regenerating vigor. Barbarians! That is to say, travelers marching toward the future Rome, going on slowly no doubt, each generation advancing a little and then halting in death, but others continue forward all the same. We have, we Barbarians, a natural advantage. If the upper classes have culture, we have much more vital heat."[3]

Whatever can be said against the histories of Michelet and of Carlyle, there is no doubt that they possess something that much of analytic history has lost. They maintain a sense of drama and, above all, a concern for the little person of the street. If it was Carlyle's view of the Revolution, and particularly of the Reign of Terror, that it was God's revenge on a society that had abandoned His Law, or if Michelet had seen the people as the incarnation of all that was good and virtuous in French society, both men, for better or worse, had placed a peculiar stamp upon the history of the French Revolution. They captivated, even mesmerized, the reading public with their dramatic story. Somehow the public would stay with Carlyle and Michelet, while the professional historian, burrowing away in his own specialized research, would lose public interest almost entirely.

There were still others who shaped the popular view. Who would forget the characters of *A Tale of Two Cities* by Charles Dickens? Who would forget the wine-shop of Madame Defarge with her bread knife a foot long, or the rumble of the tumbrils to the Place de la Revolution, or the vision of the women of Paris chatting and knitting as they heard the knife strike the block.[4] Here in the history of Carlyle or in the novel of Charles Dickens was history at its most dramatic— violence, mass executions, the epitome of human tragedy.

But was it history? Other novelists as well as popular historians have used the French Revolution to raise exciting issues of political philosophy and even "social psychology." In the novel of Anatole France, *The Gods are Athirst*, we see the tragic figure of Everest Gamelin, a convinced Jacobin, propelled by an idea that leads to self-doubt and eventually self-destruction. The purge, the eradication of the last enemy plot, the elimination of the last opponent of the republic, cleansing the body politic—it is all here displayed in dramatic form.[5] And what a setting for the tragic conflict of principle and friendship, of the titanic battle between two men, Robespierre and Danton—one the incarnation of uncompromising principle and the other, the more easygoing way of opportunism and compromise. Put another way, the novelist contrasts Maximilien Robespierre the incorruptible, the puritan, the purifier, and Georges Danton, the organizer, the orator, the breezy, lustful lover of this life. What better setting to discuss the age-old problem of the efficacy of radical reform and revolutionary change! The issue was later drawn in Peter Weiss's famous play, *Marat-Sade.*[6] Here the Marquis de Sade gives the classic arguments against revolutionary change. He argues that the unbounded expectations of ordinary people can never be fulfilled; only disillusionment and suffering must follow. For those who see in Marat the hero of the play, he is nonetheless a tragic hero for the chorus continues to cry, "Marat, we are poor. And the poor stay poor. Don't make us wait anymore. We want our rights and we don't care how. We want our revolution now." But the "Herald" has the last word: "The revolution came and went, and unrest was replaced by discontent." No doubt the Reign of Terror is a mine of the great themes of literature and drama, used and misused again and again.

But what was the Reign of Terror really? Can the historians clear away the veil of passion and drama and see the events in better perspective? We are told historians are equipped for this. They are presumably prepared by years of professional training to stand apart from current events about them, to be free from anachronism, free from political bias, free from temperamental inclination, free from stylistic popularization, and free from emotional commitment. Surely historians should be able to tell us just what happened and why. However, as we all know, such a dispassionate reconstruction of historical events is not possible. Historians have not been unbiased, uncommitted, or untouched by the world about them. Each has seen the Terror of 1793–94 in his own way. Often unconsciously, they have tied it to their own politics, to their own life style, to their own personal historical philosophy, leading them to look upon this history in a certain way.

Alphonse Aulard said: "Go to the sources, say nothing that is not supported by the sources, and footnote everything." But such an austere professional code is not enough in the face of such a momentous year in the history of Western Civilization. The very drama, scope, and, above all, obscurity of the Reign of Terror too readily serves current "causes" and present problems. History can be therapeutic, a bag of tricks, a source of legal precedents for any argument. The fact of the matter is the historian, like any human being, must tangle with many preoccupations, public and private, political and psychological, professional and temperamental. He or she is seldom neutral or uncommitted. My purpose is to show how and why historians have changed their views about this year in history and, what the Terror now means to us in 1976. And if in the end we seem no closer to the truth today than Carlyle was in 1837, then perhaps at least we have learned something about how historians go about their trade, how approaches to a subject can change (and perhaps improve) and how the multifaceted prism of history can be viewed again and again over time, hopefully, in sharper focus and understanding. For some of us it can be said more simply: What new secrets and surprises does *Clio*, the muse of history, have in store?

First, let us clear away a few stubborn myths and misconceptions about the Reign of Terror. The Reign of Terror represents only one year in a decade of revolution. It is the year from June 1793 to July 1794. For many historians, this is not the most important year of the French Revolution. For many, the years from 1789 to 1791 fixed the most permanent institutional features on a new France, and those from 1799 to 1801 modified, but did not destroy the foundation built a decade earlier. The attraction of the years, 1793–94, which we call the Reign of Terror, lies in the fact that it was the most violent period, the one which raised the greatest hopes and the greatest fears of what revolution might become.

By the end of 1792, the French Revolution had been in progress three years. Unlike the republican experiment in America, the French Republic was unable to develop in isolation. It had real and present enemies. No understanding of the Reign of Terror is possible without full recognition of the enemies threatening the new Republic from without and within. By the beginning of 1793, France was at war with every major power of Europe including England, Holland, Spain, Prussia, and Austria. The enemy was indeed at the gates. Nor was the "enemy from within" a figment of the imagination of the republicans. The *emigrés*, those who had left France to seek foreign allies, had friends everywhere; not only most "aristocrats" but half of the clergy of France were opposed to the new republic. The loss of this clerical support meant that many peasant villages followed their priests into passive if not active opposition to the new regime. But by early 1793 there were fresh reasons for alarm. Robert Palmer in his book, *Twelve Who Ruled*, captures these tensions succinctly: "War, inflation, hunger, fear, hate, sabotage, fantastic hopes, boundless idealism, and the horrible knowledge for the men in power that if they failed they would die as criminals, murderers of their king, and the dread that all the gains of the Revolution would be lost, and the faith that if they won, they would bring Liberty, Equality, and Fraternity into the world."[7]

But let there be no mistake about it. This was a dictatorship, a dictatorship of a committee of twelve to be sure, but a dictatorship nonetheless. And in the course of the year that followed, this dictatorship tried and executed some 40,000 French citizens for what it termed "treason." There is also no doubt (even among the most diverse historians) that as the Terror progressed, "due process under law" disappeared from the courts of France. This is not to say that all of the 40,000 were unjustly condemned to death. Indeed, over half of the 40,000 were captured with guns in their hands fighting against the new republic. But it is to say that "trial by jury," the cross-examination of witnesses, and all that comes under the term "due process of law" disappeared by the spring of 1794. Under the new, harsh "law of suspects" people could be tried for mere suspicion of insufficient loyalty to the state. The guillotine, that new efficient method of execution, was established in every important square in every provincial capital of France, as well as in the most prominent quarters of Paris. Its purpose was preventive as well as retributive; that is, it was to deter enemies of the republic and encourage its friends. Requiring from each "citizen" certificates of residence, certificates of civicism, and an increasingly harsh civic conformism, the Reign of Terror was indeed a regime of fear. Modern historians, whether on the political left or right or in the center, do not deny the dictatorial aspects of this regime. Where they differ is over the causes and justification for this year of dictatorship and what the Terror meant for the future of French and even Western history.

* * *

Now let us change the focus of this paper for a moment from the year of the Terror in the French Revolution to some very important political events in France almost one hundred years later. In 1871 France underwent its fourth major revolution since the great Revolution of 1789. Out of that revolution and the Commune that followed, there issued slowly and painfully, but ultimately successfully, the Third French Republic. After many years of struggle and doubt, it was not to be a republic born of high idealism, but, as the French would say, *faute de mieux*, "the government that divides us least." The Third Republic was not a "social republic." It was not a regime concerned about the urban or rural poor or with social legislation for the new working classes. It was nonetheless a parliamentary regime concerned with the defense of civil rights and with the defense of small as well as large property. It was in many ways a negative regime, anticlerical, antiauthoritarian, and antibigness.

In these political circumstances, one of France's most famous historians, Alphonse Aulard, was raised and wrote his history. His work has become one of the great milestones in the writing of the history of the French Revolution. Aulard's family came from what we would call the middle class. His father was an inspector of secondary education, a high school supervisor. Having a strong respect for education, he saw to it that his son received a good university education—no doubt at some family sacrifice. Aulard was an able student and became a well-known professor, not only of history but of literature as well.

Alphonse Aulard was, in nineteenth-century terms, a political liberal. He believed in freedom of speech and press, constitutional government—the liberalism of John Stuart Mill; he believed in the Third

Republic, and there seems little doubt that he did what he could in his own professional career to make that Third Republic a viable regime. In part, his interest in the French Revolution was conditioned by his desire to give the Third Republic a parliamentary tradition. At the same time he was a good nationalist and hoped to find in his history of the French Revolution a kind of therapeutic nationalism and public spirit that he felt was lagging in the France of his own day. Finally, Aulard stood in that tradition which regarded history as the highest of human culture, the foundation of political science, and, above all, the basis for what nineteenth-century optimists called "progress."

But it would be false to say that a man like Aulard used history simply to bolster a sagging national ego and to create a parliamentary tradition. Aulard was also working in Paris at a time when methods of history were changing and sources of history becoming better organized at the national archives and libraries of Paris. Aulard himself contributed to this change of method as well as to the editing of fresh new sources of the French Revolution. Hence, Aulard must not be regarded as a man concerned with indoctrination. Here again we see the historian as a political man and, at the same time, a man trained to be careful about his generalizations and careful not to misuse history. Aulard's training had made him aware of changes in evaluation of scholarship, of the evolution of all the "sciences," and of the transitory character of facts and ideas. As he said himself, "The definitive of today is the provisional of tomorrow."

It is not irrelevant also to recall that Aulard was a great teacher. For him the good life intellectually resided not in the retention of details but in the power of analysis and in what he called the *esprit de finesse*. He never called down a student for not knowing a thing or a fact. As he said, "If he does not know it, it's perhaps because he has a bad memory and maybe that he had not time to learn it. There are so many things to learn." There was in Aulard, more than in most teachers, an intellectual compassion, a generosity of attitude. Nonetheless, he was demanding, for he insisted that history must be an analysis and not simply a good story, and that facts alone were not enough. As he said time and time again, "Estimate the value of a historical fact in terms of its degree of influence upon the evolution of an individual, a group, or society that is being studied." All facts are not of equal interest, and the historian must decide which are relevant and important and which are not.

Despite his stern code of professionalism, Aulard believed that the Revolution must be treated with sympathy. He said himself, "He who does not sympathize with the Revolution sees only the surface. In order to understand it, it is necessary to love it." In 1901 Aulard published his well-known *Political History of the French Revolution*.[8] As the title suggested, it was intended to treat the political aspects only. Like so many historians, he said quite frankly, "I cannot do everything. I cannot know all of the essential sources. The sources of economic and social history of the Revolution are dispersed and difficult to get together. I shall concentrate on the political sources, the speeches, the reports, the newspapers, the parliamentary debates composed by the Revolutionists themselves." His history turned out to be what the English called Whig history, the history of political progress toward republic and democracy where political institutions and political leadership weigh most heavily.

What, in brief, did Aulard say about the Reign of Terror? First of all, he was not happy about the Terror and did not consider it the essential message of the French Revolution. He admitted begrudgingly that the Terror was necessary, but certainly the figure of Robespierre was abhorrent to him. Why was the Terror necessary? Circumstances of foreign and internal war made it necessary. The Prussian invasions of 1792, the revolt in the provinces of 1793, and the treason of some of its most important generals made it necessary for the Republic to centralize its power in Paris and establish a dictatorial committee. In short, his was the "thesis of circumstances." Circumstances made the Terror necessary. Fortunately, it did not last long and the Revolution could get back "on the track," so to speak, toward liberal development which was very much Aulard's own political preference. Perhaps Aulard was too anxious to forget, if not ignore, the unsavory aspects of the Reign of Terror. His knowledge of everyday life among the lower classes of Paris was minimal. Furthermore, he edited mountains of documents, official documents, and acts of the Committee of Public Safety and other revolutionary committees, and it may well be that in reading over these official acts he became more impressed by national issues and running a war than by everyday local conditions and the lot of the Parisian populace. I am not trying to damn Aulard with faint praise. He was, after all, the greatest French historian of the French Revolution in the first decades of this century. But in retrospect, because of his politics and his scholarly choices, his work lacked a social dimension and his interpretation of the Reign of Terror suffered from this deficiency.[9]

* * *

Now let us turn to one of Aulard's most able pupils, Albert Mathiez. For like Aulard in the first decade of the twentieth century, Mathiez was to become perhaps the most important French historian of the Revolution in the 1920s. No two more different men could be imagined than Aulard and Mathiez. The differences range from their social origins to their professional careers, from their temperaments to their political philosophies. Mathiez was raised in a poor peasant family in Upper Savoy, and there was something about Mathiez that always reminded one of his rural, peasant origins. Mathiez made his way up the hard way; by scholarships, by dogged work, he made his way up the slow ladder of provincial universities. But it was a long time before he ever could get close to the capital—and Paris, for the historian of France, is the Mecca of the sources of French history, especially of the French Revolution. Moreover, Mathiez never obtained the famous "chair" in the French Revolution at the Sorbonne, the honor so coveted by historians of the Revolution.

It can be understood, therefore, why Mathiez was a somewhat difficult person. Frustrations, both social and professional, probably made him personally "difficult" and very dogmatic on certain issues. He revolted against his teacher, Aulard, and later became a rather dominating master of students. Unlike Aulard, whose compassion and understanding of students was legend, Mathiez drove his pupils, making them more disciples than comrades in research. Part of the revolt of Mathiez against his professor stemmed from domestic politics and the regulated economy during World War I. Mathiez regarded Aulard's "liberal" philosophy as superficial and even fraudulent. He identified Aulard with the Third Republic and its incapacity or un-willingness to provide social legislation for the working classes. He was still young at the time of the Russian Revolution in 1917 and, as many of his generation, he found an inspiration in that Revolution. Mathiez died before the infamous Stalin purges of the 1930s, so that Russia's revolution still held promise in his lifetime for many intellectuals like himself.

Given all of these influences, Mathiez was a different historian. Of course, he subscribed to the same professional code as his professor. He compiled and edited new collections of documents. He observed the rules of evidence. His history is still professional history, but it is marked by a different interpretation of the French Revolution and the Reign of Terror. Unlike Aulard who saw the Terror as an unfortunate aberration, Mathiez saw the Terror as the very center of the Revo-lution. For him the Terror was much more than a dictatorship ne-cessitated by the circumstances of war. To Mathiez, the Terror, particularly in its last stages, was an effort to redistribute wealth to the poorer classes of French society. There was no doubt that Mathiez saw the Revolution as an example of class struggle. He wrote about his own work, "In the early period of my studies the idea of associating the historical movement with the 'class struggle' was not a dominant conception to which I subordinated other explanations, but already the social conflict was attracting me. . . . If I had the time and the space I would explain why history such as Aulard understood it is a polemical history for the profit of a 'party' and why little by little I freed myself from his influence to arrive at a more 'objective' view of things. . . . Thus I rejected the Republican defense politics of Aulard and his [political] friends, who did not wish to draw attention to the conservative role of the bourgeoisie, [and reveal] the misery of the people who were duped [by the conservative middle class]." Yet the Marxism of Mathiez was not a straightjacket for his work. No doubt such phrases as the "premature dictatorship of the proletariat" and his enormous effort to make Robespierre into the hero of the Reign of Terror leave many of us unsatisfied. On the other hand, Mathiez looked at the Terror from below for the first time. He drew attention to social aspects of the Revolution that had not been studied seriously before. He recognized that there was a political pressure group in Paris known as the *sans culottes* who, whether a "premature proletariat" or not, were nonetheless an important political force shaping the events of 1793 and 1794.

In the eyes of Mathiez, Robespierre had recognized the plight of the poor of Paris. Robespierre and the Committee of Public Safety had understood that the policies of free trade were the policies of the "proprietary class." Price control, the efforts to redistribute the property of the "suspects" among the poor, the first social insurance program, and even proposals for universal, free public education were much more than the expedients of wartime. This was the beginning of a "social republic." For Mathiez, all of this would be lost by the reaction of Thermidor (July, 1794). The "property-conscious bourgeoisie" would regain the reins of power and cancel all price controls and social legislation. The consumer, especially the near-subsistence consumer, would be sacrificed on the altar of "Free Trade" and profit. Now this is quite a different picture than the Thermidorian reaction of Aulard, for whom it was a welcome relief from an oppressive dictatorship.

Running through Mathiez's interpretation of the Reign of Terror is not so much the cadence of Karl Marx as a peculiar view of popular democracy, sometimes merging into an almost semi-mystical or romantic "collective will." Furthermore, Mathiez saw something more in the religious cults of the Reign of Terror than crass expediency. He saw in them a kind of substitute religion in which Robespierre himself played a singular role, a deeply felt civic religion—with its own liturgy, saints, and moral rules. Mathiez, it seems, was more influenced by the democratic mysticism of Michelet than by the class war of Karl Marx. But whatever his limitations as a "scientific" historian, Mathiez had turned scholarly attention toward a new stratum in French society, the "little people" of Parisian society.[10]

* * *

For over twenty years after the death of Mathiez in 1932, his views on the Reign of Terror tended to predominate among liberal as well as socialist historians of the Reign of Terror. Details and emphases might vary, but the role of the "little people" in Paris, the *sans-culottes*, and their identification with the Jacobin Party and its leader, Citizen Robespierre, was the accepted truth about the Reign of Terror. But unfortunately, the *sans-culottes*, presumably the "common people" of the street, still remained a vague, omnibus "mass." It was a social group sometimes seen as a proletariat, sometimes as a "pre-proletariat"; at other times it was the poor of Paris, or it was simply labeled "Jacobin." Although attention was now more centered on the city of Paris and on domestic issues, historians still concentrated on "official history," that is, the legislation—laws, debates, speeches, and committee work of the National Parliament. But now they included such issues as price control, rationing, social security programs, and efforts at public education—all of which seemed to demonstrate the social consciousness of the Jacobin Party and of its leader, Maximilien Robespierre. It would seem that for many historians in these years both before and after World War II, Robespierre had become a benefactor of the poor of Paris—hero of the downtrodden—and, for some historians, the first leader of an urban proletariat. Postwar Eastern European scholars suddenly found him interesting. His speeches and writings found publishers in such unlikely places as East Berlin. In 1958 there was even a historical conference celebrating the 200th anniversary of the birth of Citizen Robespierre. Not every historian attended—many could not quite forget the guillotine and 40,000 executions—but it was a sign of the times in French historiography and in international politics.

Then in the late 1950s another shift occurred in the historiography of the Reign of Terror. A group of historians who had been busily burrowing into the police records of the French archives began to delineate more clearly the actual profile of the *sans-culottes* of the streets of Paris in 1793–94. There is no doubt that this group of historians had a cohesion that did not spring entirely from its common interest in "history from below." There seems little doubt that the Cold War, which was blowing "hot" in the early 1950s (Korea), was not irrelevant to the views of this new "school" of French history. At its worst, international historical conferences representing this school had an unfortunate way of referring to American scholars (among others) as "bourgeois imperialists," unworthy to be social historians of the Reign of Terror. We were too biased against the "proletariat" and against a "social" or "peoples' democracy." Despite this unfortunate dogmatism, the new "school" made a real contribution to the history of the Reign of Terror, not by its obvious ideological preferences, but by its assiduous work in turning up new sources of French history. The most important member of this new school is Albert Soboul. It was Soboul who moved beyond the official parliamentary record that even Mathiez had not really abandoned, and made his way into the police files and, above all, into the section meetings (the 48 subdivisions or wards of Paris) bringing the *sans-culottes* to life for the first time.

What were they really like? First, *sans-culotte* simply means "without knee-breeches." As Robert Palmer has commented, it is not that they *rejected* them; they simply had none. The long trousers were the badge of a certain income level, a certain standing of people normally confined to manual work and limited education. The *sans-culottes* in 1793 represented perhaps 100,000 individuals in a Parisian population of about 600,000. They were concentrated in the eastern quarters of Paris, particularly in the famous Faubourg St. Antoine, the location of the infamous Bastille prison. The *sans-culottes* were not the dregs of society, the vagabonds, and beggars of a floating population. On the contrary, they were almost all residents of their wards and more than three-fourths of them were shopkeepers and artisans who owned some property, or at least the tools with which they worked. Only about one-fourth were wage-earners in the modern sense of the word. This was the first surprise for historians who were looking very hard for an "urban proletariat." The *sans-culottes* were made up of all kinds of people, including shopkeepers, small merchants, artisans, porters, water-carriers, domestic servants, café waiters, wig-makers—working people, but not Marxist "workers." But the term *sans-culottes* also denoted a people in a very special state of political action and excitement. This *political* state captures the principal characteristics of this group during the Reign of Terror. Not that these people were unconcerned with such economic issues as the price of bread and cost of living, but their economic interests and their levels of income were surely less important to them than their political aspirations and desire for social esteem.

The Revolution had opened new opportunity and new expectancies for these people. They had been active in the famous "days" of the Revolution. The storming of the Bastille in 1789, the storming of the royal palace in 1792, and the manifestation of force in June 1793 had given the *sans-culottes* a sense of political importance. They took equality seriously. They no longer accepted a subordinate position in social relations. They could not bear arrogance or disdain, and they did not like so-called "cultured speech." They had a distinct dislike for anything that smacked of "aristocracy." They made a virtue of their long trousers. They wore a red cap which symbolized their belief in social equality and republicanism. They carried a pike, which was not so much a weapon as a symbol of republican belief. In their every-day speech they preferred to address each other as *tu* rather than *vous*, a familiar form as if they were all school friends or brothers and sisters. They loved to go out on the *grands boulevards* where they had never dared to show their faces before the Revolution and have a good Sunday walk. They enjoyed a new-found sense of pride and dignity. They were "somebody."

Their economic ideas were rather undeveloped. They took a very negative view toward wealth, especially concentrated commercial wealth. They hated speculators of all kinds and especially speculators in food supplies. But they did not object to private property providing it was fairly equally distributed. They placed a high value on work with one's hands and on the skills of the artisan. It must not be thought that they did not believe in the work-ethic. They were probably just as distrustful of the beggar as they were of the "idle aristocrat." In some ways their beliefs resembled the Jeffersonian ideal, each man his plot of ground, his workbench, and each man his independence and dignity. But unlike Jefferson's rural democracy, theirs was an urban setting. They favored small properties, small business, small employers, small workshops. Some have called their ideal the paradise of the green-grocer. They were anticapitalists in the sense that they were afraid of bigness and especially of the world of finance, which they only dimly understood. But their anticapitalism did not spring from the consciousness of being proletarians (or wage-slaves) in the Marxist sense. On the contrary, it could be said that they had such a great respect for private property that they believed that everyone should have some, but not too much. And their whole view of property and of capital had nothing to do with production—their view was actually an obstacle to economic growth—but everything to do with notions of social and political equality.

The political views of the *sans-culottes* amounted to direct democracy. They took the notion of political participation very seriously indeed. Here was a group of hard-working shopkeepers and artisans who were willing to spend five or six evenings a week after work at political meetings. Their active political participation was as high as 20 percent (average 10 percent) and was sustained throughout almost a full year of the Revolution. Even by modern standards such political participation is extraordinary! In addition to their regular political meetings, they were willing to do committee work, to serve in vigilante committees against "suspects," to regulate the price of bread, to prevent hoarding, and to aid the war effort. They publicly chastized and ridiculed "shirkers" and maintained an intense patriotism. Furthermore, they were prepared to march in the streets to make their views known in times of political crisis. No doubt scarcity of food affected their political activity, making them particularly prone to panic and fear as well as to high expectations. However, it would be wrong to see them as a fundamentally violent group. If they were rough people without much education, their violence, when it did occur, was not indiscriminate. They were genuinely afraid of a counter-revolution and this fear was not unfounded. Remember this was war-time, and there were enemies from within as well as from without. In 1793 it was not at all clear who would win—and to lose would mean a return to kings, bishops, and nobles—to privileges, inequalities, and social distinctions. Their attitude toward public execution by the guillotine may shock us today, but for them it was the popular "ax" which was to bring fear into the hearts of the counterrevolutionaries. And for some it was even considered the "scythe of equality" which would force the grain-hoarders and speculators to bring bread on the market.

Now what was the relationship between this group of *sans-culottes* and the Jacobin Party? The interpretation of Mathiez no longer applied, for Soboul and his school had discovered that the interests and goals of the *sans-culottes* and those of the new Jacobin establishment were not the same. After Robespierre and his group of lawyers and politicians had seized power, they saw no more need for street agitation. Robespierre on numerous occasions thought it incomprehensible that there should be disorder once he, the leader of the people of Paris, had gained executive power. But Robespierre and the Jacobin Party recognized that they had a constituency and they made an effort to deal with this important pressure group. Hence they proposed legislation which would control bread prices and distribute the land of the "suspects" as part of a program to respond to the demands of the *sans-culottes*. The point is that the *sans-culottes* movement was an independent one—separate from the Jacobin clubs—and that it soon became disillusioned with Robespierre's program. First, the demands of *sans-culottes* for a system of free public education were not fulfilled by the government of Maximilien Robespierre. In fact, it seems that the Jacobin government was not even interested in providing buildings for such schools. Moreover, the Jacobin government found it more practical to deal with large war contractors rather than respond to the *sans-culottes'* demands for small industrial shops. The Jacobins seemed to favor "bigness" in organizing the war effort. More decisive, the Jacobin government did not find it "convenient" to have the *sans-culottes* meeting every day of the week, petitioning and hounding the government for new legislation, and generally maintaining high political tensions in the east side of Paris. They saw this activity as unnecessary agitation and troublemaking. It is an interesting reflection of the determined political activism of the *sans-culottes* that, when the Robespierre government permitted no more than one meeting per week, the *sans-culottes* designed special political clubs of their own and continued to meet every day of the week. But the main point is that the Jacobin government attempted to depoliticize and "manage" the *sans-culottes* movement. It aroused suspicion further by drafting the younger street leaders into the army. As the year 1793–94 advanced, the *sans-culottes* became disenchanted with their Jacobin leadership and in the summer of 1794 failed to support Robespierre when he needed them.

Robespierre emerges from Soboul's research as an "establishment petit-bourgeois." Fallen from his role as a leader of an emerging Parisian proletariat, Robespierre now becomes the enemy of that emerging class—retrograde—fighting against the "wheel of history." Yet Soboul has been careful and thorough about his research, so that despite his own political leanings and his avowed Marxist history, it is quite clear that this is not a proletariat in any Marxist sense at all. That is why Soboul himself refuses to call the *sans-culottes* a "class." But it is quite clear from the facts of the case that though this is no Marxist class it is nonetheless a social group marked off from its social superiors by differences of dress, manners, mode of speech, eating and drinking habits, amusements, living quarters, lack of servants, availability of leisure, degree of schooling and a whole cluster of habits, attitudes, and what we call, generally, a style of life. What Soboul has done, perhaps inadvertently, is to expose a whole layer of society in all its diversity and to present the facts that belie his own theory of history. Fortunately, the Marxist framework and conclusions of Soboul's work can be easily removed from the body of his research. The result is a splendid exposure of the *sans-culottes* as they really lived and functioned in that year of the Reign of Terror.[11]

* * *

And so the Reign of Terror has returned again to the people. Indeed, it was much more than a government that responded to the immediate circumstances of external war and internal threat. The Jacobin government was constantly under political pressure from the *sans-culottes* of Paris. The Jacobin Party responded by attempting to control this political constituency and ended by losing its sympathy and support. This gives us a somewhat different picture of Maximilien Robespierre and the Jacobin dictatorship. Where he has been seen in literature as the mad dictator, or by the school of Aulard as a man suffering from a species of paranoia, or by Mathiez as the hero of the proletariat, he has now become something of a ward politician with all the problems that such men have in maintaining the loyalty of their constituency. At the same time, he was forced to become a war leader and to depend upon other elements of society to pursue that titanic struggle. No doubt,

Robespierre did show signs of what modern psychiatrists call "paranoia," though some historians like Robert Palmer would label it extreme nervous fatigue. All of this is not to excuse the acts of Robespierre, particularly in the last months of the Terror, but it is to reduce him to more human proportions and make him and the Jacobin Party more understandable.

Another benefit of the kind of research pursued by historians such as Soboul and many others in England and the United States as well as in France has been to reemphasize historical complexity and capture the human responses of a layer of society once considered anonymous and mute. Studies have been made by other historians about individual *sans-culottes* leaders such as Jacques Roux (the defrocked priest) and Jean Santerre (the brewer), back-street leaders, and of other lesser men who would never have seen the light of history were it not for this kind of painstaking local research.[12]

In a strange sort of way we are back again with Jules Michelet and even Charles Dickens. But instead of seeing an amorphous mass called the "People," we now discern human beings in all of their colorful individuality—groping, feeling, striving, blundering, and trying again. For although there was much more to the French Revolution than the *sans-culottes*, they still remain central to our understanding of the Reign of Terror. And the *sans-culottes* emerge no longer as the dregs of society manipulated by "outside agitators," or the repository of all that was virtuous in the French Revolution, but rather as very ordinary human beings who for a moment in history had political importance. A contemporary professional soldier had this to say about them:

> The *sans-culotte* is a man who always goes on foot and who lives simply, with his wife and children . . . on the fourth or fifth story. The *sans-culotte* is useful. He knows how to plow a field, how to hammer, and saw, how to cover a roof, make a pair of shoes. And since he works, you are sure not to find him at the café. . . . In the evening, he goes to the meeting of his Section, not powdered, not scented, not booted in the hope of being noticed by all citizenesses in the galleries, but in order to support to the utmost the right sort of resolutions.[13]

This is an idealized portrait no doubt, but an enormous improvement over Carlyle's "monstrous mob."

Having come full circle from Carlyle, Dickens, and Michelet to Albert Soboul and a new school of historians "from below," is this the final cycle of interpretations of the Reign of Terror? The history of this controversy should make us doubt it. My point is simply to demonstrate that the "influences" that play on historians, ranging from their personalities and times to their political philosophy and theories of historical change, can lead to radically different interpretations of a historical period or event. Yet this is not necessarily an obstacle to valid, meaningful history. For if the code of the historian is observed, a code demanding respect for the sources, an honest, complete reporting of the facts, and adherence to the "rules of evidence," *Clio*, the muse of history, will not be violated. In fact, the "outside influences" may be a blessing in disguise.

NOTES

[1] Thomas Carlyle, *The French Revolution, A History*, 3 vols. (London, 1870–71) Book III, ch. I, p. 150.

[2] Ibid., p. 153.

[3] Jules Michelet, *The People*, Translated with an introduction by John P. McKay (Urbana, Ill., 1973), p. 18.

[4] Charles Dickens, *A Tale of Two Cities*, Works of Charles Dickens vols. 50–51 (New York, 1872–73).

[5] Anatole France, *The Gods Are Athirst*, tr. by Mrs. Wilfrid Jackson (New York, 1928).

[6] Peter Weiss, *The Persecution and Assassination of Jean Paul Marat As Performed by the Inmates of the Asylum of Charenton under the Direction of the Marquis de Sade*. English version by Geoffrey Skelton, verse adaptation by Adrian Mitchel (New York, 1966).

[7] Robert R. Palmer, *The Twelve Who Ruled; The Year of the Terror in the French Revolution* (Princeton, 1941), p. 5.

[8] Alphonse Aulard, *The French Revolution, A Political History, 1789–1804.* 4 Vols. Tr. by Bernard Miall (New York, 1910).

[9] J. L. Godfrey, "Alphonse Aulard," in Bernadotte E. Schmitt, ed., *Some Historians of Modern Europe, Essays in Historiography by Former Students of the Department of History at the University of Chicago.* (Chicago, 1942). I am heavily indebted to this excellent article, as well as to the bibliography in the footnotes.

[10] Albert Mathiez, *The French Revolution*, tr. by Catherine Alison Philips (New York, 1928); Frances Acomb, "Albert Mathiez," in Bernadotte Schmidt, ed., *Some Historians of Modern Europe*. See also James Friguletti, *Albert Mathiez* (Paris, 1975).

[11] Robert R. Palmer, "Popular Democracy in the French Revolution," *French Historical Studies*, vol. I, no. 4 (1958) pp. 445–69; Albert Soboul, *The Parisian Sans-Culottes and the French Revolution, 1793–1794*. Tr. by Gwynne Lewis (Oxford, 1964).

[12] See as one example, Richard M. Andrews, "Justices of the Peace of Revolutionary Paris, September 1792–November 1794 (Frimaire, Year III)", *Past and Present*, No. 52 (1971): 56–105.

[13] Richard Cobb, *A Second Identity, Essays on France and French History* (London, 1969) p. 108.

A BIBLIOGRAPHICAL NOTE ON "HISTORY FROM BELOW" IN MODERN FRENCH HISTORY   The best treatment of the "Reign of Terror" in English is by Robert R. Palmer. His *Twelve Who Ruled* (Princeton, 1941) has withstood the test of time remarkably well. See also his *Age of Democratic Revolution* (Princeton, 1959, 1964) for the broader context of the events in Paris from 1793 to 1794. Another interpretation of the Terror can be found in Crane Brinton, *A Decade of Revolution* (New York, 1934). See especially Brinton's short bibliographical essay on Aulard and Mathiez. For specialized aspects of the Terror and the entire revolutionary period, see the French journal, *Annales historiques de la Révolution française*. The most complete one-volume bibliography of the decade of the French Revolution is Jacques Godechot, *Les Revolutions, 1770–1799* "Nouvelle Clio" (Paris, 1963). Very useful as a manual and a bibliographical guide is the most recent edition of Leo Gershoy, *The French Revolution and Napoleon* (New York, 1964).

Robert Palmer in his review article, "Popular Democracy in the French Revolution," *French Historical Studies* vol. I, No. 4 (1958), 445–69, presents an excellent summary of the work of Albert Soboul and his "school" on the *sans-culottes* of Paris. The works of this "school" include Albert Soboul, *The Parisian Sans-Culottes and the French Revolution, 1793–1794*. Tr. by Gwynne Lewis (Oxford, 1964), an abridgment of Soboul's thesis first published in 1958; George Rudé, *The Crowd in the French Revolution* (Oxford,

1959) and *Paris and London in the Eighteenth Century* (New York, 1971); Käre D. Tonnesson, *La Défaite des sans-culottes* (Oslo, 1959); Walter Markov, ed., *Jacobiner und Sans-Culottes* (Berlin, 1956). This "school" regards itself as "Marxist," but its interpretation of the *sans-culottes* is not an orthodox Marxist interpretation. They have been characterized as "more Marxist than Marx," but this is hardly the first time the disciples have misunderstood the master.

"History From Below" has not been limited, of course, to studies of Paris during the French Revolution, although it is not surprising that historians with socialist sympathies have been attracted to it. But the main thrust of French historiography, especially since World War II, has been toward preindustrial European history and over very long periods of time—several centuries. Rural society has been the focus of many detailed monographic studies by members of the now well-known "Annales School." Although urban history has not been totally absent from this research, it has played a lesser role until quite recently. That is one reason why North American and English historians of France have had a special contribution to make here.

Jeffry Kaplow's two books are efforts to recapture the daily existence and "mentality" of the laboring poor in two urban centers. *Elbeuf During the Revolutionary Period* (Baltimore, 1964) and *The Names of Kings: The Parisian Laboring Poor in the Eighteenth Century* (New York, 1972), if "Marxist" in inspiration, are not simplistic studies of the "class war," nor abstract arguments about the "relations of production." Real people emerge. Of broader scope is Olwen Hufton, *The Poor of Eighteenth-Century France* (Oxford, 1974), a superb piece of descriptive social history, gripping without becoming sentimental. Richard Cobb has written four books in English on the "little people" in both urban and rural settings. They are *The Police and the People* (Oxford, 1970); *Problems of French Popular History, 1789–1820* (Oxford, 1969); *Reactions to the French Revolution* (Oxford, 1972); *Paris and the Provinces, 1792–1802* (Oxford, 1975). Whatever Cobb's books may lack in synthetic quality, they make up for in their unique grasp of the personal and the concrete historical situation.

Although urban history is still a comparatively new field of research in France, four pioneering works deserve special mention. Two are studies of provincial cities before the Revolution of 1789: Pierre Deyon, *Amiens capitale provinciale: Étude sur la société urbaine au XVIIe siècle* (Paris, 1967) and Maurice Garden, *Lyon et les Lyonnais au XVIIIe siècle* (Paris, n.d.). Two others focus on Paris in the nineteenth century: Louis Chevalier, *Classes laborieuses et classes dangereuses à Paris pendant la première moitié du XIXe siècle* (Paris, 1958) and Adeline Daumard, *Les Bourgeois de Paris au XIXe siècle* (Paris: Flammarion, 1970) to which should be added Daumard's collaborative study of four French cities, *Les Fortunes françaises au XIXe siècle* (Paris, 1973). Insofar as studies of social groups have been placed in urban settings, urban history has not been neglected in France. Histories of the mercantile communities of Nantes by Jean Meyer, of Marseilles by Charles Carrière, and of Bordeaux by Francois Crouzet have informed us a great deal about the social and economic life of these port cities. Finally, Phillipe Wolff, medievalist at the University of Toulouse, is editing an important series of general histories of French cities from their Gallo-Roman origins to the present. They serve to remind North American historians especially how much of the history of European cities is preindustrial—even pre-Renaissance—yet as complex and dynamic as a nineteenth-century metropolis. Urban history is not to be identified with industrialization, however important their interrelationship is today.

In the urban history of post-revolutionary France, North American historians are making important contributions, approaching the urban milieu partly from an interest in labor history, long burdened with political and ideological polemics among those French historians who have written about it. Americans also bring a bag of sociological "tools" and an interdisciplinary awareness that their French colleagues sometimes lack. The following books are samples of what we can expect in the years to come: Robert J. Bezucha, *The Lyon Uprising of 1834* (Cambridge, Mass., 1974); Joan W.

Scott, *The Glassmakers of Carmaux* (Cambridge, Mass., 1974); Charles Tilly, Louise Tilly, Richard Tilly, *The Rebellious Century, 1830–1930* (Cambridge, Mass., 1975).

Urban-labor history today is much more than a study of labor organization and a review of the "standard of living" question. It embraces "popular culture" in the broadest sense, touching folklore, low-life literature, the popular press, demography, the family, rural-urban migration, "work," "leisure," diet, deviance, crime, prostitution, public health, education, city planning, and "utopian protest" from the quasi-mystical to the rational. French urban history is at long last coming into its own with a fresh interest on both sides of the Atlantic. It promises a wider scope for "History from Below" and invites comparisons with other countries and other cultures.

THE ONENESS
OF SOUTHERN LIFE

Joel Williamson

In the Southern part of the United States, we are two—and yet, we are one. In the South, we are two cultures, one black and the other white, and yet we are one culture. That is the essence of our Southern lives, a tension-laden contradiction, an apparent impossibility which is the root of our being. Black is black, and white is white, but ever— or almost ever—the twain have met. We have met, partly of choice, partly of necessity, for we have been married by this Southern soil, by this geography, and the centuries of time in which we have lived here together. White is white, and black is black; but, if one looks closely at the history, one sees that white is also black, and that black is also white, and that both are one. Two worlds in one, a duality that is also, paradoxically, a unity. At one level the two worlds are in conflict, at another they are in harmony. Apart and together, hating and loving, this tension has been our tribulation and our history, and it seems almost to be our destiny. It is a history unique on the face of this earth and one of inestimable value, for us, in the South, and for others.

What we have come to in the South is a way in which two very different people of the world have come together, and each has found its separate way together. It is a precious example in a world in which belted[1] and booted commandos with automatic weapons and strings of handbombs assault the totally vulnerable flesh of "civilians." It is a useful experience when some Christians roll bombs into the lives of other Christians with the seeming casualness of gentlemen on the bowling green. All over the world today, we are seeing and suffering from intolerances of vast magnitude—religion against religion, race against race, and yet, always, people against people. We suffer wars in which the victors lose, and the losers lose also; wars that are too often fought by terrorists pretending to be soldiers, booted and belted inside as well as out, ready to blast the innocent bodies of children. Such inhumanity is insanity; and if it is sane, we should all embrace insanity. No cause is worth a slaughter of innocents—of our future selves.

Historically, how has it happened that we have arrived at an end in the South in which there is a white culture and a black culture that are yet one? I hope not to alienate anyone, but black culture in the South is whiter than it would confess, and white culture is blacker than it knows. This is true because what has happened in the South is a continuous symbiosis between black and white. Black has consumed white and fed white, and white has consumed black and fed black, each giving to each, even as each has taken from each. The process has proceeded simultaneously so that it is really impossible to say which came first. But for now, and purely for the purpose of attempting to understand what has happened, let us first look at the more fully researched side of the equation in which black people are seen as becoming white.

Through enslavement, the interpretation would run, through the crossing of the Atlantic in the infamous "middle passage," and in the careful system of acculturation called "seasoning" in which the African was married to the plantation system and learned to survive in the New World, the process of depriving the black man of his natural culture and of pumping European, English, and English-American culture into the void proceeded very far. When the first black child was conceived, and born, and bred in America, a cultural mutation occurred. That child and his brothers and his sisters who came after were lost to Africa far more than were their parents. No man can know precisely what his father knew, and the life experience of a black born

slave in America was vastly different from that of an African born
free. Each succeeding generation in America, by its very birth, moved
a quick step further away from the primal culture of the black heart-
land. During the remainder of their lives, they drifted toward whiteness.

White Americans of the Revolutionary generation paused to consider slavery, and then in a very spotty and gingerly way moved beyond
to ponder the meaning of blackness in people. In a sense they coped
with slavery. North of Mason's and Dixon's line, one state after
another either acted to end slavery immediately or to put it upon the
path to gradual extinction. By federal action, slavery was prohibited
in the entire territory north and west of the Ohio River. Ultimately,
white people in the free states would outnumber and overpower white
people in the slave states. In this way the nation met the problem of
slavery, but clearly they could not cope with the problem of blackness
—they could not give blackness a definite meaning in their human
universe. In the South, after a tentative move toward emancipation in
the turn of the century years, leadership faltered. The result was a
drifting, a drifting which was abruptly halted by Nat Turner's insur-
rection in black belt Virginia in 1831. There had been rumors of insur-
rection previously, but before Turner one could always choose to
believe that such were the hysterias of the timid. Nat Turner with fifty-
seven whites left slaughtered in his wake made it undeniable that it
could happen here. It had happened here. With that traumatic experience, the broad current of race relations in the South wrenched up and
out of its former channel, like a great river disrupted by some giant
catastrophe, and poured out upon the landscape in a rushing and
seemingly desperate search for a new place for blacks and a new order
for society. The ultimate result was that the white society changed
itself, became something quite different, to adjust to the black presence.

In and after the 1830s, in the last three decades of slavery, a paradox
occurred in race relations in the South. Even as white society came
to impose a more rigid police control over blacks, it also moved across
the race line to touch blacks with unprecedented intimacy. In the
"hard-soft" period of late slavery, whites worked diligently, desperate-
ly, and, one must say, brilliantly, to build a place for blackness in
their religion, in their philosophy, in their science, economy, literature,

and in their families. In their ideal world, Southerners were fantastically successful in this endeavor, and their success was still rising when the war came. Emotionally speaking, in the thirty years before the war, the South had progressed from relative confusion and despair to order and optimism. On the eve of conflict, Southern thought was well along the road toward a novel and highly integrated system. Ultimately, this culture forged an image of the black man with which it could comfortably live, and it created an abundance of institutions which worked steadily to make the image real.

Essentially, the image made the Negro a child in the white family, an adult body with a child's mind and heart, at the same time appealing and appalling, unthinkingly affectionate and unwittingly cruel, at once potentially a social asset and a liability. Held by the white man's power, locked in the white man's embrace, a perpetual childhood was the ideal role imposed upon the Negro. It was a role to flatter the white man's image of himself as a kindly parent. The white role, ideally, breathed paternalism and its image was that of aristocrat. The black part came to be called Sambo. And Sambo came to be vital to the South because he not only denied Nat Turner and gave "massa" back his life, but he gave him beauty and white soul as well.

Sambo was a man who never was. He was a creature of the white mind, a prescription for psychic survival day by day—or, perhaps, rather, night by night—with a terror which might otherwise drive one over the edge of sanity. Seen from the black side of slavery, playing Sambo was part of a program for physical survival. When the white world panicked into a color conscious hysteria (which it did recurrently), Sambo was a mask behind which a black man might at least live rather than die. Cast-down eyes, shuffling feet, soft words, and the proper address were white invented signals to signify that this black man meant no violence. Indirectly, the role saved blacks from physical damage. But it functioned more directly to save whites themselves from wild and murderous behavior that would have destroyed their own self-flattering, complementary roles, a behavior that would have destroyed their beautiful selves.

Still there was more to the Sambo role than simple submissiveness. It called upon black people to be like white people because if blacks were like whites, then whites had nothing to fear from blackness. Thus Sambo was acculturated, thus Sambo was integrated—and he was here to stay. Africa was no longer his home. Survival depended upon his being white-like, or seeming to be so. And yet, there was a limit to the whiteness allowed blacks. If blacks were too white, they would threaten the neat bipolarity which lay at the roots of a growing Southern culture. In this way, black people were held suspended between two worlds where they could be neither perfectly white, nor yet perfectly black.

Of necessity and of volition, black people generated a culture which was neither African nor white American—it was another country. As scholars, we have only recently begun to perceive the nature of that culture, a part of the other side of the symbiotic equation. It is yet like a ship coming to port. We see the masts rising upon the horizon and we are making our estimates. We are beginning to catch glimpses of an early slavery that was not as tightly organized and set as it later became. Peter Wood, in his book so aptly entitled *Black Majority*, depicts an early slavery in South Carolina that is so loose as to suggest to him the term "unfree" instead of slave. He sees Africans coming to the colony in such numbers as to almost—culturally speaking—overwhelm the whites and impress the whole with their stamp.[1]

Stepping back and surveying the whole of the black experience in America in the antebellum period, it is possible to see black culture as made up of four inputs.

First, a part of black culture was the direct result of slavery. Slavery had its special regimes of work, for instance, and these contributed to a black life style. Northerners who came early to the Sea Islands of South Carolina during Reconstruction noted that blacks went to bed early and rose early, that they swore little and drank less, and that blacks sang in the fields as they worked.[2] A part of black culture was generated by slavery, but a part was generated by opposition to slavery. Somewhere, somehow, black people convinced white people that they could labor only three-fifths as effectively as white workers, a peculiar fraction which found its way into the United States Constitution. Slaves were very capable of dissembling, of "puttin' on massa," and became highly adept at the art. Again, when Northern missionaries came to the Sea Islands during the Civil War, they moved—or they were moved by the blacks themselves—all too quickly into the roles of parents to the childlike slaves. After all, the whites did have the whip hand: Southern whites, literally, before the war, and now the Yankees, materially. Black Islanders proved no less skillful at putting on the new masters from the North. Two black women, who had been house servants as slaves, came through the lines and found comfortable berths serving Northern school marms in Beaufort. They let the Northern white ladies know that they relished their company because, as they said, it "seemed like they couldn't be happy without white ladies 'round."[3] What they meant was that they could not be happy without being around the good things in life which affluent white women usually enjoyed. A man who had been a coachman as a slave became coachman to the wife of Mansfield French, one of the missionaries. French had been a leading abolitionist for years before the war. Driving in Beaufort one day, Mrs. French and the coachman heard an early— and as it turned out premature—announcement of emancipation. Mrs. French clapped her hands and bounced for joy, praising the Lord repeatedly. The coachman was noticeably less elated at his alleged emancipation, and she asked him how he felt about it. "Most beautiful Missus," he replied, "onspeakable." "But why don't you say Hallelujah as I do?" she asked. "I am burning inward, madam," he answered, from behind the mask.[4] This was precisely what she wanted to hear; but she could not have said it so well herself. Shortly the blacks on the Islands had persuaded Northerners that the truth was what the missionaries had come to prove—that is that the blacks were really white, that they would retool to become independent yeoman farmers almost instantly, and that they would make an excellent market for Yankee manufactures to be bought with Southern raw materials. The most perceptive Yankees, like the most perceptive Southerners, saw through the mask and knew the game. Some grew angry, others played it. "Jim and Judge both lying up today," wrote planter Tom Chaplin in his diary on May 21, 1857, a busy season in the planting year, "they will have their time out."[5] A part of black culture was deceiving the masters, taking small delights where it found them.

Not all black people were slaves, of course, and a second part of black culture consisted of the way free blacks responded to the white world. Again one could make a division between the acceptance of whiteness by free negroes and their rejection of it. Free Negroes, most of whom were mulattoes, were uniquely well situated to share white culture. Often, they were well educated, well-to-do, and indeed much closer kin to whites than to blacks. The free mulatto community operated as something of a conduit for white culture flowing into the larger black community. Yet, free Negroes were seen as black by the white community and held strictly at arms length. Inevitably, free blacks would build a culture that was at war with the source of their rejection; they would build churches, and schools, and clubs that existed against the white world rather than in simple imitation of it.

Black culture also grew out of the frontier afforded by the New World environment. The geography, the climate, the flora and the fauna of the South were not African. Each locale in the South—the swamp, the Sea Islands, the tidal rivers—had its own natural logic and the African in America, no less than the Englishman in America, had somehow to come to terms with it. And so they did and made of it a new home for themselves. The love of the land, the fondness for the place of their birth and breeding was a trait of Negroes in the South as it is perhaps of all peoples. White Southerners, so specially possessive of the land themselves and so idolatrous of the legalities of ownership, could hardly contemplate, much less understand, and still less sympathize with the feelings of Negroes about their mutually natal soil. Most black people lived with a large number of other black people on plantations. It was they who trod its paths by day and by night. With their hands and their feet they had closely mapped its surface, and with their bodies they had registered its heat and cold. On the large plantations and in the more remote, sparsely settled areas where the white man was most seldom seen, black people met the land and created life styles that had least to do with blackness of skin.

Without doubt, a fourth part of black culture in the American South was African in its origins. But the real question is not whether the African legacy has survived into modern times. Certainly it has. Nor even is it a matter of how much of it has survived. The real historical problem is how the African heritage was transmuted in the American environment; how it was changed by slavery, by the African's personal blackness in a white world, and by the novel physical setting. That problem is every bit as difficult as defining European survivals in white culture. And it is more difficult because the black experience was refracted through slavery and through a reigning moral code in which black, sometimes, meant bad. There is a peculiar and distressing insensitivity in the argument that blacks have to "make it" in America just as the Irish, the Italians, and we other immigrant groups have done. Would that it were so simple. To dismiss the distinctive black experience in this facile way, one has to ignore the white man's special perception of blackness in humans, and his reaction to that perception. If blacks have rotted at the doorstep of the white tower in America, it is not because they take a perverse pleasure in giving their lives to offend white nostrils. It is, rather, because of the exclusiveness of the social world the white man made.

The Negro, then, is the person the white man made; but, also, the white man is the person the black man made. As whites invaded black life with a new intensity in the middle of the nineteenth century, they not only changed blacks, they were changed by blacks. Whites then and later would have been vastly resentful at the suggestion that blacks had educated them, so proudfully intent were they on educating the blacks. Without attempting to catalogue the entire range, it seems fairly clear that whites learned much from blacks in language, literature, and religion, in music and manners, and in cuisine and conjuring. It is probably not too much to say that a significant amount of the African heritage that survived the slave South did so on the white side of the racial line. Southern whites would have passed beyond resentment and into outrage at the idea of themselves being Africanized. But it was true, and the debatable question is not whether or not Southern whites carry traces of Africa in their culture. It is how much of it do they carry.

White people adopted and adapted not only African survivals from Negroes, they also continually drew from the ever-full springs of a rising black culture to fill the cups of their lives. How black is Southern white religion? How much of black spirituality is there in Southern Christianity? Did not the Southern church become fundamentally different from that of the North because of the black presence? If so, that might account in some degree for the continued secession of the Southern church even after slavery was dead and the union remade. From where, after all, does Southern Baptist and Southern Methodism come? There are so many ways in which Southern whites learned from blacks that we could never call the complete roll.

An obvious carrier is the black "mammy." Overlooked is the—for want of a better term—black "daddy." No one has yet studied the manner in which Southern children in the slave period were reared, or the effects that process might have had upon the adult. But we do know that upon the large plantations typically, the older slave women over-saw the young slave children, and that often white children shared the life of the blacklings until puberty, when separation began. Many Southern whites later claimed a close childhood association with some adult who was a slave. Usually it was a "mammy" they claimed, but now and again some white son of the master class found his mentor in a dark hero, some black and accomplished Nimrod who tutored the boy in the lore of field and stream. Further, it is possible that upper-class Southerners learned their reputedly exquisite manners from their close association with blacks. This theory would argue that blacks were subject to such sudden, violent, and sometimes arbitrary punish-ments from whites that they developed a supersensitivity to the thoughts and moods of others, an interest and a talent which they conveyed to the whites about them. It might well be that black mammies and daddies were the prime movers in generating and transmitting Southern manners.

Language also illustrates much of what has been said; that is, that the culture of each race fed upon the other. A quick index into language exists in the names that people take. Rather obviously blacks in America took Western names. Sometimes it happened that African names sounded like a Western name, and the transition was rather easily made. On the plantations of the deep South, blacks typically had only a given name. The given name generally reflected three sources of Western culture—they were classical like Scipio or Bacchus, or Phoebe; they were Biblical like Elijah or Sarah; they were British like Jim or Elizabeth. On large plantations it might sometimes happen that a baby girl might be given a name already in use—such as Jane. Shortly the child might come to be identified by reference to her mother Sarah. She might come to be known as "Sarah's Jane," as distinguished from, say, Phoebe's Jane. In time Sarah dies and gradually the possessive dissolves. Sarah's Jane becomes Sarah Jane, melodious and euphonic, an appealing and appropriate double name. No social scientist will ever prove it, but it might be that the well-known Southern white affinity for double names is something taken from slave culture, from black culture. It is different, it is beautiful; and because it is beautiful, it is valuable.

Interestingly, one can do the same for black men and white. The idea of the all prevading black matriarchy in slavery and afterward is challenged in part by the truth that black males born on the plantation were often enough identified by reference to their fathers rather than to their mothers. Thus, black Henry might come to be identified through his father as John's Henry. Again, in time the possessive gives way and John Henry moves on to gain fame if not fortune in the railroad industry. Double given names for Southern white men occur less frequently than for Southern white women. But during most of my life in South Carolina, I lived two doors away from John Tom. I was in school with Joe Ed, my son plays with a boy called Hugh Merl, and I don't watch a television show that features a Jim Bob. Not so beautiful as feminine double names I concede, and I applaud the relative scarcity of the use.

As always in race relations in the South, what one sees on one side of the race line can be seen balanced on the other side. Thus, in relation to names, one can easily flip over and do the black side. In freedom, black people chose to drop the classical names of slavery. Bacchus, Scipio, and Caesar disappeared. But Biblical and British names continued to abound. Further, honorific names appeared. Black men sometimes took names like Captain or Major, Senator or Judge. Perhaps most interesting were the last names they chose. Washingtons and Lincolns were plentiful, and every color except black was frequent. Not a few took the names of their late masters. Sometimes, they did it in part from love, sometimes they did it because the name was respected. I think most often and for the most part they did it because it represented their most intimate community—the people of the plantation into which they had been born and reared, the land upon which they had lived their lives. When a black takes the name Heyward, or Aiken, or Coffin, or Chaplin, he is reflecting the way in which slaves identified themselves conveniently by saying, "I'm one of Mr. Heyward's people." In freedom when he takes the family name Heyward, it really is descriptive because Heyward's people are his people, and the Heyward plantation is truly his home.

Ultimately, the process was probably much more intricate than each race simply teaching the other. It seems inevitable that the exchange and the change were continuous. Whites taught blacks Christianity, for instance, but blacks lost something and added something in the translation, spirituality perhaps, which they then fed back to the whites, who also lost something and added something, and so on perpetually until what we have are two cultures in symbiosis. White culture fed off black and grew and changed, and black culture fed from white and grew and changed. Finally, it is possible to speak of two cultures, one white and the other black, but it is also proper to speak of a fusion of cultures.

We in the South, black and white, bought our experience dearly. We have walked separately and together through the vale of tears, and we have passed separately and together through the valley of the shadow of death. And now while it seems that we are emerging upon the other side, we should fear evil, and we should take care to preserve the dearly bought fruit of our suffering. We should save ourselves, separately and together, for our own sakes, and for the sake, insofar as it can be, of our sadly suffering fellow man. Let us gracefully learn to avoid cultural imperialism as we are learning with scant grace—and slowly—to avoid economic and political and military imperialism. Let us pass beyond toleration of difference to a sensitivity to the value of other people's lives and to an appreciation of the style of their living. What we have built in the South between black and white has a potential as a model in that effort. What we have, even now, is much too valuable to be melted into a middle Americanism even if America would accept that. We must preserve and improve our culture, even if a world would not see it. In the South we have a way, and I have faith that we also have a will to continue and to improve the way.

NOTES

[1] Peter H. Wood, *Black Majority: Negroes in Colonial South Carolina From 1670 Through the Stono Rebellion* (New York: Alfred A. Knopf, 1972).
[2] Willie Lee Rose, *Rehearsal for Reconstruction: The Port Royal Experiment* (Indianapolis: The Bobbs-Merrill Co., Inc., 1964), pp. 101–2, and *passim*. See also: Joel R. Williamson, *After Slavery: The Negro in South Carolina During Reconstruction, 1861–1877* (Chapel Hill: University of North Carolina Press, 1965), pp. 303–4.
[3] Rose, *Rehearsal*, p. 131.
[4] Ibid., p. 167.
[5] Ibid., pp. 138–39.

BIBLIOGRAPHICAL NOTE   The definitive study of black culture in the Sea Islands of South Carolina during the transition from slavery to freedom is Willie Lee Rose, *Rehearsal for Reconstruction: The Port Royal Experiment* (Indianapolis, 1964). Ms. Rose's "Notes on Sources" is a masterly coverage of the sources, both published and unpublished, upon the topic. In particular for the subject of this essay, one might consult the section in those notes entitled "Works on Sea Island Negro Culture and Religion." Joel Williamson's book, *After Slavery, The Negro in South Carolina During Reconstruction, 1861–1877* (Chapel Hill, 1965), was in the process of publication at the time that Professor Rose's study appeared. The first chapter of that monograph deals with the Sea Islands during the war. Subsequent chapters frequently refer to matters in the Islands during Reconstruction.

PART II

ARTICLES

THE CRISIS

IN URBAN SOCIOLOGY

Edward G. Armstrong

Nearly forty years ago the complaint was first heard that "in the rich literature on the city we can look in vain for a theory of urbanism presenting in a systematic fashion the available knowledge concerning the city as a social entity."[1] Twenty years later another sympathetic investigator of urban sociology remarked that "no subtlety of perception is required to determine that the contemporary American theory of the city is in crisis."[2] The problem was the nonexistence of a comprehensive theory of urban life. Attention was given to one issue such as ecological form or another such as mental illness while other aspects of urban life and urban living as a whole were left unquestioned. In late 1975, another survey of urban sociology confirms that "the intellectual crisis confronting urban sociologists" is still with us. Once again the problem focused upon is the "inadequacy" of urban theory and once again the reaction of the urban sociologists is to move away from main-line sociological issues. Today, their choices include specializing on urban policy and community planning.[3]

The obvious question is, "Why is urban sociology in a perpetual state of crisis?" To a large extent, the assessment of urban sociology's present moribund condition must be based upon how the discipline developed over time. The ultimate solution, if one exists, to the problematic status of urban sociology rests on an appreciation of the difficulties sociologists experienced in their early confrontation with the phenomenon of urban life. My goals are three-fold: (1) to describe contemporary urban sociology in terms of its theoretical assumptions and methodological limitations; (2) to analyze the ideological framework of the history of urban sociology; and (3) to report on recent challenges to this framework. My thesis is that the crisis of urban sociology is a profound example of the crisis of contemporary sociology itself.[4]

URBAN SOCIOLOGY DEFINED

Urban sociology is a discipline concerned with developing systematic, reliable knowledge about the urban situation by means of sociological research techniques. Although there are different positions taken by various groups of urban sociologists with regard to the particular area of substantive concern and the particular techniques of analysis, the set of possible alternatives is quite limited and forms what can be called the paradigm of normal urban sociology.[5]

To remain distinctively "urban" sociologists, sources of theoretical effort must include one or more of the following topics:[6] (1) Adoption of the city and urbanism as a frame of reference. Attention must be given to the conditions of existence of the association of individuals who are living in the city or becoming urbanized. This association of individuals is problematic or at least different in itself; (2) Acceptance of the rural-urban dualism. Modification of this typology includes a theory of social change and cultural development that employs a rural-urban continuum; (3) Explanations of changes in the urban environment that focus upon the process of urbanism itself. Descriptions of the economic, geographic, historic, and political context of a city provide interesting background information. However, such information is independent of the immediate explanatory framework.

To remain sociologists, sources of empirical data must include one or more of the following research techniques: (1) *The demographic method.* The demographic method is thought by many to be the approach best suited for urban sociology.[7] It consists of the comparative examination of recorded statistical information collected, in most cases, by government agencies. Rates of urban growth may be the basis for inferences about such characteristics of the urban citizens as age, sex, income, and family size. (2) *The survey method.* This is the most popular research procedure in sociology.[8] Here, the goal is to generalize about a population on the basis of results obtained by means of questioning a segment of the population about attitudes or behavior. The epistemological justification for the sample survey is probability theory. (3) *Participant observation.* The method of participant observation has been "more closely identified with the study of communities than any other method of research."[9] This technique involves the participation of the researcher in the daily lives of the people in order to gain insights that may lead to a basic understanding of the group or situation. The consequences of the use of this technique are the subject of a certain amount of disagreement: for some, the research is an end in-itself; while for others, the technique's sole purpose is to stimulate research hypotheses that can be more properly questioned by means of a more "scientific" method. Choices would be limited to the methods mentioned above.

In their everyday research activities, urban sociologists do not question and do not present a rationale for adhering to the theoretical and methodological limitations imposed upon them by the normal urban sociology paradigm. Such an explanation is uncalled for because it is generally understood that this is the way urban sociologists proceed. A review of the development of the paradigm can constitute nothing less than a total review of all the assumptions discoverable within the history of urban sociology. However, such a complete survey, because of the complexity and the number of works that would need to be mentioned, is impossible. One way of clarifying this development is to select a basic and central aspect of the paradigm and trace its progress. It appears to me that such an idea is readily available. This is the "primary group ideal."

The "primary group ideal" implies the acceptance of a basic assumption on the nature of social reality and a basic judgment on the nature of urban living. Social reality is seen as an integration of individuals linked together by their shared membership in intimate face-to-face association and cooperation. Such association and cooperation is usually called the primary group.

THE "PRIMARY GROUP IDEAL" IN URBAN SOCIOLOGY

In a famous discussion of the images employed by urban sociologists, Anselm Strauss remarked that "urban sociologists had allowed their ideological commitments profoundly to affect their research."[10] A problem is that such a statement fails to draw a certain distinction that must be evoked in a very cautious way. This is the difference between ideology in the sense of value judgment and ideology in the sense of weltanschauung. The former meaning denotes sets of prejudices, biases, and self-serving doctrines. This is the realm of personal preferences, perceptions, and feelings. The latter meaning includes categories of reasoning, the conceptual world, and the system of propositions expressing a world of ideas. Ideology, in its first meaning, refers to believing what you want to believe. The second meaning refers to paradigmatic aspects of thought and therefore refers to believing what you can not help but believe.

Urban sociologists, among others, have often been accused of being prejudiced against the city. In addition, they can be charged with being ideological in the second sense of the word. However, the point must be made that a critique along these lines is not necessarily a form of vulgar Marxism or mechanical sociology of knowledge in which all ideas are seen as mere "representations" and in which epistemological relativism seems the only recourse. We must keep in mind what has become known as the genetic fallacy.[11] A genetic fallacy is committed by one who judges the veracity of a statement on the basis of the characteristics of the individual making the statement. The discovery that certain individuals "hate cities" does not lead to the conclusion that their work is biased. The disclosure that others see their work as a study of the changes within the primary group does not lead to the conclusion that this is a limitation corrupting the nature of social reality. At most, we can hope for a correlation between certain views on the city and certain ways the city has been treated analytically. With this limitation in mind, we can examine urban sociologists with regard to the two different types of ideology. In doing so, I hope to evince that the "primary group ideal" is a key paradigmatic aspect of urban sociology and that it is something quite different from a simplistic manifestation of an anti-urban bias.

THE ANTI-URBAN BIAS

Sociology has always been more popular in America than in Europe. In fact, the distinctive field called "urban sociology" had its origins "in the translation of European sociology into the context of the American colleges and universities in the early years of the century."[12] Thus, attention can be given to the individuals who figured prominently in the ascendency of both sociology and urban sociology in America with the knowledge that these individuals formed the basis of the urban sociology enterprise in general. These individuals had similar backgrounds and as the Hinkles summarize, each was "tutored in the ideals of a frontier social democracy and the personalized intimacy of agrarian society."[13] The early American sociologists came from rural and strongly religious backgrounds, achieved academic respectability in publicly supported Midwestern universities, and directed classroom and professional attention to ameliorating what they considered a social evil—the conditions associated with urbanization such as unemployment, crime, family instability, and race relations.

The notion of social evil was not simply used metaphorically. The motivations of members of society were considered the ultimate root of social phenomena. Existence of the problems themselves was enough to demonstrate that the persons had strayed from moral standards. This, in turn, was enough to convince the early sociologists that knowledge must be put to the service of finding out why individuals act in certain ways. David Matza supports the view that early sociologists were incapable of separating their standard of morality from their work by examining early examples of urban sociological research such as *West Side Studies* which were sponsored by the Russell Sage Foundation in 1914. Throughout the studies there are references to

the "perversion" of life and the destruction of the "normal development" of human society in the city. As Matza stresses, "the virtual
absence of moral life is taken as a cardinal feature of the West Side."[14]
For early sociologists, the city was a social and a moral evil. The study
of the city was an exercise in social pathology.

There is thorough documentation that the early urban sociologists
were by no means unique among American intellectuals. In 1823,
Jefferson wrote that cities were filled with vice while rural life was
"rational, moral and affectionate." A famous straightforward summary of the anti-urban bias in American history is provided by
Hofstadter. The agrarian society of early America reacted to the increased urbanization by clinging to what Hofstadter calls the "agrarian
myth." This is the belief that because of its close communion with
nature, rural life is moral, civic, and religious. In fact, the early urban
sociologist may not be unique among intellectuals in general. B. I.
Coleman demonstrates the all-pervasiveness of anti-urbanism in nineteenth-century British thought.[15]

Thus far, the anti-urban bias has been viewed as if it were reducible
to a simple equation: a scholar's rural background plus increasing
urbanization yields a bias against the city. Hardly anything is this
simple and the Whites are certainly correct when they say that anti-
urbanism can not be treated in a "monistic way." The Whites hold that
"the American city has been caught in the crossfire of two powerful
antagonists—primitivists and sophisticates." Romanticists preferred
the wilderness while the intellectual saw the city as a failure because
it did not provide "organic social relations" and "social intelligence
and face-to-face human relationships."[16] In fact, in certain instances
the "antagonists" combined features of both primitivists and sophisticates. The "primary group ideal" became a paradigmatic element in
urban sociology at the point in time when investigators of the city no
longer preferred living anywhere but the city.

THE PRIMARY GROUP IDEAL

The idea of the primary group was popularized by Charles H.
Cooley. Cooley stated that the simplest way of describing the primary
group is to "say that it is a 'we'."[17] Individuals identify with each other

and share a common mentality. The primary group is primary in many ways: (1) It is the basic building block of human society, for individuals become socialized only through their membership in such groups. (2) It is indispensable to all human relationships because only within primary groups do individuals gain the psychological support needed to carry on their day-to-day activities. (3) It is the basic element in all other social groups. The social system or society, the most inclusive group, is a set of parts in mutual functional interaction. The parts are institutions which in turn are sets of primary groups. (4) It is the first place to begin the examination of society and the place to look for the causes of social problems. (5) If dissolved, society would be destroyed and if changed, society's foundation would be weakened. It is at this point that the judgment on the nature of the city comes into play. The city is a place in which the primary group has been changed or is being destroyed.

Social theorists have been preoccupied with the "primary group ideal" since the earliest stages of social thought.[18] However, twentieth-century sociologists rarely go beyond the work of Cooley for the historic basis for the idea of the primary group. It is virtually impossible to find a basic sociology text that does not refer to Cooley's work in chapters on socialization and on the group. As an investigator of Cooley's general sociological orientation concludes, "within the generation of the founding fathers of American sociology, perhaps no one has more contemporary relevance for or exerted a greater influence on the discipline than Charles Horton Cooley." This is important because Cooley's notion of the primary group is a clear manifestation of an anti-urban bias, or what C. Wright Mills has called Cooley's "Christian-democratic version of a rural village."[19] There may be some difficulty in employing a concept in a "value-neutral" way if the anti-urban bias is inextricably interwoven into the initial formulation of the concept.

Cooley's importance to the development of urban sociology cannot be challenged. In fact, Cooley's dissertation was one of the first studies of urban transportation.[20] However, urban sociologists see their intellectual heritage as resting upon the work of social theorists other than Cooley. Each of these scholars employs the "primary group ideal," yet denies that he is classifiable as anti-urban. The most important individuals in the history of a specifically "urban" sociology and the central figures in the formulation of the normal urban sociology paradigm are Tönnies, Durkheim, Weber, Park, and Wirth.

1. FERDINAND TÖNNIES

Ferdinand Tönnies (1855–1936) published *Gemeinschaft und Gesellschaft* in 1887. Formulations presented in this work are still used in urban sociology. The renowned James S. Coleman employed the concepts outlined by Tönnies to the investigation of community disorganization and conflict, while theoretical viewpoints developed in recent urban sociology texts use Tönnies as a starting point.[21]

Gemeinschaft and gesellschaft are types of groups. They are differentiated according to the relationship of human wills which is defined as "an inherent whole which unites in itself a multiplicity of feelings, instincts, and desires." Gemeinschaft is based on natural will. Individuals understand, sympathize with, confide in, and depend upon each other. There is a "similarity of work and intellectual attitude." Gesellschaft is based on rational will. Individuals are strangers, feel antipathy and mistrust toward each other, and are slaves to each other. Their consciousness corresponds to their membership in a particular conflicting class.[22]

Tönnies concluded his theory with a description of the two contrasting periods of human history. A period of gesellschaft follows a period of gemeinschaft. Each of these had different forms of external social organization. Summarizing Tönnies' outline, we have:

A. Gemeinschaft
  1. Family life = concord.
  2. Rural village life = folkways and mores.
  3. Town life = religion.

B. Gesellschaft
  1. City life = convention.
  2. National life = legislation.
  3. Cosmopolitan life = public opinion.

The only form of external social organization that seems out of place is public opinion. This connotes, at least to me, a rather mild form of social control. However, this is not Tönnies' meaning of the term. For Tönnies, public opinion is the consciousness of the upper classes. There is a tendency for public opinion to turn into a justification of despotism against the lower classes. The irresistible police power of the upper classes can be used to curb the impulses of the masses. Tönnies stated, "City life and Gesellschaft condemn the common people to decay and death."

It certainly appears the Tönnies preferred the gemeinschaft type group. It is difficult to imagine that one could be neutral when one describes dependence in a gesellschaft as "typically exemplified by servitude, slavery and the like," and as resulting from "a completely weak will" such as found in "hypnotized persons, sexual slavery, and the like."[23] Yet, Charles Loomis remarks that "although critics accused him of recommending Gemeinschaft as good and condemning Gesellschaft as bad, he disclaimed any such intention." Disregarding his manner of description, Tönnies did not believe that gesellschaft was an unhealthy or abnormal state of the human group.[24]

2. EMILE DURKHEIM

Emile Durkheim (1858–1917) is one of the most cited authors in contemporary sociology.[25] For Durkheim, "social life is above all a harmonious community of endeavors, when minds and will come together to work for the same aim." Society itself is the source of all morality and the social order is equated with the moral order.

The basis of social life is called consensus or integration or, most often, solidarity. Solidarity varies along two dimensions: the intensity and the multiplicity of points of attachment that hold the individual to the group. Durkheim discovered two types of solidarity upon which types of societies are based. Mechanical solidarity is rooted in the similarity of individuals' minds and consciences. An absolutely homogeneous group emanates from this form of cohesion. Mechanical solidarity is, of course, characteristic of rural groups. Organic solidarity is based on differences. This unity is called organic for it is similar to a "system of different organs each of which has a special role, and which are themselves of different parts." Accordingly, collective conscience and individual conscience are divided. The sole source of solidarity is the division of labor.

Although organic solidarity is a "normal phenomenon," it is historically secondary. It is a product of social evolution or growth.[26] Many negative consequences result from this process that did not exist in groups based on mechanical solidarity. Joachim Israel specifies what Durkheim considers the most important of these problems: the disruption of social solidarity due to "the lack of moral norms governing economic life, a lack due to the discrepancy between the slow development of the production process." This is the state of anomie.[27]

Anomie or normlessness is a condition prevalent in modern societies that disrupts solidarity. Durkheim went on to discover that suicide rates increase when the society has only weak regulation over the individual; for example, businessmen become disoriented during booms and depressions, and divorced people suddenly are uncontrolled by others. Both of these groups tend to be constituted of urban residents. Durkheim called this phenomenon anomic suicide.[28]

The analytical procedures used by Durkheim in the study of suicide are basically the same as those used by many contemporary urban sociologists: the multivariate analysis of demographic data. As Hanan Selvin points out, "the methodology of *Suicide* is important to those now engaged in empirical research." By means of a highly sophisticated methodology, Durkheim collected empirical data that dramatically supported the rise of anomie, that is, the decline of the primary group in urban situations. Although it may be true that "Durkheim's conservativism significantly limited his perception of society," the argument could be made that the weight of his data imposed just such a conservativism upon him. Although sociological literature comprises a vast number of changes in the meaning of the concept of anomie, the "primary group ideal" remains incorporated into every change.[29]

3. MAX WEBER

Max Weber (1864–1920) is another urbanist often cited by contemporary sociologists. He is the author of *The City*, a book-length article published in 1921. Early investigators of urban sociology regard this work as the first attempt to formulate a systematic theory of urbanism.[30]

Except for the very first page of *The City*, Weber kept the primary group ideal removed from his comparative analysis of the history of the city and the urban community.[31] For our purposes, attention must be directed to this first page. Here, Weber explains why he refuses to define the city as "a colony so extensive that personal reciprocal acquaintance of the inhabitants is lacking." The reason is simple: "this impersonality was absent in many historical localities possessing the legal definition of cities."[32] We are on firm ground in assuming that this statement implies that Weber sees this impersonality present in many contemporary cities.

Weber, however, distinguished two types of solidary social relationships. One type is called communal. This is defined as an orientation of social action "based on a subjective feeling of the parties, whether affectual or traditional, that they belong together." It is only insofar as there is this feeling that there is a genuine community. Examples of communal relationships are the family, erotic encounters, religious brotherhoods, and military units. The second type of relationship is called " 'associative' if and insofar as the orientation of social action within it rests on a rationally motivated adjustment of interests of a similarly motivated agreement." Examples of associational relationships are market exchanges and voluntary associations based on self-interest or motivated by certain social issues.

The communal relationship is the "most radical antithesis of conflict," while the associative relationship very often consists in conflict and competition.[33] The associative relationship is based on a rational orientation in which others are seen as means for the successful attainment of one's own ends. This form of relationship characterizes modern capitalistic society. In this society the irresistible force of economic acquisition is an "iron cage" in which individuals are trapped.[34]

The relationship between the modern city and modern capitalistic society is complex. Both are products of increasing rationality in human affairs. Yet, neither is a "mere" product. For example, the modern city is a prerequisite of the technical and economic conditions of machine production which in turn determine the lives of those who are born in the city. For the first time we have a strict reading of the "primary group ideal" that can not be linked in even the most superficial way to a personal anti-urban bias.

4. ROBERT PARK

Robert Park (1864–1944) was the "most influential member" of the University of Chicago Department of Sociology, the intellectual center of American sociology prior to World War II. Park's particular interest was urban theory and research and he is the author of "The City," an article that appeared in 1914 and *The City*, a book published in 1925.[35] These are "classic" works in American urban sociology. Park was the leader and his work may still be the leading influence in American urban sociology.[36]

The Chicago school of sociology had one dominant theme. This was the quest to make sociology scientific. In his *Introduction to the Science of Sociology*, Park stressed that sociology was a "natural science" in that it verifies hypotheses by means of "observation and experiment" for the purpose of establishing universally applicable "natural laws and generalizations." In fact, as the Hinkles note, one of the reasons Park became interested in the city was that he believed that the city offered a convenient laboratory for the science.[37]

Some earlier American sociologists saw the city as morally and socially evil and used the term pathological to describe features of city life. The city was viewed as unnatural. Park purged the concept of pathology from urban analysis, substituting instead the idea of social disorganization. Although Park saw the city as a source of social disorganization, the city was just as normal and natural as rural localities.

Park used the term social disorganization to indicate that scientific sociology was different from the highly speculative discourse that had been going by the name of sociology. His belief was that this idea was more scientific than that of pathology and further delimited a realm specific to sociologists. Use of the term pathology was often limited to those who viewed sociology as a subfield in or a development of biology. However, the substitution of terms did not represent any substantial change in the way the urban situation was described.

For Park, the village is the fundamental type of society. A village is "a product of the spontaneous and unreflective responses of individuals living together in intimate, personal, and face-to-face relations." Order is maintained by common sense and intuition. In the city, old forms of communication and control are greatly diminished. The individual undergoes a process of "individualization" and the society becomes a mere "constellation of social atoms" or synonymously, the society becomes disorganized. As Park stated: "It is probably the breaking down of local attachments and the weakening of the restraints and inhibitions of the primary group, under the influence of the urban environment, which are largely responsible for the increase of vice and crime in great cities." Yet, Park recognized that the urban situation is complex and not all those living in the city are subject to such weakening of restraints. Here he has in mind the "professional people," those who are "keenly alive to the interests of their profession."[38]

5. LOUIS WIRTH

Louis Wirth (1897–1952) was a student of Park and a professor at the University of Chicago. He wrote the most famous discussion of the theoretical and methodological foundations of urban sociology. His article has been the subject of a book-length analysis.[39]

Reviewing the history of urban sociology, Wirth found only two studies, Weber's *The City* and Park's *The City*, that at least approximate a systematic theory of urbanism. Yet, neither established a framework upon which scientific research might profitably proceed. It was Wirth's goal to formulate a number of sociological propositions that would provide just such a framework. Having examined the available research on the urban situation, Wirth concluded that a theory of urbanism must treat at least three variables: "(a) numbers of population, (b) density of settlement, (c) heterogeneity of inhabitants and group life." The descriptions of each variable and the demonstrations of their interrelationships clearly relate to the "primary group ideal." Furthermore, and this is a point overlooked in subsequent considerations of Wirth's project, each variable is linked to a particular research strategy.

Although Wirth considered them separately, it is important to keep in mind that all three variables are complementary. Combining numbers, density, and heterogeneity we have the definition of the city as a place where a large number of different people live in rather close contact. With this in mind, we can examine each variable in the order Wirth presented and add to this Wirth's view of the proper research techniques for their scientific study.

a. *Size.* Wirth stated, "The multiplication of persons in a state of interaction under conditions which make their contact as full personalities impossible produces that segmentalization of human relationship." Beyond a certain limit, the members of the community cannot come to know one another. The urban resident, although having an extraordinary number of contacts, finds that the contacts become more and more impersonal. People are less dependent on others and their knowledge of others is fractionalized. As Wirth summarized: "This is essentially what is meant by saying that the city is characterized by secondary rather than primary contacts." In fact, Wirth accepted Durkheim's notion of "anomie" as the best way to speak of the nature of the social relationships that are caused by a large number of people assembled in one place.

Size provides the empirical basis for the way of studying the city known as the "ecological perspective." Wirth believed that the following factors are related to the size of the city: patterns of land use, nature of the physical structures, transportation, public utilities, and "many other phases of the physical mechanisms of the city." Also, size determines the proportion of people from different ethnic and racial groups found in the city and the scope of the services rendered by the city. One can see a number of hypotheses derived from this description. As Wirth recognized, with the use of this type of data, "we are able to operate with fairly objective indices, [and] it becomes possible to arrive at quite precise and generally quantitative results."

b. *Density.* Tracing his position to Darwin and Durkheim, Wirth stated, "an increase in numbers when area is held constant (i.e., an increase in density) tends to produce differentiation and specialization, since only in this way can the area support increased numbers." Place of residence and place of work become separated. The technological nature of work demands people with different skills and different personalities. Accordingly, "the close living together and working together of individuals who have no sentimental and emotional ties foster a spirit of competition, aggrandizement, and mutual exploitation." What happens then is that formal organizations must take the place of traditional associations. Formal control is needed to prevent disorder. Formal educational and recreational institutions replace those that were traditionally based on the family.

The method based on the density factor is called the study of urbanism "as a form of social organization." The transfer of socially significant activities to specialized institutions, the central result of increased density, can be associated with many variables all of which "can be substantially verified through objective indices." Examples include "the weakening of bonds of kinship, and the declining social significance of the family." In turn, these phenomena can be measured by the number of working mothers, lodgers in the household, postponed marriages, childless couples, and couples with fewer children.

c. *Heterogeneity.* Wirth held that "wherever large numbers of differently constituted individuals congregate, the process of depersonalization also enters." As the cities developed and as the economy expanded, a premium was placed upon efficient performance rather than personal qualities. People became linked by a "pecuniary nexus" and a "purchasability of services and things has displaced personal relations as the basis of association."

Heterogeneity is the basis for the final approach called the study of the "urban personality" or the perspective that sees urbanism "as a set of attitudes and ideas, and a constellation of personalities." Heterogeneity is the major factor in explaining depersonalization. Depersonalization is defined as a lack of "consistency and integrity of the personalities." Wirth listed seven variables that are signs of depersonalization and for which "indices are available." These are "personal disorganization, mental breakdown, suicide, delinquency, crime, corruption, and disorder."[40]

This brief precis makes evident that Wirth did provide a framework of propositions and a set of research questions that are mutually implicative. It should also be clear that both his theory of urbanism and his sociological research program rest on the "primary group ideal." Although Wirth "was far too much an urban type himself to find any comfort in . . . anti-urbanism," his vision of the city as the number one enemy of the primary group is a return to pre-Weberian urban sociology. As Sjoberg notes, Wirth refused to see the city as a phenomenon "molded by the social system of which it is a part."[41]

There is one final point on Wirth that can only be touched upon here. This is the question of the research hypotheses he established and the way in which he assumed they would be examined. As Wirth was proud to announce, each question could be answered by objective indices that are either readily available or easily formulated. It is legitimate to wonder if the hypotheses and in turn the framework of propositions were selected because of the ease with which they could be made into statistical-scientific statements. It may be reasonable to entertain one hypothesis rather than another because it is easier to operationalize, or because operational indices already exist. However, allowing elements, and only such elements, that can or have been been operationalized into one's framework of theoretical propositions appears at best tautological and at worst solipsistic.

The "primary group ideal" is a point of major attention in the works of Tönnies, Durkheim, Weber, Park, and Wirth; and the work of these scholars forms the intellectual foundation of contemporary urban sociology. Without question, treatments of urban anomie, social psychological alienation, and the difficult search for community in the city are based on this negative conception of the "primary group idea."[42] Urban sociologists, in turn, have influenced many impressionistic accounts of the isolation and loneliness of city life.[43] The "scientific support" afforded the "primary group ideal" by the urban sociology enterprise may be at least partially responsible for the view of the city that predominates the American value system. Further, this view may be responsible for the crisis in urban sociology.

CHALLENGES TO THE "PRIMARY GROUP IDEAL"

Agreeing with Thomas Kuhn, Friedrichs contends that scientific paradigms "are shattered as fundamental anomalies between hard, raw, empirical data and paradigm-derived theories, rules, and procedures appear and persist." Disaffection with the "primary group ideal" has existed in urban sociology for some time. However, it is only within the last two years that the problem inherent in the basis of urban sociology has been recognized by the general sociological audience. As Kuhn states, "if awareness of anomaly plays a role in the emergence of new sorts of phenomena, it should surprise no one that a similar but more profound awareness is a prerequisite to all acceptable changes of theory."[44] Presently, my goal is to mention certain of the early challenges to the "primary group ideal" and to offer hypotheses as to the reasons the early challenges were unacceptable to the urban sociologists. Furthermore, and most important of all, the recent challenges to the "primary group ideal" are summarized. It is these challenges that bring a "more profound awareness" to urban sociology that there are major difficulties within one of its basic paradigmatic elements.

BASIC AWARENESS OF ANOMALY: THE OBSERVATION STUDIES

It is not my intention to survey the history of sociology and to discover studies that demonstrate that the primary group is alive and well in the urban situation. However, certain famous discussions that draw this exact conclusion are in need of a certain amount of consideration.

The classic participant-observation study in sociology is William Foote Whyte's investigation of lower-class, Italian, street-corner boys in Boston.[45] Although Whyte discovered that there are numerous differences among the gangs, one thing remained constant. The gangs were not disorganized and the members were not without primary group support. In fact, Whyte's study is often used to demonstrate the vital importance of primary group membership in society. Some years later, Herbert Gans lived in a similar Italian neighborhood in Boston and replicated Whyte's findings. The general inhabitants of the neighborhood had a strong sense of community and numerous in-depth personal ties with their neighbors.[46] Moving away from Boston and the Italian subculture to Washington and the black subculture, we find similar conclusions. Elliot Liebow observed that the social world of the ghetto is a complex series of differentially structured primary group relationships. Far from being alone in the world, the typical man on the street corner is involved in a whole network of personal interactions. Most recently, we have Gerald Suttles' participant-observation study of four ethnic groups in Chicago. Specifically mentioning Park and Wirth, Suttles concluded that those envisioning the disappearance of the communal qualities of city life are "wrong."[47]

It is rather interesting that the large number of studies that support the existence of personality in the urban situation have been disregarded by mainstream urban sociology. Speculating upon the reasons for such oversights, I would suggest that the methodology used in the studies was simply not deemed adequate. Participant observation studies unique phenomena. One can not generalize from the results, for the research itself is essentially idiographic. As we have seen, the foundation of urban sociology presupposes the natural science model. Therefore, urban sociology is monothetic. At most, the observational studies should have given the urban sociologist a hint that the applicability of the "primary group ideal" may be limited to particular situations.

PROFOUND AWARENESS OF ANOMALY: THE EMPIRICAL STUDIES

During the past two years (1974–1975) two articles have been published in a major sociology journal that challenge the "primary group ideal." Both are based on the multiple regression analysis of survey research data, the standard tool of "scientific" sociology.

In one study, Kasarda and Janowitz investigate community attachment in mass society. Their goal was to test various hypotheses concerning the outcome of living in an urban area. They included in their scheme the Tönnies and Wirth hypothesis that the outcome of city living involves "a substitution of secondary for primary contacts, a weakening of the bonds of kinship, and a declining social significance of the local community." As Kasarda and Janowitz state, "For the most part, the coefficients speak for themselves. Increased size and density of a comunity do not weaken kinship ties and the significance of the local community. Nor is there a substitution of secondary for primary group relations in the large, dense community." In the other study, Hunter tests the hypothesized loss of community as expressed in the works of Tönnies, Durkheim, Weber, and Wirth. Hunter discovered that there is neither a decline of the local community as a unit of primary social interaction nor is there a lessening of the sense of community in the city. Hunter noted that in the urban community there are a number of forces that exist to maintain community solidarity. For example, city residents are "involved in creating and maintaining a more formal structural embodiment of community—a local community organization."[48] The work of Kasarda and Janowitz, and Hunter, leave the urban sociologist with no recourse but the acceptance of the tenuousness of the "primary group ideal."

CONCLUSION

Insofar as urban sociology focuses on the "problems" of city life, it must inevitably confront the "primary group ideal." This is the domain of inquiry that has led a specifically "urban" sociology into respectable eminence. Agreeing for a moment that urbanism as a way of life is not the isolated existence it is made out to be, the problem becomes one of delimiting an area of specialization for the urban sociologist. If the urban sociologist studies issues other than urbanism, say, certain general sociological questions within a city, he could not be characterized as an "urban" sociologist by what he studies. If the urban sociologist studies the city as a whole, involving himself with questions of policy and education, he could not be characterized as a sociologist. In this case he could be called an "expert on urban affairs." As such, he would be forced to deal with a vast number of circumstances of a non-sociological nature.[49]

Predicting the turn urban sociology will take is difficult. It is possible that the challenges to the "primary group ideal" will simply be forgotten. Perhaps the "primary group ideal" will join the anti-urban bias and be justifiably called "an image that will not die."[50] Another possibility is that urban sociology will be reduced to an atheoretical collection of bits of empirically gathered data or a mere set of a vast number of propositions in need of clarification and qualification.[51] Finally, urban sociology may remain in its present condition and await the resolution of the paradigmatic conflicts currently occurring in general sociology.

NOTES

[1] Louis Wirth, "Urbanism as a Way of Life," *American Journal of Sociology*, 44 (July 1938): 1–24. Reprinted in *Louis Wirth on Cities and Social Life* [ed. Albert J. Reiss, Jr.] (Chicago: University of Chicago Press, 1964), p. 67.

[2] Don Martindale, "Prefatory Remarks: The Theory of the City," in Max Weber, *The City* (New York: The Free Press, 1966; original edition, 1958), p. 9.

[3] Rosemary Mellor, "Urban Sociology in an Urbanized Society," *British Journal of Sociology*, XXVI (September 1975): 276, 280.

[4] The crisis of sociology has been documented by Alvin W. Gouldner, *The Coming Crisis of Western Sociology* (New York: Basic Books, 1970); Robert W. Friedrichs, *A Sociology of Sociology* (New York: Macmillan, 1970); and Larry T. Reynolds and Janice M. Reynolds, eds., *The Sociology of Sociology* (New York: David McKay, 1970).

[5] The idea of "paradigm of normal sociology" is borrowed from Friedrichs, op. cit., p. 11. Friedrichs, of course, borrowed the idea from Thomas Kuhn, *The Structure of Scientific Revolutions* (Chicago: University of Chicago Press, 1962).

[6] I have expanded Mellor's, op. cit., p. 280, description of urban sociology.

[7] Jack P. Gibbs, ed., *Urban Research Methods* (Princeton, N.J.: D. Van Nostrand Company, 1964), is a text dedicated solely to the application of the demographic method to the study of the city. See also Leo F. Schnore, ed., *Social Science and the City* (New York: Praeger, 1968), for a similar emphasis.

[8] Derek Phillips, *Knowledge from What?* (Chicago: Rand McNally, 1971), p. 3, points out that over 90 percent of the studies in the major sociology journals employed the survey method.

[9] Dennis E. Poplin, *Communities: A Survey of Theories and Methods of Research* (New York: Macmillan, 1972), p. 276.

[10] Anselm L. Strauss, "Strategies for Discovering Urban Theory" in *The American City: A Sourcebook of Urban Imagery*, [ed. Anselm Strauss] (Chicago: Aldine, 1968), p. 525.

[11] Abraham Kaplan, *The Conduct of Inquiry* (San Francisco: Chandler, 1964), p. 12.

[12] Rosemary Mellor, op. cit., p. 280.

[13] Roscoe C. Hinkle, Jr., and Gisela J. Hinkle, *The Development of Modern Sociology* (New York: Random House, 1954), p. 2.

[14] *West Side Studies* (New York: Russell Sage Foundation, 1914), pp. 40, 60; Quoted in David Matza, *Becoming Deviant* (Englewood Cliffs, N.J.: Prentice-Hall, 1969), p. 20; David Matza, p. 18.

[15] Quoted in Morton and Lucia White, *The Intellectual Versus the City* (Cambridge: Harvard University Press and The M.I.T. Press, 1962), p. 19; Richard Hofstadter, *The Age of Reform* (New York: Vintage, 1955), pp. 24–25; B. I. Coleman, *The Idea of the City in Nineteenth-Century Britain* (London: Routledge and Kegan Paul, 1973).

[16] Morton and Lucia White, op. cit., pp. 222, 225, 223.

[17] Charles Horton Cooley, *Social Organization* (New York: Shocken, 1962), p. 23. (Originally published in 1909.)

[18] Plato, for example, believed that only the city-state was morally self-sufficient. A good life implied participation in the life of the city-state. Plato saw the decay of the city-state begin by the break-up of the communal way of life of the ruling class. See Book VIII of *The Republic*. Also, Rousseau declared, "Unfortunately, there is no such thing as home education in our large towns. Society is so general and so mixed there is no place left for retirement, and even in the home we live in public." See *Emile* (New York: E. P. Dutton, 1961), p. 351.

[19] Roscoe C. Hinkle, "Charles Horton Cooley's General Sociological Orientation," *Sociological Quarterly*, 8 (Winter 1967): 5; C. Wright Mills, "The Professional Ideology of Social Pathologists," *American Journal of Sociology*, XLIX (September 1943). Reprinted in Reynolds and Reynolds, op. cit., p. 136.

[20] Charles Horton Cooley, *The Theory of Transportation* (Ph.D. diss., University of Michigan, 1894).

[21] See James S. Coleman, "Community Disorganization and Conflict," in *Contemporary Social Problems* [eds. Robert K. Merton and Robert Nisbet] 3rd ed. (New York: Harcourt Brace Jovanovich, 1971), especially pp. 664–67, and see also, Peter H. Mann, *An Approach to Urban Sociology* (London: Routledge and Kegan Paul, 1965).

[22] Ferdinand Tönnies, *Community and Society* (New York: Harper and Row, 1963), pp. 103, 43, 256.

[23] Ibid., pp. 231, 230, 242.

[24] Charles P. Loomis and John C. McKinney, "Introduction" to F. Tönnies, op. cit., pp. 2–3.

[25] Mark Jay Oromaner, "The Most Cited Sociologists: An Analysis of Introductory Text Citations," *American Sociologist*, 3 (May 1968) and B. J. Keeley, "Use of Reading Lists for the Graduate Students in Sociology," *Sociology and Social Research*, 18 (July 1964).

[26] Emile Durkheim, *The Division of Labor in Society* (New York: The Free Press, 1960), pp. 338, 148, 129–30, 181, 353. (Originally published in 1893).

[27] Joachim Israel, *Alienation from Marx to Modern Sociology* (Boston: Allyn and Bacon, 1971), p. 144; Emile Durkheim, op. cit., p. 368.

[28] Emile Durkheim, *Suicide* (New York: The Free Press, 1951), pp. 246–54, 258. (Originally published in 1897.)

[29] Hanan C. Selvin, "Durkheim's *Suicide*: Further Thoughts on a Methodological Classic," in *Emile Durkheim*, ed. Robert A. Nisbet (Englewood Cliffs, N.J.: Prentice-Hall, 1965), p. 113; Lewis A. Coser, *Continuities in the Study of Social Conflict* (New York: The Free Press, 1967), p. 155; For an extended treatment of the development of the concept of anomie, see Marshall B. Clinard, ed., *Anomie and Deviant Behavior* (New York: The Free Press, 1964).

[30] Mark Jay Oromaner, op. cit., and B. J. Keeley, op. cit.; Max Weber, *The City* (New York: The Free Press, 1966); Louis Wirth, op. cit., p. 67.

[31] The city was simply defined as a market. An urban community was a market that was at least partially autonomous politically and an association with its own laws. See Weber, op. cit., p. 81.

[32] Ibid., p. 65.

[33] Max Weber, *The Theory of Social and Economic Organization* (New York: The Free Press, 1964), pp. 136, 137.

[34] Max Weber, *The Protestant Ethic and the Spirit of Capitalism* (New York: Charles Scribner's Sons, 1958), p. 181.

[35] Lewis A. Coser, *Masters of Sociological Thought* (New York: Harcourt, Brace, Jovanovich, 1971), p. 357; Robert E. Park, "The City," *American Journal of Sociology*, 20 (1914–1915), reprinted in Robert E. Park, *Introduction to the Science of Sociology* (Chicago: University of Chicago Press, 1921), and, *The City* (Chicago: University of Chicago Press, 1925).

[36] Sylvia L. Thrupp, "The City as the Idea of Social Order," in *The Historian and the City* [eds. Oscar Handlin and John Burchard] (Cambridge: The M.I.T. Press and Harvard University Press, 1963), p. 130; Peter I. Rose, *The Subject Is Race* (New York: Oxford University Press, 1968), p. 9 argues that Park is still the leading sociologist in the field of race relations. It very well may be that the same holds true for urban sociology.

[37] Robert E. Park, *Introduction*, pp. 11, 12; The Hinkles, op. cit., p. 34.

[38] Robert E. Park, *The City*, pp. 107, 106, 114; Robert E. Park *Introduction*, p. 312.

[39] Louis Wirth, "Urbanism as a Way of Life," *American Journal of Sociology*, 44 (July 1938): 1–24; R. N. Morris, *Urban Sociology* (New York: Praeger, 1968).

[40] Louis Wirth, in Albert Reiss, op. cit., pp. 69, 71, 79, 78, 73, 74, 80, 76, 82.

[41] Don Martindale, op. cit., p. 38; Gideon Sjoberg, *The Preindustrial City* (New York: The Free Press, 1960), p. 15.

[42] See E. Digby Baltzell, ed., *The Search for Community in Modern America* (New York: Harper and Row, 1968), for an extensive bibliography. See also David W. Minar and Scott Greer, eds., *The Concept of Community* (Chicago: Aldine, 1969), especially the sections on "The City as a Community," and "Social and Personal Consequences of Change;" Also: Robert Nisbet, *The Quest for Community* (New York: Oxford Uni-

versity Press, 1953); Maurice R. Stein, *The Eclipse of Community* (Princeton: Princeton University Press, 1960).

43 For example, Alvin Toffler, *Future Shock* (New York: Random House, 1970), pp. 87–90, for his discussion of "modular man" and his review of Wirth's discussion of urbanism. See also, Philip Slater, *The Pursuit of Loneliness* (Boston: Beacon, 1970), and, Vance Packard, *A Nation of Strangers* (New York: David McKay, 1972).

44 Robert W. Friedrichs, op. cit., p. 23; Thomas S. Kuhn, op. cit., p. 67.

45 William Foote Whyte, *Street Corner Society* (Chicago: University of Chicago Press, 1943).

46 Herbert Gans, *The Urban Villagers* (New York: The Free Press, 1962). See also his article "Urbanism and Suburbanism as Ways of Life: A Re-Evaluation of Definitions," in Arnold Rose (ed.), *Human Behavior and Social Processes* (Boston: Houghton Mifflin, 1962).

47 Elliot Liebow, *Tally's Corner* (Boston: Little, Brown, 1967); Gerald D. Suttles, *The Social Order of the Slum* (Chicago: University of Chicago Press, 1968); Gerald D. Suttles, *The Social Construction of Communities* (Chicago: University of Chicago Press, 1972), p. 8.

48 John D. Kasarda and Morris Janowitz, "Community Attachment in Mass Society," *American Sociological Review*, 39 (June 1974), 328, 336; Albert Hunter, "The Loss of Community: An Empirical Test Through Replication," *American Sociological Review*, 40 (October 1975), 547.

49 This appears to be the position taken by Scott Greer in *The Urbane View: Life and Politics in Metropolitan America* (New York: Oxford University Press, 1972).

50 For example, Michael Lewis, *Urban America: Institutions and Experience* (New York: Wiley, 1973), p. 16, declares that one of the basic assumptions of the sociological study of the city must be "the need for improving the lot of men in urban society." See Jeffery K. Hadden and Josef J. Barton, "An Image That Will Not Die: Thoughts on the History of the Anti-Urban Ideology," in L. H. Masotti and Jeffery K. Hadden, eds., *The Urbanization of the Suburbs* (Beverly Hills, Calif.: Sage Publishing, 1973).

51 Just such a position can be found in Claude S. Fischer, "Urbanism as a Way of Life: A Review and an Agenda," *Sociological Methods and Research*, 2 (November 1972), and, "Toward a Subcultural Theory of Urbanism," *American Journal of Sociology*, 80 (May 1975).

ORGANIZATION THEORY:

Implications for Behavior of

Metropolitan Councils of Governments*

Gerald A. Starr

For many years students of urban affairs have clung to the notion that the American metropolis suffers from excessive fragmentation of the political system and therefore needs some sort of mechanism for centralized policy making. There have been accordingly many attempts to establish centralized government over metropolitan regions; usually the attempts met failure. In the hope of gaining some measure of rationalization of the urban policy process, a different and more politically palatable solution eventually came to be advocated. The reformers' arguments proved persuasive—at least in Washington—and with the assistance of strong federal backing, in the past decade the council of governments (COG) has become the characteristic instrument of urban regionalism.

Councils of governments are "multi-functional voluntary regional associations of elected local officials or of local governments represented by their elected officials."[1] COGs provide "an areawide mechanism for key officials to study, discuss, and determine how best to deal with common problems. This mechanism is not a government, as it has no mandatory financing and enforcement authority. Instead it

* This work was originally prepared for delivery at the annual meeting of the Georgia Political Science Association, Savannah, January 31, 1976.

is a continuing agency to furnish research, plans, advice, recommendations, and coordination."[2] In most cases the COG is structured so as to give all member general-purpose governments equal representation and voting weight, regardless of member population.[3]

In practice, the primary role of most COGs revolves around the formulation and application of functional and comprehensive plans for the region. Such plans may be drawn by the COG's staff, by consultants, or even by other planning agencies. Once adopted by the members of the council, however, they hopefully will serve to direct and channel the course of urban development. It is here that most COGs exercise what little influence they possess. Regional councils, which have been designated as "clearinghouses," review and comment upon applications for federal grants-in-aid for projects and programs. The idea is that federal agencies will be attentive to clearinghouse findings as to whether the subject of funding conforms with regional planning; if the areawide body has given disapproval, the application will presumably be denied. There is no guarantee, however, that the clearinghouse's recommendation will be honored; local jurisdictions thus are not actually compelled to fall in line with the regional plan.

Since the review-and-comment procedure and simple moral suasion comprise the whole armory of COG weapons in the battle for centralized policy making, one might well expect councils to be rather ineffective tools for the advancement of metropolitan unification. And that is the way things have turned out. As far back as 1966, in fact, the Association of Bay Area Governments is said to have recognized "that a voluntary association of cities and counties was unable to make and implement comprehensive regional plans."[4] The empirical evidence gathered over the years since then generally sounds the same theme, although only a small sampling of the literature can be presented here.

Charles Harris, after studying seventy-four councils of governments, concluded the organizational features which made them essentially confederations for debating rather than acting upon controversial issues prevented COGs from disturbing the status quo supported by established interests.[5] The 1969 survey by the International City Management Association indicated COGs were greatly dependent on fed eral support and guidance; councils were influenced by federal funding patterns to involve themselves with physical development and functional planning to the detriment of confronting controversial social issues.[6] Melvin Mogulof studied seven COGs in metropolitan areas around the country and reluctantly concluded that none of them were effectively redistributing resources.[7] The councils he studied were beset by a myriad of problems: "The image of the COG we mean to convey is one of a beleaguered organization, surrounded by unsure federal partners, unwilling local members and a barely awakening state government."[8] In an extensive study of regionalism by the Advisory Commission on Intergovernmental Relations (ACIR), deficiencies were noted in federal program participation, relationships with other area-wide bodies, and citizen involvement in regional matters.[9] Most important, COGs were ineffective in bringing their plans to fruition: ". . . local governments considered implementation of comprehensive and functional plans to be the most serious problem facing regional councils."[10]

The picture which emerges from the literature shows COGs are not meeting the objectives which they were originally designed to pursue. Most councils of government are weak institutions, buffeted about by the conflicting expectations and demands of federal bureaucrats, planners, and local officials. They have generally been unable to build firm public support or even public recognition. They have accomplished relatively little toward implementing the plans they generate. Although they were supposed to advance regional harmony, many councils have been split by persistent controversy over organizational means, purposes, procedures and structure. Councils of governments, in sum, have not fulfilled the hopes their authors held for them.

Since COGs' performance has been so disappointing, we might well wonder if there could not have been some means for evaluating their potential before we invested so much in them. Could we have exercised better foresight and acted more prudently? Could we have become more sure of the outcome before proceeding to establish hundreds of voluntaristic regional planning and coordinating agencies across the nation?

The thesis of this paper is that such questions can be affirmatively answered and with a reasonable degree of confidence. Councils of governments are not a wholly unique organizational phenomenon. They have experienced what may be unusually severe stresses for public agencies, but in the need to recognize, deal with, and attempt to come to terms with objects in the environment they share with other organizations a set of common needs for viability and achievement of objectives. If councils of governments do have the capacity to mediate successfully stimuli coming from the environment and develop appropriate responses based upon some acceptable behavioral code, they should like other organizations achieve a stable and profitable existence.

It is submitted that we should analyze and evaluate COGs in terms of the relationship just described. If we are to gain a better understanding of what we may reasonably expect from councils of governments, we should see COGs as organizational theorists do: as social organisms with a systemic relationship to surrounding institutions, with regularized patterns of action and subject to the same organizational needs experienced by other such social systems. This paper represents an attempt to apply to COGs just such an analysis based on organization theory and offer some predictions as to what they can become.

Any one of a number of theoretical approaches could be used to analyze councils of governments but space permits only one to be discussed in this paper. The perspective rather selectively relied upon here is structural-functional theory as expounded by Talcott Parsons.[11] No claim is made that his concepts are the "best" ways of describing organizational behavior; certainly no one would suggest that Parsonian theory is easy to apply to empirical situations. It is used here because his concepts have been widely adopted (and adapted) in social science literature, the theory is extensively developed and widely known, and his work is highly congruent with the systems approach for understanding social system behavior popular today. In addition, Parsonian theory has already been demonstrated to have utility as a theoretical "window" by which we can examine and understand the functioning of urban regional organizations.[12]

The portion of Parsons' scheme with which we shall be concerned bears on his idea that any organization—any social system, in fact—has to satisfactorily perform certain activities or tasks in order to persist over time without fundamental alteration or destruction.[13] He finds there are four such "functional imperatives" for system viability. "Adaptation" pertains to the acquisition and deployment of system resources. "Goal-attainment" is the achievement of organizational purposes. "Integration" provides internal harmony. "Pattern-maintenance" establishes regularized patterns of behavior that serve to stabilize and give continuity to the system's interrelationships. The last function is also called "latency"; it thus accounts for the last letter of the familiar AGIL acronym. Again, the four functional requisites comprise the scope of necessary system activities. Therefore, if for some reason a system cannot adequately perform some function and the satisfaction of that imperative is in deficit we can regard that system as fatally handicapped in its efforts to pursue its designated objectives and maintain its structural integrity.

The first function, adaptation, involves the organization's adjustments to the internal and external situation necessary for it to pursue its objectives. A system must adequately procure, produce and mobilize "generalized facilities," i.e., system resources of all kinds, as required to meet its needs. Resources include "land"—resources closely committed to the organization on a long-term basis—labor, capital, and "organization"—the proper arrangement of the other three factors of production.

The satisfaction of the adaptation function in COGs is in some ways aided by their status. To a large extent the tasks of procuring the factors of production are done for them. "Land" is obtained by grants of formal authority and responsibility as governed by statutory provisions for areawide agencies, and generated by the councils' charters of incorporation and by-laws. COGs thus enjoy intangible but very real assets of an enduring character. Procurement of personnel resources is also largely taken care of automatically: government members of the COG are selected through the elective mechanisms of their respective jurisdictions; technical personnel are gained from the ranks of the planning and managerial professions. The task of obtaining capital is considerably aided by the largess of the federal government.

Two-thirds of urban regional councils responding to an ACIR survey reported that for each of three recent years over half of their revenues came from federal grants.[14]

But it is also apparent the COGs have some problems with respect to the factors of production. We have already noted the marked limitations in council authority to enforce regional policy. The recruitment of personnel resources from two very different perspectives carries the potential of persistent friction between governing boards and their employees. While politicians want to minimize the involvement of COGs in local affairs, planners have a vested interest in expanding agencies' roles. Many staff members want COGs to exercise a veto power over matters before them, and perform line functions as well as the usual staff duties.[15] Council directors feel they should have a major part in determining council objectives and achieving agreement upon them.[16] Washington's generosity in funding regional bodies also creates problems. The ACIR concluded massive federal assistance "has transformed areawide confederalism from a wholly independent undertaking to a largely federally financed surrogate for metropolitan government."[17] Such a dependency relationship is quickly perceived by political officials and reinforces their fears that councils of governments are federal weapons for intruding upon properly local matters. Since Parsons' factor of "organization" involves the proper relationship of land, labor, and capital, we should therefore anticipate it to be unfavorably affected by problems with the other factors. The persistent concern of COGs with structural reorganization—in 1973 more than a third of councils surveyed were considering some form of reorganization[18]—seems to be just such evidence that the adaptive function is inhibited in councils of governments.

Goal attainment is defined by Parsons to be the reaching of some desired state of affairs which is different from the extant condition. Parsons categorizes organizations as those collectivities which are distinguished by primacy of orientation to the attainment of specific goals; organizations are society's most effective means for meeting desired purposes. The goals of an organization, moreover, cannot in the ordinary case be defined or chosen without intervention or at least acquiescence by the larger system (e.g., the metropolis; American political culture) of which the organization is a differentiated part. A goal is a "product" consumed by the larger system. If the larger system rejects such a product, we can say that there is a "disposal problem" for the organization. The analogy to the firm and its marketplace is obvious. But public organizations likewise have "products" which must be exchanged for resources from the environment. Since ordinarily there is no marketplace to regulate the relationship, public organizations often are governed by elected representatives which represent the citizen consumers' preferences. The governing board of a COG likewise serves as a conduit for public satisfaction or dissatisfaction with the regional council.

Goal-attainment, Parsons believes, is especially related to decision-making processes. And councils of governments are peculiarly decision-making organizations. In a real sense, decisions are the "products" they supply. While some decisions primarily have an internal referent—assigning responsibilities to the executive director, or allocating voting weight within the governing board, for example—other decisions, such as those pertaining to regional policy, are primarily external in impact. Of course, controversial questions of area policy can and do carry into the internal affairs of the council.

Attaining the designated goals of regional planning and plan implementation is the most conspicuous failure of COGs. William Timmins studied the planning process and product of forty-eight regional agencies. "Our central findings are that their growth has far outstripped the quality of their planning"; Timmins concluded, "that available management tools, especially systems analysis, have not been adequately employed; that their full potential is still far ahead. . . ."[19] The ACIR survey of member officials found "local governments considered implementation of comprehensive and functional plans to be the most serious problem facing regional councils."[20]

Such failures can be readily explained by the organizational circumstances in which COGs find themselves. As we noted above, the goal-product of an organization must be consonant with the values of the larger system. Such consonance in COGs is powerfully enforced through the device of having representatives of local governments sit on council governing bodies. The governing board "imposes the conditions governing the processes of disposal and procurement" and "is also part of a wider social system which is the source of the 'meaning,' legitimation, or higher-level support which makes the implementation of the organization's goals possible."[21]

The significance of this is that local officials are not usually oriented toward the goal of centralized, rationalistic policy making. Rather, they prefer that the COG do what is minimally required to maintain the flow of federal funds to area governments, but otherwise observe the status quo of metropolitan political structure and resource allocation. Thus if councils were to vigorously pursue a comprehensive planning and policy implementation role they would by offending their governors' parochial values, jeopardize their locally derived funding, their support from key members, and eventually their survival.

Councils of governments, like all organizations, naturally seek to avoid or minimize stress. In Edward Banfield's trenchant words, "organizations . . . are not like salmon; they much prefer sterility to death."[22] As a result, in the effort to remain viable systems they must scale down their ambitions and displace regionalistic goals in favor of less controversial ones, such as service activities for member governments. To be more exact, they wind up with two sets of goals, one "official" and the other "operative."[23] Official goals pertain to area-wide planning and policy making; the true goals serve to check the development of the council as a regional institution.

Integration, the third functional imperative, has to do with the internal processes by which a system's components are established and kept in a state of unity thereby preventing natural centrifugal tendencies from destroying the integrity of the system. Successful integration requires the existence of sufficient supportive commitment from members of a system; the "problem" of integration is that of creating and maintaining such a spirit of solidarity. Members must demonstrate some degree of self-subjugation in the interests of the larger collectivity and accept roles which are supportive of the system's other functional requisites. Since for almost any system there are other and competing role demands and obligations on members, system integration must be steadily nourished.

Integrative processes in councils of governments are seen in the form of activities which serve to enhance the spirit of solidarity and cooperation. A key to such activities is stress upon the whole organization's interests—often in the name of regionalism—rather than on those of an individual member or subgroup. A spirit of solidarity is evidenced on the part of a political official by his or her willingness to subordinate the interests of the jurisdiction in favor of the regional collectivity. This might take the form of support for increases in dues assessments for the COG, or perhaps the acceptance without protest of decisions which promote areawide objectives even at some detriment to the member's jurisdiction.

But in examining the concept underlying councils of governments, one is immediately struck by the intrinsic potential for organizational conflict, i.e., disintegration. The basic rationale for a COG is that it provides a formal mechanism for regularly bringing together elected officials so they can compatibly discuss common problems and jointly decide upon avenues for coordinated action. But of course, there is no reason a lessening of differences of opinion will necessarily result. Instead, the very opposite outcome may occur if council meetings serve to fan the flames of disagreement by raising and aggravating disruptive questions. Points of conflict within the region's governments may be exacerbated simply by their presentation to the council. Cleveland illustrates the point. It tried to use its COG as a forum to present the problems of inner-city residents, only to find that suburban communities refused to share Cleveland's concern for the urban poor. "The Cleveland case," says Frances Friskin, "suggests that greater understanding does not necessarily lead to greater desire to cooperate. In fact, the reverse can and did happen."[24]

The joining of central cities and suburban communities in COGs means regional agencies have an ever-present source of dissension. Although many regional council directors report there has been little conflict over specific issues between core and suburban interests,[25] the fact that most councils apportion voting weight equally among their members indicates the presence of a source of irritation for central cities already less content with their representation.[26] With respect to smaller governments, observers have noted a widespread suburban distrust, even fear, of the central city.[27] Especially in COGs serving the larger SMSAs, matters such as assessment of dues, fear of dominance by a single jurisdiction or a coalition of jurisdictions, and voting arrangements have been controversial issues.[28] Even non-membership in the council can be troublesome, since "to the extent that the COG does not include the cities and towns and/or counties of the metropolitan region it may serve as a barrier to the normal cooperation which might exist among the several jurisdictions of the region."[29]

We can also see that the clearinghouse role for federal aid presents another source of potential disruption for COGs. Relatively few grant applications are actually rejected by clearinghouses, yet local representatives may still feel uneasy over the chance, however slight, that a screening agency may help interrupt the flow of grants-in-aid. Thus COGs are put under an irresolvable strain—at the same moment, they must discharge their responsibilities in rejecting wasteful or ill-planned facilities and programs, yet they must also be careful not to upset the officials who have the final say on policy. "COGs are kept busy, on the one hand, trying to demonstrate to federal authorities that they are worthwhile investments, and, on the other, reassuring local units that they constitute no threat to them."[30] Short of complete harmony of viewpoints among the two sides, there is no way for COGs to reconcile the opposing preferences of their two "publics."

The planning responsibilities of most councils of governments also generate conflict. It is difficult to think of a metropolitan area which does not contain jurisdictions with widely varying tastes, needs and resources. Planning for a relatively heterogeneous region will certainly be far more difficult than planning for a single, relatively homogeneous community, and of course even the latter task is extremely demanding in its complexity.[31] The pattern of political fragmentation and overlapping authority, the narrow perspectives of planners, the uncertainties in the planning process, and the inadequacies of means for plan implementation have been seen as compelling almost certain failure of the comprehensive planning process.[32] Attitudinal dimensions will also vary. Orientations toward planning as a concept or process will differ between communities that reflect the "public-regarding ethos" and those communities where the "private-regarding" ethic prevails.[33] Officials who see local government as "an instrument of community growth" are likely to differ sharply from the office holder who prefers governments to be a "caretaker" or "provider of amenities."[34] In planning activities as with the other sources of tension just described, it is clear the integration function (as it would relate to a healthy area wide agency) will be retarded. The natural tendency to minimize organizational conflict again leads to retreat from regional guidance.

The fourth function which Parsons holds to be necessary for system viability is pattern-maintenance, or latency. This relatively passive phase serves to restore the qualities dissipated in the energy- and resource-consuming phases of adaptation and goal-attainment. Potential disruptive tensions must be diverted or quelled, and motivational and cultural patterns must be renewed, if the system is to continue to devote itself to its primary objectives. Observance of this function does not actually mean the organization is literally dormant, but rather that there is an absence of unified action for the purposes of system adaptation, goal-attainment and integration. The system does not undergo change and is therefore said to be "latent."

Pattern-maintenance is primarily an internally directed function, since the object is maintenance of the value patterns of the system. Furthermore, there must be a certain degree of uniformity in such values. Pattern-maintenance serves to constrain value differentiation.

But latency has an external aspect, too, in connection with the overriding importance of relating a system with its environment. As we have already seen, it is necessary that the system's value patterns and goals be complementary to those of the larger universe of systems. In organizations this external aspect of the pattern-maintenance function is the special province of what Parsons calls the "institutional" or "community" level of the system. This segment is positioned in the interface between the system and its surrounding objects, and operates to "mediate" the system with its environment.

Pattern-maintenance in COGs, as in other social systems, is not a phase where things are "done." There is no overt change in the state of the system. But by subtle means the continuity of the organization is being advanced and its stability is being strengthened. Pattern-maintenance is manifested, for example, when members assume "peacemaker" roles during council disputes, or when they offer statements which assert that regionalism poses no threat to traditional local government values, i.e., argue that COGs are "legitimate."

With respect to councils of governments, however, the process of pattern-maintenance is inhibited by the presence of several factors. First, COGs conform very well to the definition of "partial" social systems. Kaplan, addressing this point in his structural-functional study of Metropolitan Toronto, explains, ". . . The partial or segmental system controls only a small part of the behavior of its members, may lead the members only in areas deemed appropriate to that system, must compete for the member's attention and loyalty with a number of other systems, and cannot make extensive use of social control mechanisms without provoking a reduction in the members' commitment to the system."[35] Because they suffer from the weakness of partial systems, COGs, like Metro Toronto, experience considerable difficulty in laying claim to the loyalties and attachments of their members.

Another problem stems from the fact that the key subsystem of a council of governments is its governing board. This panel is composed of officials who owe primary obligations and responsibilities to jurisdictions which may well be in conflict not only with the COG, but with each other. When differences arise between the council and its member governments, the representatives of those governments are not likely to assume the side of the council. They are much more likely to repudiate the policy at issue and attempt to demonstrate their loyalty to their elective constituencies.

In addition to the difficulties apparent in obtaining the loyalty of political officials, we should recognize the potential problems with regard to the professional staff who bear much of the burden of advancing regionalism. COGs are structured so as to subordinate professional planning advice to political judgments. Planners who work in this context may experience the frustrations often experienced by specialists who find their values differ from, and their suggestions rejected by, their organizational superiors.[36] They may be led by their education and experience to believe they best understand the nature of regional issues and would, therefore, expect to exercise some power in dealing with them. When political considerations intrude upon planning decisions—as they often do—such influences are seen by planners as somehow "unprofessional,"[37] but they are not cued as to how to respond to them. There is no normative theory for the planning discipline which instructs the planner whether he should be a political agnostic, an adviser to political decision makers, or a political activist.[38] It is not surprising therefore that COG directors usually do not believe they should perform the role of conflict resolver.[39] The result, again, is inhibition of pattern-maintenance processes. In this fourth functional imperative, as with the others, councils are handicapped in becoming strong, viable instruments of regionalism. Had such limitations been better considered, had organizational analysis been applied to test the concept of councils of governments before so much had been invested in the device, it appears we would surely have been much more cautious in turning to COGs in hopes of reshaping the metropolis.

But Americans are a people attached to the notion that institutional forms can be devised to overcome any such drawbacks as have just been described. If a public agency does not perform as expected and intended, we reorganize incessantly in the belief that eventually the correct structural arrangement will be discovered and the then revitalized agency will proceed to discharge its duty. In a demonstration of this attitude, metropolitan reformers have recently turned to a "new, improved" COG known as the Umbrella Multi-Jurisdictional Organization (UMJO). In calling for the creation of these strengthened regional agencies, the International City Management Association (ICMA) explains UMJOs would differ from COGs in that the proposed agencies "would be composed of state and local government representatives with the latter having at least three-fourths of the membership. Local governments would be required to become members. But deliberations would be governed by a dual voting system including population-weighted voting on certain issues, with the specific procedure to be spelled out in the state legislation or left to individual councils. . . . This reformed regional council then would be a comprehensive planning, coordinating, programming, servicing, and limited implementing body."[40]

Another prestigious affirmation of the UMJO approach has come from the Advisory Commission on Intergovernmental Relations, which calls for these more muscular COGs to be the basis of a new "Substate Districting Strategy."[41] In their plan, UMJOs would be "prime contractor" for all substate regional activities, would receive grants-in-aid and revenue sharing funds, and would review not only applications presently screened under the A–95 procedure but all major capital facility projects as well. It would control or govern special districts. Upon an affirmative vote of members and area population it would assume operational and revenue-raising functions. Under the ACIR proposal either existing COGs could be the nucleus of UMJOs or new organizations might be formed.

UMJOs are obviously remarkable institutions—as close as one can get to metropolitan government without calling it such. They go far beyond previous concepts of voluntaristic areawide planning and coordinative agencies. One wonders how those mayors who unhappily called enfeebled COGs "new layers of government" would react to UMJOs; they would surely be dismayed and probably speechless. But even assuming that sufficient impetus exists to impose UMJOs on unwilling local governments, we must still ask whether they can reasonably be expected to perform as the ICMA and ACIR hope and intend. If this question is left unasked, we may be doomed to repeat our disappointing experience with councils of governments.

Following the thesis of the preceding sections of this paper, it is submitted that by analyzing UMJOs in the light of organization theory we can do much to answer the question of their ability to overcome environmental hostility toward regionalism. The balance of this paper therefore briefly examines the capacities of this latest proposal for metropolitan centralization, again relying upon Parsonian theory for the conceptual framework. Parsons has concerned himself with this issue of organizational potency. Put very simply, he holds that four conditions must be satisfied if organizations are to generate power to influence objects within the environment.[42]

The first condition is the institutionalization of a value system which legitimates organizational goals and the principal goal-attainment patterns or methods. We have already seen that COGs suffer in this respect; in the usual case they have proved unable to overcome existing localistic value systems which deny them legitimacy as part of the metropolitan decision-making process.

And regarding UMJOs, there seems to be no reason to expect them to be any more successful in this respect. Indeed, the UMJO device will offend the localistically oriented values of the typical city or county politician even more than does the COG. The intensity of objection and resistence to UMJO concepts and operating principles will increase in proportion to the perceived capacity for such institutions to disturb local autonomy.

The second condition for organizational potency requires regulation of the system's procurement and decision-making processes through universalistic rules. Parsons reasons that through adherence to uniformly acceptable means of doing things the system establishes the validity of its claims to loyalty and cooperation from its members. But unfortunately there are situations where there are no universalistically accepted rules. For example, there is no "universal rule" concerning the division of power between large and small jurisdictions within a council of governments. Both the one-city, one-vote principle and the population-based voting rule can be defended on practical as well as philosophical grounds, and consensus regarding the best method is an unlikely event. In this connection, it is significant that the ICMA left the issue of voting procedure in UMJOs rather ambiguous: they would use population-weighted voting on "certain issues, with the specific procedure to be spelled out in the state legislation or left to individual councils." This seems to be an admission that the ICMA could not decide the question; we can be rather sure on the basis of continuing intra-COG friction over representation of large versus small cities that UMJOs will not (at least not permanently) settle the question either. We can predict continuing controversy over decisions reached by such debatable means, and stubborn resistance to implementation of policies reached by what at least some member governments will consider to be an unfair procedure.

Parsons' third condition requires that there must be command of rather detailed and regular support from persons whose cooperation is needed. We have noted COGs' deficiencies in this regard. Probably UMJOS would do somewhat better—any institutions exercising as much formal authority as they are proposed to exercise will surely gain the loyalty (or at least constant interest) of many political figures. An UMJO would be such a significant factor in its metropolitan political system it would acquire its own "courthouse crowd." Also, by containing all jurisdictions within the area, it might enjoy more comprehensive support in the sense it would appear to be more representative. But the point should not be pressed too far. UMJOs, like COGs, will be governed by persons whose primary and presumably internalized obligations will be to other institutions which elected them and whose interests may well be in conflict with areawide objectives. As long as reformers attempt to fashion metropolitan government out of a confederation of local governments and their officials, we may expect the dominant value base to be the one which originally enjoyed the members' allegiance.

The fourth condition for power Parsons postulates requires the system to exercise command over "necessary facilities"—especially financial resources. COGs suffer in this regard because a large portion of their funds come from federal sources, which is uncertain in amount and timing, and much of the balance comes from voluntarily collected local assessments. UMJOs would have more reliable sources of funding, and they would exercise their own taxing powers. This could perhaps be the source of considerable tension since an UMJO might well be perceived by local governments as intruding upon their revenue sources. Even so, with regard to the fourth condition, more than with any other, UMJOs appear to have a clear advantage over councils of governments.

There is an aspect of UMJOs, however, which has a bearing upon all the foregoing analysis. The greatest distinction between COGs and UMJOs lies in the grant of coercive powers which reformers wish to give the new agencies. Governments would be required to become members, and city halls and courthouses could be forced by the regional authority to follow its prescriptions. By moving from voluntaristic regionalism to compulsory regionalism, the advocates of UMJOs propose to move them close to true metropolitan government.

We might ask, however, whether in view of the link between organizational potency and legitimacy of organizational goals and processes such authority can be realized in practice. American government is replete with examples of agencies which could not effectively exercise powers formally permitted them. Lyle Yorks, writing perceptively of the situation in which federal regulatory commissions find themselves, observes that "command has generally played a limited role in the maintenance of social order. It is most effective when employed only against deviants rather than when used as the principal instrument of control. This suggests that general compliance is best motivated by something other than fear of sanctions. It must be obtained through general consensus that the regulation is correct or through positive incentives utilized in a fashion that motivates compliance."[43]

No one would say that officials of local government think of themselves as "deviants" from the customary American political order, which traditionally prizes the "government closest to the people." We can be sure, on the other hand, that many will see regional agencies—especially of the new UMJO variety—as deviants from American political tradition and culture. If UMJOs are established and if they vigorously move toward unification of metropolitan policy making, we can safely predict rather massive resistance to implementation of decisions they reach. Implementation of decisions, says Parsons, must "be 'motivated' by some sort of 'demands' in the community that the measures in question be carried out; if this is in deficit, the administrative process runs into all sorts of difficulties . . . which coercive powers alone are not adequate to cope with."[44] The deficit he speaks of is obvious with respect to UMJOs.

One final point should be made. It will have been observed by the reader that running all through this analysis of problems facing both councils of governments and umbrella multi-jurisdictional organizations is the idea that environmental resistance to regional objectives deprives them of organizational legitimacy and accordingly restricts their ability to shape the urban environment. It takes time, the partisans of regionalism will argue, for areawide agencies to establish and cultivate such favorable climates of public and political opinion. Given sufficient time, it will be said, COGs (or UMJOs) will succeed in enlisting support for their cause.

Perhaps they will. In any event, within a few years the question whether councils of governments or any organizational descendants of them can overcome metropolitan fragmentation will be answered. But there is a danger in simply awaiting the passage of time to find out how this great urban experiment comes out—a risk that goes beyond the prospect of mere waste of time and resources. The allowance of time for organizational evolution to see what happens may be harmful in itself. There is a tendency in organizations to increasingly routinize their behavior over time.[45] Maturity is usually accompanied by less dynamism of purpose and action, not more. In the process of "becoming" there is the very great likelihood that regional councils will become bureaucratized. And although bureaucracies are well suited for some purposes, they seem to be the antithesis of what regional councils should be if they are to aggressively cope with complex and fast-changing urban issues.

Signs of bureaucratization are already present in COGs today. Greater attention is being given to procedural matters, staff manuals are being written, retirement plans are being debated and adopted. COGs compete with each other, not in terms of how well they reallocate resources among communities or to what extent they check urban sprawl, but in the attractiveness of their annual reports. Eventually, the process of bureaucratization itself may stunt the drive toward regional planning and action and may cause the slow but inexorable withdrawal from vital but controversial matters. Even the critics of "another layer of government" would probably prefer that the destiny of regional councils of governments prove to be something more than another layer of impotent bureaucracy.

NOTES

[1] U.S. Advisory Commission on Intergovernmental Relations, *Substate Regionalism and the Federal System*, 6 vols. (Washington, D.C.: U.S. Government Printing Office, 1973), vol. 1: *Regional Decision Making: New Strategies for Substate Districts*, p. 50. This is the most extensive and penetrating study of regional councils. Further references to the first volume will henceforth appear as ACIR, vol. 1.

[2] John C. Bollens and Henry J. Schmandt, *The Metropolis*, 2d ed. (New York: Harper & Row, 1970), p. 365.

[3] ACIR, vol. 1, pp. 80, 82.

⁴ Victor Jones, "Bay Area Regionalism: Institutions, Processes, and Programs," in U.S. Advisory Commission on Intergovernmental Relations, *Substate Regionalism and the Federal System*, vol. 2: *Regional Governance: Promise and Performance* (Washington, D.C.: U.S. Government Printing Office, May 1973), p. 106.

⁵ Charles W. Harris, *Regional COGs and the Central City* (Detroit: The Metropolitan Fund, Inc., March, 1970). His reservations about COGs' potential are also stated in his "Regional Responses to Metro-Urban Problems: Councils of Governments" (a paper prepared for presentation at the 1972 annual meeting of the American Political Science Association).

⁶ Urban Data Service, B. Douglas Harman, *Councils of Governments: Trends and Issues* (Washington, D.C.: International City Management Association, February, 1969). The extremity of COGs' dependency on federal funding patterns is indicated by the finding of one researcher that less than five percent of COGs surveyed had undertaken any action without federal funding support. See John Allen Bielec, "Metropolitan Regional Council Decision-Making: Public Program Selection, Environmental Influence and Executive Rationality" (Ph.D. dissertation, University of Maryland, 1972), p. 443.

⁷ Melvin B. Mogulof, *Governing Metropolitan Areas* (Washington, D.C.: The Urban Institute, 1971), p. 7.

⁸ Ibid., p. 16.

⁹ ACIR, vol. 1, p. 102.

¹⁰ Ibid., p. 122.

¹¹ Among the more prominent works by Talcott Parsons which the reader may wish to consult are *Toward a General Theory of Action* (Cambridge: Harvard University Press, 1951; reprinted in paperback by Harper Torchbooks, New York, 1962); in collaboration with Robert F. Bales and Edward A. Shils, *Working Papers in the Theory of Action* (New York: The Free Press of Glencoe, 1953); *Structure and Process in Modern Societies* (New York: The Free Press of Glencoe, 1960); *Sociological Theory and Modern Society* (New York: The Free Press, 1967). Articles which explicitly deal with organizations are "A Sociological Approach to the Theory of Organizations," *Administrative Science Quarterly*, 1 (June 1956): 63–85; 2 (September 1956): 225–39; and "Some Ingredients of a General Theory of Formal Organization," in Andrew W. Halpin, ed., *Administrative Theory in Education* (Chicago: Midwest Administration Center, University of Chicago, 1958). These two articles were reprinted in *Structure and Process in Modern Societies*. Parsons' attention is focused on a particular kind of formal organization in "The Mental Hospital as a Type of Organization," in Milton Greenblatt, Daniel J. Levinson, and Richard H. Williams, eds., *The Patient and the Mental Hospital* (New York: The Free Press, 1957). A full bibliography through 1967 of Talcott Parsons appears at pp. 539–52 of *Sociological Theory and Modern Society*. Readers unfamiliar with Parsons' thought are advised to first consult some guide to the theory, such as Max Black, ed., *The Social Theories of Talcott Parsons* (Englewood Cliffs, N. J.: Prentice-Hall, Inc., 1961); William C. Mitchell, *Sociological Analysis*

and *Politics: The Theories of Talcott Parsons* (Englewood Cliffs, N. J.: Prentice-Hall, Inc., 1967); or R. Jean Hills, *Toward a Science of Organization* (Eugene, Ore.: Center for the Advanced Study of Educational Administration, 1968).

[12] Harold Kaplan, *Urban Political Systems: A Functional Analysis of Metro Toronto* (New York: Columbia University Press, 1967). My "Organizational Functions and Conflict in a Regional Council of Governments: An Application of Parsonian Theory" (Ph.D. dissertation, University of Oklahoma, 1975), from which this paper draws heavily, also discusses the uses of this theory for analyzing system needs and characteristics.

[13] Much of Parsons' earlier work concerns another set of concepts dealing with system behavior characteristics called the "Pattern Variables," but limitations of space do not permit their inclusion in this analysis.

[14] ACIR, vol. I, p. 88.

[15] Ibid., p. 105.

[16] Urban Data Service, Laurie S. Frankel and Walter A. Scheiber, *Characteristics and Administrative Relationships of Regional Council Directors* (Washington, D. C.: International City Management Association, October, 1973), pp. 14–16; Jean Gansel, "Regional Council Directors: Perspectives of External Influence," *1974 Municipal Yearbook* (Washington, D. C.: International City Management Association, 1974), p. 55.

[17] ACIR, vol. I , p. 52.

[18] Urban Data Service, Frankel and Scheiber, p. 22.

[19] William Montana Timmins, Jr., "An Analysis of Planning by Regional Councils in the United States" (Ph.D. dissertation, University of Utah, 1972), p. 205.

[20] ACIR, vol. I, p. 122.

[21] Parsons, *Structure and Process in Modern Societies*, pp. 63–64.

[22] Edward C. Banfield, "Ends and Means in Planning," in Sidney Mailick and Edward H. Van Ness, eds., *Concepts and Issues in Administrative Behavior* (Englewood Cliffs, N. J.: Prentice-Hall, Inc., 1962), p. 77.

[23] The distinction is explained in Charles Perrow, "The Analysis of Goals in Complex Organizations," *American Sociological Review* 26 (December 1961): 859–66.

[24] Frances Friskin, "The Metropolis and the Central City: Can One Government Unite Them?" *Urban Affairs Quarterly* 8 (June 1973): 417.

[25] ACIR, vol. I, p. 98; Gansel, pp. 51, 54.

[26] ACIR, vol. I, pp. 88, 118.

[27] Harris, *Regional COGs and the Central City*, and Royce Hanson, *Metropolitan Councils of Governments* (Washington, D. C.: Advisory Commission on Intergovernmental Relations, August, 1966).

[28] ACIR, vol. I, pp. 100, 104; Gansel, pp. 51, 54.

[29] Harris, "Regional Responses," p. 8.

[30] Henry J. Schmandt, "Intergovernmental Volunteerism," *The Regionalist Papers* (Detroit: The Metropolitan Fund, Inc., V), p. 8. Mimeographed, forthcoming. Cited in ACIR, vol. I, p. 110.

[31] See Graham S. Finney, "The Intergovernmental Context of Local

Planning," in William I. Goodman and Eric C. Freund, eds., *Principles and Practice of Urban Planning* (Washington, D. C.: The International City Managers' Association, 1968). The many determinants of land use patterns are discussed in F. Stuart Chapin, Jr., *Urban Land Use Planning*, 2d ed. (Urbana: University of Illinois Press, 1965).

[32] John Friedmann, "The Future of Comprehensive Urban Planning: A Critique," *Public Administration Review* 31 (May/June 1971): 315–26.

[33] David C. Ranney, *Planning and Politics in the Metropolis* (Columbus, Ohio: Charles E. Merrill Publishing Company, 1969), p. 147.

[34] Oliver Williams, "A Typology for Comparative Local Government," *Midwest Journal of Political Science* (May 1961): 150–64.

[35] Kaplan, *Urban Political Systems*, pp. 18–19.

[36] See Robert K. Merton, *Social Theory and Social Structure*, 1968 enl. ed. (New York: The Free Press, 1968), chaps. 8 and 9.

[37] Ranney, p. 148.

[38] Ibid., pp. 147–50.

[39] ACIR, vol. 1, p. 91; Urban Data Service, Frankel and Scheiber, p. 9.

[40] David B. Walker, "Substate Districting and a Reformed Regional Council Strategy," *Public Management* 56 (January 1974): 7.

[41] In addition to the Commission's recommendations as stated in ACIR, vol. 1, chap. 11, the reader may find concise statements of the Commission's views in David B. Walker and Carl W. Stenberg, "A Substate Districting Strategy," *National Civic Review* 63 (January 1974): 5–9; 15; and in the ACIR *Information Bulletin* No. 74-2 (February 1974).

[42] See Parsons, *Structure and Process in Modern Societies*, pp. 42–43.

[43] Lyle Yorks, "Nader's Raiders and the Regulatory Process: Some Observations and Comments," *Atlanta Economic Review* (November/ December, 1974): 32–33.

[44] Parsons, *Structure and Process in Modern Societies*, p. 77.

[45] See, for example, the processes described in Anthony Downs, *Inside Bureaucracy* (Boston: Little, Brown and Company, 1967).

SCIENCE AND THE CITY:

Some Political Implications*

Nicholas Henry

"Science and the City" is a new and modish academic field. Bibliographies devoted to it are available,[1] at least one major university has a graduate course called "Science and the City" (Purdue), and the federal government has produced a number of publications on the topic.[2] Ekistics, the "science of human settlement," has a journal dedicated to it, and the "Experimental City" is a focus of increasing scholarly concern.

Because the field is only a few years old, its development can be traced fairly easily. From all accounts, it was inaugurated with a "Summer Study on Science and Urban Development" at Woods Hole, Virginia, in 1966. Robert C. Wood, former Undersecretary of the Department of Housing and Urban Development (HUD) and a political scientist, provided the catalyst for the conference. Carroll notes that the Woods Hole symposium was ". . . an attempt by HUD to publicize and to generate support for its planned research activities as well as an attempt to gain advice from knowledgeable people. It was also an attempt to create an image of itself as a department attuned to the

* My thanks to Mr. Mark Schwartz of Arizona State University for his constructive suggestions in the writing of this essay. Final responsibility for the piece is, of course, mine.

forward-looking politics of middle-class ideology and vested economic interests with which its predecessors generally were associated." Woods Hole articulated a growing, if relatively small, inclination in Congress to support research and development in housing and urban studies. Although monies had been appropriated for these purposes from 1948 through 1954, appropriations either were not requested or were denied from 1955 through 1962. Since then, however, urban social research has been funded on an expanding basis.[3]

Scientific research for the city is occurring at the local level too. There is a growing tendency for cities to hire industry-based research firms to study their problems. California officials recently asked their state's aerospace industry to study areas of local concern. New York City has engaged the RAND Corporation for urban research. This has led the RAND Corporation to open a branch devoted strictly to studying New York City's problems. New Haven has contracted IBM to design a metropolitan information system.[4]

In addition, municipally supported, in-house centers, have been established for scientific advice on urban affairs. Five of the fifty largest American cities have such centers (Chicago, Los Angeles, Oakland, New York, and Seattle), but the popularity of the idea may be waning. Sapolsky observes that ". . . over one-third of the science advisory units formed by state and local governments have either fallen dormant or have been disbanded . . . very few of these advisory units have survived an election that brought about a change in administration."[5]

Apparently, the major interest in the relation of science to urban regions lies at the national level. Such major figures in urban affairs as former Undersecretary Wood and John W. Gardner of the Urban Coalition appear to perceive urban science as a national enterprise. Sapolsky has noted that the better scientists prefer the prestige of federal as opposed to state or local appointments. Emerging as the undisputed centralizing force of urban-applied research and development is HUD. Carroll calls HUD "the focal point of the movement. . . ."[6]

Consequently, social research may be an important resource for government. Nevertheless, the impact of scientific technology on the present urban polity seems of pre-eminent importance. In analyzing this impact, the ". . . issue is not the survival of the system per se, but the survival of the system in a form consistent with essential democratic values—individual liberty and opportunity, numerous centers of political power, effective constraints on centralized control, local initiative, and local freedom of choice within broad constitutional restrictions."[7]

The hypothesis presented in this paper is that demographic shifts, the administrative political structure of cities, the evolution of scientific expertise, and the emergence of federal concern over the urban condition may congeal and significantly undermine the concept of corporate government at the local level. Further, if this should occur, it will do so through the efforts of city administrators themselves. No radical changes in the political structure will be necessary for the undercutting of local self-government to happen. The advantageous position of the federal government will lead to a quiet usurpation of local government's functions.

A number of scholars have observed a demographic trend that was confirmed by the 1970 census: people are leaving the cities and clustering around their legal limits.[8] Willbern has written: "There seems little to block an endless expansion of urban or semi-urban ways of life over vast areas of the countryside outside our traditional city limits. . . . The more urban we become, the more shaky becomes both the concept and the reality of the city."[9] Webber thinks that we are in the midst of "a post-city age." Besides demographic trends, there are additional factors that contribute to the decline of the concept of the city. Higher education, which opens its doors ever wider, reduces local identifications. Rising real incomes, which permit long-distance travel and communication, and the concomitant expansion of personal awareness, also undermine the notion of a local community.

This latter phenomenon implies that communication and transportation technologies have and will continue to promote a post-city age. Technological developments in these fields

. . . are likely to be accelerated dramatically by cost-reducing improvements in transportation and communications technologies now in the research-and-development stages. (COMSAT Communications, high-speed ground transportation with speeds up to 500 m.p.h., TV and computer-aided educational systems are likely to be powerful ones.) . . . Our compact, physical city layouts directly mirror the more primitive technologies in use at the time these cities were built. . . . If currently anticipated technological improvements prove workable, each of the metropolitan settlements will spread out in low-density patterns over far more extensive areas than even the most frightened future-mongers have yet predicted.[10]

The spectre of a vast, coast-to-coast Los Angeles blanketing the country brings with it, of course, altered political patterns. Scheiber observes: "Our metropolitan areas, sprawling as they do across city, county, and state boundaries, have, with only a few exceptions, no single voice with which to speak and no forum with which to resolve their internal differences. If new areawide policies or programs are to be adopted, this can be done only by the harrowing tug-and-pull of attempting to achieve consensus among a large number of frequently feuding baronies with diverging views as to what their true interests are."[11] Scheiber's description of the present state of urban areas as "baronies" is appropriate yet unpleasant. A number of students have tried to project alternative scenarios concerning the structure of urban politics in the future. For purposes of this essay, the literature in this field may be categorized into corporate conceptions of the city, territorial conceptions of the city, and amplification of the urban status quo.

Corporate analyses of cities accept as axiomatic the preservation of local self-rule. Willbern has typologized these studies into those which advocate a return to the status quo ante, those which espouse suburbia, and those which predict a community form called "metro."

A return to the status quo ante (or what Willbern calls the "preservation of cities") is urged by such writers as Jane Jacobs and William S. Whyte, Jr. They want to restore a sense of community by massive but intelligent urban renewal programs, and by discouraging the use of automobiles that ply through cities from the suburbs.

Suburbia, as advocated by Robert C. Wood, reestablishes the urban community in a less densely populated form. Suburbs form around professional, religious, ethnic, and class preferences. The "New Towns" movement is, in many ways, an embodiment of this notion.

"Metro" refers to local efforts to seek the urban community anew by annexing the governmental units that surround the city. Willbern lists five forces that generate Metro: economies of scale, spillover effects (e.g., of air pollution), crisis, "multi-level participation" in governance (i.e., the smaller political units tend to rely on the larger ones for services), and the effects of professionalization.[12] The idea of Metro is important because it establishes a political structure that is considered essential in order for urban technologies to be used to their fullest capacity, and yet still retain the values of corporate cities. Gardner has stated: "It is a mistake to suppose that [centralization] would weaken our greatest cities. It would strengthen them to be nerve centers in a farflung and varied pattern of human settlements in which vitality is distributed through all parts of the system. The great cities, have certainly not been strengthened by the centripetal forces operating in recent decades."[13] Advocacy for the "regional city" generally is premised on the notion that, by matching a real administration with urban functions, needed changes can be wrought with less friction. Unfortunately, this point remains moot. There are, at this writing, three major "Metros": Nashville, Miami, and Indianapolis. No one, to date, has noticed a withering away of urban political conflict in any of these cities.

Starr, in this regard, makes a most pertinent point relative to New York.

> Earnest citizens in America even in New York—have held up
> the idea of regional government as a misty, glamorous objective;
> a Valhalla of good government. Many of these gentlemen have
> forgotten that New York City has, for seventy years now, offered a
> practical demonstration of the possibilities and difficulties of a
> regional government that exerts exclusive general power over what
> were once independent municipal, village, and county authorities.
> Instead of speculating on how regional government *might* work,
> one can see how New York *does* work—or doesn't.

Starr goes on to argue that political struggles are just as pronounced in New York as elsewhere—if not more so. The mayor of a regional city is most effective when he assumes "the more-or-less neutral status of umpire" in order to balance inner-city needs with outer burough pressures.[14] But politics will always remain preeminent.

While the cause of Metro engenders widespread support, the near absence of regional cities leads one to pessimistic conclusions concerning its practicality as a tool for urban change. One scholar writes that not only are the odds against Metro developing on a national scale, but that it might not even meet its theoretical promise: "A new, metropolitan-wide, self-governing community is likely to be a will-o-the-wisp in most circumstances, beckoning the crusader, but rarely if ever obtained. The substructure existing now in the territorial units, primarily counties, will hardly serve as the vehicle for truly integrated communities. . . ."[15]

Less popular among American urban analysts is the notion of a territorial as opposed to corporate city; i.e., one ruled from afar. Nevertheless, Caldwell has contended that "cities no longer can be governed solely from within their own boundaries," and that the corporation has lost its suitability as a device for governance because cities do not conform to a viable community in an ecological sense.[16]

Most scholars who appear to support territorial cities are not so explicit. Those who bemoan the reactionary presence of local politics, generally speak vaguely of introducing reasons and rationality into the urban milieu. Stover provides a suitable example in this respect: ". . . public officials and the public must be prepared to give up inhibiting governmental forms, practices, and laws when these are not essential to the protection of the public interest [sic.]. Fragmented jurisdictions, complex processes of administrative review, and codes tied to a particular stage of technological development must all be reexamined. . . . When necessary, they must be changed . . . the level of politics must be raised."[17] The dream of raising the level of politics in order to effect urban change implies raising the policy-making process from its local environs to the national level.

Because Metro appears to be a popular but unlikely panacea for urban ills, and because the territorial city appears to be unpopular among Americans, amplification of the municipal status quo seems the most probable political development. The size of the problem plus the human and political tendency towards inertia seem to be further proof that the status quo will be the "wave of the future."

Municipal status quo has meant Scheiber's "baronies"; that is, a system of local pluralistic countervailing pressures in Galbraith's sense. "This suggested local model for local government recognizes that most Americans are in reality members of overlapping communities, and that it is difficult if not impossible to attach their communal loyalties to a single unit of government."[18]

Accepting this model and its growth, one may construct a scenario that will involve at least the following developments. There will be the expansion of opportunities for popular participation—and for personal frustration. The recent Bell and Held study of New York City concludes that "there is more participation than ever before in American society, particularly in the large urban centers. . . ."[19] Our scenario must then deal with the problem of too many competing voices and demands for the political apparatus to listen to.

An additional development will be the reduction of in-house expertise in urban governments. As local jurisdictions proliferate, their capacity to economically support and to professionally motivate able urban administrators will diminish. Price has noted: "Perhaps it is inevitable that the present geographic pattern of central cities and suburban municipal corporations will persist, since the resistance to metropolitan consolidation is so tremendous. If so, it seems clear to me that the city as such will not have a corps of personnel who have either the responsibility or the technological or intellectual capacity for thinking about the big problems, or working out their solutions."[20]

Finally, both these phenomena will contribute to a third—the deceleration of urban innovation. Bell and Held observe that not only does increased participation slow the decision-making process, but that participation itself is "a deeply conservatizing institution" after the decision is made, "for, like property, it gives people a stake in the decision that becomes binding on all."[21] And if Price's contention is at all accurate, then the possibility of a creative leader fusing the energy emanating from all these new political participants is reduced considerably; the urban leadership pool will decline with the geographic and bureaucratic splintering of urban areas. Then too, as Banfield notes in his study of Chicago, the very complexity of the post-city, urban region exercises a conservative influence on the local polity.[22]

The unhappy conclusion one draws is that the problems causing the greatest concern among urbanologists are likely to magnify: political frustration will increase, the decision-making process will grow more chaotic, municipal administration will become even less adept than it is now, and change (what many urban analysts label reform) will gear down to a snail-like rate.

The emerging literature of science and the city offers hope. The priggishness of politicians and the prejudices of the people can be overcome. The disintegration of the urban region can be reversed by the application of science and technology to the land, the buildings, the roads, the air, and to the people themselves. At least, so reads much of the literature. Perhaps some examples of its political naiveté or, more accurately, of its apolitical nature are in order. Stover, for instance, speaks of "a politics rooted in reasoned deliberation" as essential if technology is to be applied successfully to the city.[23] Harris, addressing himself to urban problems, says: "We may indeed regard the current overriding problem of our world society as a moral and cultural problem of achieving a wide consensus which will lead to political stability and social progress. This consensus can be guided by a new science. . . ."[24]

Related to this apolitical science-and-the-city literature is the yearning to flee the political obstructions of twentieth century urban sprawls, and to build anew. The writings of Buckminster Fuller and Constantinor Doxiadis display this sentiment clearly. The 1969 report from the National Committee on Urban Growth Policy analyzes the problems of ghettos, population growth, and environmental pollution, and then considers building cities "from scratch." Spilhaus's advocacy of the "Experimental City," which would stand primarily as a tribute to technology, provides an example of this theme. He writes: "There are many step jumps and innovative ideas which must be tried if we are going to get away from whittling at our people problems. Some have suggested a Marshall plan. I think a closer analogy is a space program on earth." But perhaps the most revealing statement of the genre as a whole is by Zivorad Kovacevic, Secretary General of the League of Yugoslav cities, in an address on science and urban affairs who stated that, "freedom of choice must be planned."[25]

If scientists cast a jaundiced eye toward local politics, urban politicians often view science as a useful tool, either for formulating policy or for furthering more personal ends. Sapolsky notes that ". . . political officials, while enjoying the publicity that accompanies the establishment of a science advisory group have often not found it necessary or useful to consult with these advisory groups on important public problems other than those that they believe are directly related to economic development."[26]

Nevertheless, even if local politicians misuse science (at least from the viewpoint of scientists), they are very much aware that it is the style of the age. Computers are among the aspects of science most favored by municipal officials. Goldberg reports that there were 188 urban information systems throughout the United States in 1968, and that "hundreds" more were predicted for the 1970s. By 1977, "state governments alone spent more than $107.5 million on electronic data processing and (every state government had at least one computer). . . . We must recognize the 'cognitive passion'—the factual hunger— of all government bodies. . . . The need for information gathers a momentum, a 'dynamic' of its own 'which has become independent of the needs of policy. . . .' And 'computer technology . . . extends and intensifies this passion for knowledge'. . . ."[27] But information has a dynamic process of its own. Increasingly, the intimate relationship between knowledge and power is recognized. Computer science is only one facet (if a significant one) of this intimacy.

It may be, as one scholar has argued, that we are in a "scientific superculture," an age in which knowledge and power are no longer distinct entities. A more detailed version of this contention is that:

Knowledge was always power, but it was not always the central and controlling force in society. Today it is . . . the key to understanding the implications of this new age of science is to perceive its true nature. What I have called the superculture of science and technology could with equal accuracy be described as "high information level culture." To a degree never before experienced, the critical element and basic source of power in this new age of knowledge. . . . In a society in which knowledge is becoming the most valuable commodity and most basic resource, the managers of knowledge play a critical role.[28]

If it is true that knowledge is power and that the "knowledge administrators" are by-and-large politically insensitive, certain implications for American cities must result. These implications depend to a significant degree on the kinds of knowledge introduced to the city. For analytical purposes, "urban science" (broadly defined as all knowledge acquired at a relatively high educational level that has urban applications) can be divided into three, heavily overlapping fields: professionalization, new technologies (i.e., new methods of physically renovating cities and new managerial techniques), and systems analysis.

Daland has written in an overview of "Political Science and the Study of Urbanism," that:

One of the virtually untouched areas [of study] is the relationship between municipal executive and professional groups in administration. Technical and professional groups come to municipal government with different orientations as to their role in administration and policy-making from that of the city manager, administrator, or mayor. Professional lawyers, engineers, comptrollers, city planners, personnel men, educators, and others not trained with any idea of subordination of their function to that of some overall community objective. Rather they tend to look upon their own particular subject matter as more basic, unique, independent, high level, and important that the "traditional" municipal functions considered as a lump.[29]

Daland's words still ring true more than seventeen years later, and professionalization of municipal services has had mixed effects on urban governments. Among the benefits that have been garnered from rising professionalism are the increase of technical competence, the promotion of respect for technical expertise, the enforcement of minimum ethical and technical standards, insulation from pressures to practice discrimination among clients, the avoidance of direct democratic control that would be of doubtful value in some areas, the facilitation of communication throughout particular services, greater interchangeability of personnel among governmental units, the incentive for officials to acquire more skills, the furtherance of social and technological research, the creation of in-group loyalty, and the provision of additional satisfactions for public employees.

Conversely, however, these very benefits possess their own dysfunctions for urban governments. Chief among these unintended liabilities are potential conflicts of interest between the professional group and larger publics (notably taxpayers), the presence of undue influence wielded by special publics through professional ties, insulation of the professional public servants not only from favoritism but from public control as well, the lack of internal democracy often found in professions, the limitation of public services by insistence on the maintenance of unrealistic professional standards, the diminishing of transferability of personnel among agencies due to specialized training, the lack of interagency coordination because of the particularism of professionalism, and the discouraging of local participation by the presence of a professional mystique.[30]

These dysfunctions of professionalism are more than hypothetical abstractions. They have had deleterious effects in a variety of urban settings. Kaufman's study of the New York City health centers provides a remarkable case study of administrative conflict that endured nearly half a century. Essentially, it was a matter of two schools of professionalism clashing head on: professional health officers pitted against professional administrators, fueled by jurisdictional cohesiveness, and bureaucratic rationality.[31]

Professionalism, of course, has its own politics. Few people are unaware that an expert exists for almost every point of view and, in this sense, provides no "right" answers. In an urban context, an example of this is furnished by Golembiewski's study of *The Trenton Milk Contract*. In this situation, the city's chemist and the dairies' chemist differed over whether the municipal hospital was receiving Grade A or Grade B milk. What appeared to be a simple question of measuring butterfat content was complicated not only by arguments of a technical nature, but by more significant political disputes as well. The dispute involved the incompetence of a crusading councilman, the hostility of his fellow-councilman, the dairies' belief in a political "conspiracy," and the questionable professional ethics of the city's chemist.[32]

Perhaps the most important dysfunction of professionalism, however, is the impenetrability that highly professionalized public agencies can devise as a protection from public control. Merton and others have observed that bureaucrats tend to develop a personality peculiarly their own. Their vision is constricted to the narrowly defined goals of their professional organization. Often, they become literally incapable of perceiving the larger societal dysfunctions of their operation: "A way of seeing is also a way of not seeing."[33]

Pathologies in the organization itself complicate these adverse effects of the "bureaucratic personality." The phenomenon of "uncertainty absorption" refers to the organizational tendency to regard highly tentative data as increasingly "hard," the further removed the data become from their original source.[34] Thus, "facts" of often dubious validity can be supported with great psychological assuredness by agency heads to those outside the organization. From the standpoint of organization theory, the "insulation" of public servants, the lack of interagency coordination, and the hostility of public participation in agency decision making, itemized by Willbern, are practically inevitable.

A superb example of this distortion is described by Altshuler's analysis of how an intercity freeway was located in St. Paul, Minnesota. The Highway Department actually made a very conscious decision to be inflexible with regard to the freeway's location and based this decision on rather crude cost/benefit analyses. The hard-shell of expertise manufactured by the department succeeded in resisting pressures for quite legitimate adjustments brought on by blacks (who won the only insignificant concession granted by the department). Middle-class homeowners in the St. Anthony Street area, one of the few attractive residential areas remaining in downtown St. Paul, and retailers in the central business district, also proposed relocation. The Governor even gave quiet support to these demands. The Department maintained its position despite these clamorings and the fact that an alternative route existed that would have satisfied most of their claims.[35]

In terms of professionalization, city planning is a special case. Planning is nearly as professionalized as any other urban service, but its values permit a broader professional view than do those of the other fields. George has observed that whereas planning used to exclude the urban "action system," today:

> . . . there has emerged a *politicized* concept of city planning which stresses that planning must be linked with a better understanding of the community's social structure and political processes. This concept emphasizes that planners must realize that adequate political support has to be mobilized within the community to attain the changes desired. Thus, planning activities must devote considerable attention to devising strategies for consensus-building, coalition formation, persuasion, and bargaining.[36]

In George's argument—and in Altshuler's—politics, or the "action system," simply becomes another professional problem to be solved by the intelligent application of professional techniques. The most satisfactory way to cope with uncertainty is to reduce it—to render it predictable. In the case of planning, this means "rationalizing" politics so that it more nearly matches professional values. It is planning that Willbern seems to have especially in mind when he lists professionalization as a generating force of the Metro ideal. The bureaucrat's adherence to profession standards leads to a planning conformity that transcends jurisdictional boundaries.[37]

Planning is important to the hypotheses presented in this paper because it provides an opportunity for an application of systems analysis and design into the city; both share a predisposition to see the city as a whole. Further, planning is a local profession that has the greatest likelihood of relating with national officials, in part due to a code of standards engrained by their pursuit of professionalism.

At the federal level the emphasis today is on regional comprehensive planning of urban areas. The Housing and Urban Development Act of 1968, the Public Works and Economic Development Act of 1965, the National Environmental Policy Act of 1969, recent modifications in the urban renewal program, and the new stress on urban research at HUD, all contribute toward this end of regionalization. Gardner, speaking at a Congressionally-sponsored conference, said: "Our greatest cities have lost command of themselves and their future. . . . Like a decerebrate frog, the city can twitch its muscles in response to specific stimuli, but it cannot think ahead."[38]

These factors of systems design and current federal emphases on research encourage increased dosages of urban science into city planning. Sapolsky notes that:

> Recent legislation in several science-related areas appears to indicate a growing federal interest in regional cooperation which could lead to the increased use of science and technology in meeting state and local problems. . . . Since the federal government has increasingly formulated its local assistance programs in technical terms and since it uses its experts to help evaluate the applications submitted for these programs, state and local governments must eventually begin to attain a comparable level of technical sophistication in their own operations. . . . The needs of state and local governments for federal aid would seem, then, to be a very important factor in increasing the utilization of science advice by the governments.[39]

It may be, however, that local governments will be incapable of meeting technical federal requirements for funds, as Price argues. Caldwell's thesis of the "crisis of institutional inadequacy" lends support. This, of course, will not reduce the needs of the community. The question then becomes: Who, or what, will fit the needs of the community and with what technological tools?

An immense pressure exists to fill this vacuum, not simply because technical talent is a key to the federal vaults, but because the new technologies promise so much. The participants in the Woods Hole Conference envisioned the application of new technologies (particularly computer science, management science, and new construction techniques) to such varied urban problems as new housing, rehabilitation, health services, environmental engineering, and transportation.

Without a doubt, the chief proponents of urban science and technology are situated at the national level and address themselves to national audiences, despite the fact that essentially the only people who have the authority to apply science to the city are local officials. A few of these exponents are sensitive to the unavoidable reality of local politics. Wood has noted "the political constraints which restrict the use of research results" at the municipal level.[40] Carroll has given us a pointed listing of the obstructions extant in the application of urban science: ". . . tradition and vested interest . . . overt and covert racism, jurisdictional politics, industrial and labor policies and politics, inadequate fiscal policies."[41]

These obstacles exist for a reason; local interests are threatened by new urban technologies. Already, new construction methods are beginning to encroach upon traditional modes of operation: "The number of factory-built modular housing units has increased rapidly, and now accounts for more than one-fourth of all single-family housing selling below $12,500." New technologies, such as in housing, imperil what Abrams calls the "business welfare state" at the local level. Federal urban policies have given businesses tax breaks so that many groups have a vital interest in retaining the status quo, particularly against new techniques that may render them anachronistic.[42]

In 1963, the Construction and Community Development Committee of the Chamber of Commerce of the United States vigorously denounced a proposal by the Department of Commerce (supported by the Building Research Advisory Board of the National Academy of Sciences and the White House Panel on Civilian Technology) to stimulate research in the textile and construction industry. Congress never granted approval to the proposal. "Industrial opposition to innovation in housing and various other aspects of urban development has been reinforced by organized labor's opposition based upon fears of jurisdictional and other possible changes."[43]

It is not merely vested commercial interests that are determined to reject local applications of urban science. Grass-roots political organizations may also adopt antiscientific attitudes. Muir's study of neighborhood resistance to the location of ready-made houses is an intriguing case. A pair of junk dealers in New Haven, Connecticut, bought a number of seven-year-old, galvanized iron duplexes for $75.00 each. They intended to locate sixty-five of these 20' x 48' x 10' structures in a working-class Italian neighborhood and rent them. Somehow, the houses passed the municipal fire, health, and building permit standards. But a local resident provided the political catalyst that ultimately defeated their installation: "Miss Grava did not like the prospect of the metal homes development. They were dirty and a blight to look at. In her estimation, they would attract riff-raff. They meant the possibility of disease, crime, and bodily harm. They meant lowered real estate values. Her sense of security was outraged."[44]

For roughly the same reasons, the Model Cities program has met with resistance in Indianapolis neighborhoods, despite the considerably superior appearance of the modular units that HUD officials wished to install. Gardner observed that suburbs resisted federal housing policies through the "workable program" requirement and the local veto provision of the federal public housing, rent supplement, and 221 (d) (3) programs, as well as through their zoning powers.[45]

Some federal proponents of urban technology are relatively sensitive to local politics. Wood, as Undersecretary of HUD, has said, that the implementation of technological advances in urban settings will always be subject to political considerations. Nevertheless, even Wood thinks that the United States has "a unique opportunity to master the urban environment" as a product of "flexible new legislative tools" and "new technical capabilities," among other factors.[46] Gardner, on the other hand, is more candid in advocating the need for more forceful federal measures to control urban areas. He urges federal use of the Housing and Urban Development Act of 1968 to "help open up the suburbs" to new housing technologies by restricting ". . . Federal, public, and community grants, including sewer and water, neighborhood facilities and open-space land grants, and FHA-insured mortgages to communities that are providing adequate housing for low- and moderate-income families."[47]

If local resistance to many new technologies is strong, the enthusiasm with which municipal administrators have embraced electronic data processing (EDP) and related managerial techniques (e.g., PERT, PPBS, MBO, operations research, simulation, and cost/benefit analysis coupled with the use of technical forecasting methods) indicates a major exception. There are almost two hundred urban information networks in this country, and these systems are increasing at a nearly exponential rate. Although this technology has ruffled few political feathers in its introduction to the city, its potential for altering the present urban polity is probably greater than that of any other.

There are several reasons for this massive effect. EDP stimulates centripetal political tendencies. Also while EDP maximizes hard data, it isolates decision makers from the community. EDP may undermine the role of "middle management" in cities—possibly the role of top management as well. Finally, EDP systems will burgeon qualitatively as well as quantitatively in city governance as their full potential is realized. Some of these contentions warrant elaboration. The isolation of decision makers despite greater volumes of data is the result of the same mystique that shrouds professionals. In the case of EDP professionals, the mystique is considerably more impenetrable because the technology itself requires mastery of a new language and comprehension of an unusually complex system. Those in public office who do understand the mechanics of computer science will be in an enviable position to get their way and to cover their mistakes.[48]

If the hypothesis is valid that knowledge is the surest path to power in our scientific super-culture, the rise of the urban technocrat through his command of EDP and related managerial technologies is not difficult to foresee. The technocrat will control the decision premises of the urban polity, politics will increasingly revolve around the technocrat, and the centrist tendencies of municipal administration will converge on him as their source of life sustaining data.

A side effect of EDP will be the steady displacement of managers in city government. Churchman provides a lucid explanation of this:

> . . . the middle management class of our modern society consists of information processing units. What the manager does is to take information and transfer it in various ways. . . . His goals are given; the kind of information he receives is given; the steps that need to be taken in the light of the information are given. Middle managers, in effect, are simply rather expensive computers. . . . Computer processing will get cheaper and cheaper per unit. . . . Eventually, the cost per unit will decrease below the cost of live middle manager, per unit. And there you are: pure economics will kill off the middle management class.

The analysis continues, and reaches top managerial levels as well. As EDP becomes more sophisticated, its solutions to urban problems will, in theory, be able to encompass increasingly subtle variations of decision variables.

> In fact, our top managers are very high-priced information-processors whom we, in our quaint mythology, actually believe are at the top of the human species with respect to their ability to inquire and process information. So, gradually, top management will disappear as well . . . once the internal processor gets to be capable of sensing and assimilating information, analyzing it, and coming out with optimal solutions. There will be a great age of human leisure, nice or indecent, but leisure just the same.[49]

This argument is a highly speculative one, but it is believed by many, including Herbert Simon.[50]

Besides the ethical implications raised by the possible displacement of public officials, as we know them, by a "central processor," there is an additional, more immediate moral question generated by urban information systems: the right of privacy. As urban EDP centers multiply, "pressure immediately builds for the elimination of some data and for sharing of other data."[51] This means that more information on individual citizens will become easily accessible. It is not entirely an exercise in fantasy to believe that these kinds of data—personal information—ultimately will become germane to urban decisions. This is, after all, what systems analysts must consider if they are to view all variables as "inputs" in order to secure the optimal alternative. Further, if it is valid that technology and the need to know have their own dynamic process, then these variables eventually will be secured and quantified as information bits in a huge, central analytical system.

Although systems analysis can be conceived as a separate species of urban science, it is simultaneously a synthesis of all the species. From the public administrator's point of view, systems analysis is the ultimate expression of a desire long present in the literature of public administration: the training and professionalization of generalism, and an emphasis on the "whole." As one writer states: "professionalization of those who tend to be generalists should be especially promoted."[52]

Systems analysis finds its close conceptual allies on the urban scene in planning and managerial technologies, particularly EDP and PPBS. Like professionals in these fields, advocates of systems analysis have scant respect for local political perquisites. Lessing notes that the behavior of systems analysts "is mystifying, sometimes irritating to tradition-bound bureaucrats."[53] But despite the hostility that systems analysis may provoke among older officials, the approach requires inputs from all of them:

Inherent in the use of systems techniques is the probability that the recommended approach to solving a problem will demand cooperation among a number of fragmented local, regional, and state governmental jurisdictions. Given the obsolescence of our governmental structures in the face of contemporary problems . . . this is not surprising; a virtue of the systems approach is that it follows problems, not established structures.[54]

In terms of applicability to urban sprawls, this is perhaps the chief benefit of systems analysis. As a methodology, it can be tailored most closely to the areal and functional realities of the metropolitan problem.

Jurisdictionally, however, federal officials are in the most appropriate position to apply systems analysis. Although they may be limited in terms of what they can legally do within the jurisdictions of local governments, federal officials are not contained by local political boundaries; they, more than any other public servants, can see the problems whole. This breadth of vision can be given political flesh by the centripetal tendencies of systems analysis. One of the problems of systems analysis applied at the local level has been brought out by Paul Parks: "I know that my staff of about sixty systems analysts is constantly being frustrated because they can't come to grips with the fact that there are other things that they have to look at as constraints rather than the rules of their particular field."[55] Hopefully, systems analysts at the federal level will be more aware of these constraints.

Systems analysis is not only centrist-oriented itself, but, as a synthesizer of other urban sciences, it also accents the centripetal tendencies of EDP, PPBS, professionalization, and city planning. Data gathered by one field are ingested by other fields via the computer. These same data then modify the data already present in those fields. This process of data convergence tends to concentrate all data sources at a single point, in order that each field may benefit maximally from the information provided by other fields. The governmental level at which data sources are concentrated depends on how one defines the system. But given our post-city age, the definition of an urban system demands an even wider parameter. From the standpoint of areal administration theory, federal officials are in the most logical position to manipulate variables within these parameters.

The promise of systems analysis is a starry one. If only all the proper inputs are included, the methodology can produce, for example, the best new housing technology for the ghetto, given specified social, economic, and political variables. Or, it can locate a highway in a context "best" for the economic viability of the city—or the city's social viability—or the city's political viability—or all three.

But if systems analysis emphasizes what is best in urban science, it also amplifies what is worst. As a profession and as a technology, system analysis insulates decision makers from public control—on a scale far more massive than any single profession (even planning) or technology has done heretofore. The centralizing aspects of systems analysis further this isolation. Bacon argues that urban planners and systems analysis are molded by traditional university educations in such a manner that they emerge on the city scene replete with their own version of a bureaucratic personality. The university ". . . is the institution that has most systematically rejected the feedback principle and is most likely to continue to do so. The teaching profession in general has become removed from the field of action and, indeed, has tended to distrust it. This is not a question of 'being practical'; it invokes the most essential part of idea formation."[56] Another scholar agrees, adding that the ivory tower is solidified by the bricks of "compartmentalization of knowledge" within jealous academic disciplines. For this knowledge to work towards the solution of social problems, there must be open channels of communication between teacher and urban administrator and then between the administrator and the public.

This implication concerning the utility of systems analysis for urban problems is worth developing. Carroll believes: "It is unclear whether the social and physical sciences can be melded into one science of metropolitan development. Some version of 'systems analysis' and 'systems engineering' may in time prove appropriate to the need, but so far the promise has exceeded the performance." [57] Sisson, an advocate of systems analysis for the city, also feels obliged to qualify his enthusiasm stating that systems analysis is better formulated to "study physical systems" than social systems. [58]

New York City offers an example of what it means to apply systems analysis to a polity. Starr's description of New York as a regional city is useful in this regard because the concept of region is integral to urban systems design; but Bailey's report of a systems approach to the problems of the Bedford-Stuyvesant ghetto of New York is even more revealing. In this effort, Senator Robert Kennedy mobilized architect I. M. Pei, Boston's Development Administrator Edward J. Logue, the U. S. Department of Labor, the Ford Foundation, neighborhood political organizations, the government of the City of New York, local businessmen, and others to rebuild Bedford-Stuyvesant. At the end of a year and a half, the only visible results were a handful of newly repainted houses and pronounced community discord. [59]

In defense of the project, it should be noted that funds were a major problem; only $9 million were raised, or the equivalent of about $20.00 per resident, for what is, perhaps, the national epitome of a slum. Nevertheless, politics probably had an even larger role in the effort's quick deflation; much of it centered around a municipal judge, who played with resounding success on black male fears of matriarchal dominance in the project's administration. This is not the sort of contingency that one expects to be a prominent obstacle in a systemwide program that has the best available data, the committed backing of a charismatic leader, the top urban planning talents in the country, a leading think-tank, a major federal agency, and key high-powered local political elements. But if systems analysis is indeed an inappropriate science for metropolitan areas (and it is only an "if"), this does not imply that dysfunctions of systems analysis would be negated if it were applied to cities. On the contrary, the only probable consequence would be the same dysfunctions plus governmental decisions of lower quality as a result of reliance on a misapplied (if dazzling) decision-making technique.

At this juncture, a review of the relationship between science and the city seems in order. It has been contended that we are in a post-city age due to demographic shifts, advancing technologies, and the loss of community identity through the democratization of higher education and rising real incomes. Among the principal notions forwarded by scholars to alleviate the problems caused by the death of cities and to preserve corporate government are a return to the traditional (pre-automobile) city, an enhancement of suburbia, and Metro. Of these, Metro is promising as an idea but unsuccessful as a practicality. Territorial governance of urban areas has been suggested as an alternative, but is not politically popular. It seems likely, therefore, that the urban status quo will amplify; that is, the capacity of municipal public servants to solve urban problems will decrease, political participation and frustration will increase, and innovation in solving expanding urban ills will decelerate.

Urban science is offered by a number of scientists and social scientists as a panacea for the problems of a post-city age. These proponents generally lack political sensitivity in terms of local situations. On the other hand, many local politicians and federal officials have a correspondingly naive faith in the cure-all qualities of science and technology. Linking these points of view is the emerging intimacy of knowledge and power in our scientific superculture, and the demands spawned by urban sciences for increasing quantities of data, particularly social data.

Applied urban science may be divided into three overlapping types: professionalism, technology, and systems analysis. Each has socio-political dysfunctions peculiar to it. Professionalization of a field does not signify that it will be more prone to produce "right" answers, because professionalism saddled with its own "politics of expertise" tends to produce members with narrow, distorted perceptions of reality who are insulated from public control. City planning represents a special case of professionalization because it includes politics as a professional variable, provides the basis for systems approaches to urban problems, relates easily with current federal urban programs, and paves the way for greater use of urban science at the local level.

Technology refers to superior new methods of rebuilding the city (chiefly in housing) and the new managerial sciences. National officials promote the application of new urban technologies, despite local resistence from industry, labor, neighborhood residents, and other groups. This opposition tends to magnify the impression of conservatism and administrative chaos that federal officers have of the urban polity. EDP and related management techniques have been accepted more readily by cities than have the technologies of rebuilding, but EDP in particular tends to expand the perceived need for new kinds of information, displaces human decision makers, isolates the decision-making process, and contributes toward a technocratic polity.

Systems analysis promises to meet the problems of urban sprawl, especially when applied to the profession of planning and to the technology of EDP. But because it synthesizes professionalism and technology, it magnifies their dysfunctions; e.g., political insensitivity, centricity, insulation of decision making, expansion of data files on individual citizens, the bureaucratic personality of decision makers, and technocratic political patterns. Even though systems analysis may be inflated by scientists in terms of its applicability to urban problems, these dysfunctions would not necessarily be neutralized by its inappropriateness if it were introduced to the city on a large scale.

These arguments and their supportive evidence can be reduced to the following scenario: Urban problems will intensify and multiply; many of these problems (e.g., pollution, deterioration, sprawl) will require expensive, systemswide solutions that are science based. Urban governments will grow less capable of providing science-based solutions. Urban governments will falter partly because of the chaotic effects on administration of a post-city age, and partly because of a declining base on which to support local technical talent. This local technical talent, however, will become more necessary to local governments in order to meet federal requirements for funds with which to solve their problems. The scenario becomes more dismal when we consider that federal urban research and development is already of a quality considerably higher than local technological ability, and this difference is likely to widen in the future. Thus it seems probable that federal standards for planning, managerial science, and technological sophistication in the preparation of local applications for funds will rise as local ability to meet those standards declines. As a result, informal working accommodations between local, state, and national agencies will be established in order that cities may receive both money and urban science at maximal levels. The practical effects of this will be to raise local decision making to nonlocal levels; hence, de facto territorial government.

Price hypothesizes a similar scenario. My only difference with this scenario concerns Price's contention that "we are by no means prepared to create and maintain" a corps of technologically oriented urban decision makers.[60] The corps, according to the literature on science and the city, exists and wants only to expand its decision-making parameters. The directions that new federal programs are taking comprise an important measure of its existence. It may be that the new centers of urban decision making in the United States will be in the research and development bureaus of the Departments of HUD, HEW, Transportation, and Justice.

The analyses of Price and others stop short of speculation on the patterns that extensive nonlocal decision making about local issues might take. It does seem likely, however, that control by the public of such a process would be minimal if the explanations concerning the social effects of bureaucracy and technology presented here are at all valid. By the same token, trends in systems analysis, EDP, and areal planning hint at a control of the public to a degree yet unrealized. Such control can be excused from the technocrat's point of view on grounds that it is for the "public good." But "good" is defined by highly professionalized criteria that may spring from the distorted vision of a cohesive coterie of bureaucratic personalities who receive data concerning their "system" and who are already warped by organizational pathologies.

Despite a healthy popular distrust of government from afar, Americans long have displayed an attachment for the new and novel. If science—in the forms of professionalism, housing, transportation, communication technologies, new managerial techniques, and systems analysis—can promise (as it does) to reduce violent crime, decaying buildings, choking air, and ugliness in general, the territorial administration of urban regions may be accepted as a "compromise" in the best American tradition, particularly if these problems grow more pronounced. And they will.

The environmental issue may further dramatize the popular appeal of science for urban purposes. Environmentalists have popularized the notion that man not only depends on his surroundings for life, but that man reduces his own chances for life by simplifying the natural ecology he inhabits; the more simple the ecological system, the more vulnerable it is to destruction. Cities represent the apex of man's desire to simplify natural ecosystems. In this sense, one scholar refers to a "second urban revolution" (the first one being urbanization itself) that has made cities vitally dependent on electromagnetic energy and on other cities, rather than on locally based energy sources and the immediate countryside as in the past.[61] The significance of this revolution is that if a city were deprived of energy (which it easily could be), or transportation, or communication with other cities, then it would die. The New York blackout which lasted only a brief duration, provides an example of vulnerability in an electromagnetic era. As popular awareness of urban vulnerability increases, it may develop that the American citizenry will be subjected to increased pressures to place technology in the hands of those who understand it; and the people who understand urban technology best are in the federal government. The compromise is functionally vital for the future of our living space.

The impact of environmental thinking already can be noticed in the literature of science and the city. Some writers on urban affairs now appear to use "ecology" and "general systems" as interchangeable concepts. This new emphasis may contribute to scholarly alarmism over the "decerebrate frog" we call urban areas and bring new pressures for control.[62]

Perhaps a more immediate and pertinent area of future research in political science that concerns science and the city will analyze appropriate levels of public authority for particular urban services. Bell and Held write, that "nowhere is there a detailed examination of what functions of government are best handled at what levels of government."[63] In at least one respect this kind of political science research counters the assumptions of ecology and asserts that each governmental function is discrete and can be administered separately. Ecology, which is central to the environmental approach, presumes quite the opposite—that no part of a system can operate without affecting other parts in a significant way.

It may be interesting to watch which direction political scientists choose as they investigate the implications of science and the city. If an environmental focus is selected, we may expect to see policy recommendations emerging from academia that emphasize urban technology and greater federal "participation" in local government. If structural/ functionalism is the approach, perhaps the benefits of "1400 governments" (actually, the number is closer to 90,000 in the United States) will be rediscovered. Or, perhaps political scientists may decide not to investigate the implications of science and the city at all. And this writer will have sounded the call towards deaf ears.

NOTES

[1] The Harvard University Program on Technology and Society has recently issued "Technology and the City" as No. 5 of its Research Review Series: *Science for Society: A Bibliography*, published by the American Association for the Advancement of Science, the National Science Foundation, and the Battelle Memorial Institute; it contains a section devoted to "Science and the City."

[2] The latest is *Science & Technology and the Cities*, the Committee on Science and Astronautics, U. S. House of Representatives (1969).

[3] James D. Carroll, "Science and the City: The Question of Authority," *Science* (February 28, 1969): 906, 905.

[4] Carl F. Stover, "Industry, Technology, and Metropolitan Problems," *Public Administration Review*, (June, 1967): 112–17; Carroll, op. cit., p. 904.

[5] Harvey M. Sapolsky, "Science Advice for State and Local Government", *Science* (April 16, 1968): 281–82.

[6] See Wood, "Science and the City," *Smithsonian Annual II: The Fitness of Man's Environment* (1968): 173–87, and Gardner, "The Keynote," in *Science & Technology and the Cities* (1969), pp. 1–8; Sapolsky, op. cit., p. 282; Carroll, op. cit., p. 904.

[7] Carroll, p. 903.

[8] To name two: Scott Greer, *The Emerging City* (1962) and Kenneth Boulding, *The Meaning of the Twentieth Century* (1965).

[9] York Willbern, *The Withering Away of the City* (1964), p. 33.

[10] Melvin M. Webber, "The Post-City Age," *Daedalus* (Fall, 1968): 1091–110, 1098, 1097.

[11] Walter A. Scheiber, "Commentary on Relevance of Science and Technology to Urban Affairs," in *Governing Urban Society: New Scientific Approaches*, (1967), p. 71.

[12] Willbern, op. cit., p. 70, 109–11.

[13] Gardner, op. cit., p. 1.

[14] Roger Starr, "Power and Powerlessness in a Regional City," *The Public Interest* (Summer, 1969): 4, 22.

[15] Willbern, op. cit., p. 122.

[16] Lynton K. Caldwell, "The Urban Environment as an Ecological System", *Indiana Legal Forum* (Spring, 1968): 302.

[17] Stover, op. cit., pp. 116–77.

[18] Willbern, op. cit., pp. 122 and 124.

[19] Daniel Bell and Virginia Held. "The Community Revolution," *The Public Interest* (Summer, 1969): 142, 143.

[20] Don K. Price, "Commentary on Adapting Government for Innovative Action," in *Governing Urban Society: New Scientific Approaches* (1967), p. 146.

[21] Bell and Held, op. cit., p. 177.

[22] Edward C. Banfield, *Political Influence* (1961), p. 318. Willbern argues with Banfield's contention by recalling that (a) not all governmental agencies are concerned with each act that a citizen performs and, (b) because government is not a major concern of Americans, persistent participants can secure change with relatively little opposition from fellow citizens. But the Bell and Held article would seem to counter Willbern's second reservation to Banfield's thesis, and Parkinson's Law eventually may counter his first. And, as Willbern states: "I must confess that these two observations constitute only marginal qualifications to the generalization that the more elaborate the system of units and agencies, the more difficult innovation may be." (Willbern, op. cit., p. 125).

[23] Stover, op. cit., p. 117.

[24] Britton Harris, "Commentary on Relevance of Science and Technology to Urban Problems," in *Governing Urban Society: New Scientific Approaches* (1967), p. 69.

[25] Scheiber, op. cit., p. 73; National Committee on Urban Growth Policy, *The New City* (1969); Athelstan Spilhaus, "Technology, Living Cities, and Human Environment," in *Science & Technology, and the Cities* (1969), p. 43; Zivorad Kovacevic, "Summary Views and Comments," in *Science & Technology and the Cities* (1969), p. 120.

[26] Sapolsky, op. cit., p. 282.

[27] Edward M. Goldberg, "Urban Information Systems and Invasions of Privacy," *Urban Affairs Quarterly* (March, 1970): 249, 255.

[28] Lynton K. Caldwell, "Managing the Scientific Super-Culture: The Task of Educational Preparation," *Public Administration Review* (June, 1967): 128–33.

[29] Robert T. Daland, "Political Science and the Study of Urbanism," *American Political Science Review* (June, 1957): 509.

[30] York Willbern, "Professionalization in the Public Service: Too Little Or Too Much?" *Public Administration Review* (Winter, 1954): 17–19.

[31] Herbert Kaufman, *The New York City Health Center*, (1959).

[32] Robert Golembiewski, *The Trenton Milk Contract* (1959).

[33] Robert K. Merton, "Bureaucratic Structure and Personality," in *Reader in Bureaucracy* (1952), pp. 361–71. Merton compares his idea of bureaucratic personality to "Veblen's concept of 'trained incapacity,' Dewey's notion of 'occupational psychosis' or Warnotte's view of 'professional deformation'" (p. 364). Merton is quoting Warnottes (p. 364).

[34] James G. March, and Herbert A. Simon, *Organizations* (1958), p. 165.

[35] Alan Altshuler, *The City Planning Process: A Political Analysis* (1965), pp. 17–83.

[36] Alexander L. George, "Political Leadership and Social Change in American Cities," *Daedalus* (Fall, 1968): 1200.

[37] Altshuler, op. cit., James K. Thompson, *Organization in Action* (1967), p. 13; Willbern, op. cit., p. 111.

[38] Gardner, op. cit., p. 3.

[39] Sapolsky, op. cit., p. 284.

[40] Wood, op. cit., 183–84.

[41] Carroll, op. cit., pp. 903–4.

[42] Gardner, op. cit., pp. 3–4; Charles Abrams, *The City Is the Frontier* (1965), p. 220.

[43] Carroll, op. cit., p. 908; See also: Editorial, "Lowering the Cost of Housing: The Labor Union's View," *Progressive Architect* (June, 1968): 100.

[44] William K. Muir, *Defending "The Hill" Against Metal Houses* (1955), p. 8.

[45] Gardner, op. cit., p .7.

[46] Wood, op. cit., p. 184, 178.

[47] Gardner, op. cit., p. 7.

[48] Donald N. Michael, "On Coping with Complexity: Planning and Politics," *Daedalus* (Fall, 1968): 1183–85.

[49] C. Mest Churchman, "The Use of Science in Urban Affairs," *Governing Urban Society: New Scientific Approaches* (1967), pp. 39, 40.

[50] Herbert A. Simon, *The Shape of Automation for Men and Management*, (1965).

[51] Goldberg, op. cit., p. 255.

[52] Willbern, "Professionalism in the Public Service," op. cit., p. 20.

[53] Lawrence E. Lessing, "Systems Engineering Invades the City," *Political Power and the Urban Crisis* (1969), p. 513.

[54] Stover, op. cit., p. 115.

⁵⁵ Paul Parks, "Urban Problems and Technology," *Science and the Future of Man* (1970), p. 37. Parks was the administrator of the Boston Model Cities program.
⁵⁶ Edmund N. Bacon, "Urban Process," *Daedalus* (Fall, 1968): 1171.
⁵⁷ Carroll, op. cit., p. 909.
⁵⁸ Roger L. Sisson, "Commentary on Impacts on Governmental Functions of Developments in Science and Technology," *Governing Urban Society: New Scientific Approaches* (1967), p. 107.
⁵⁹ James Bailey, "RFK's Favorite Ghetto," *Architectural Forum* (April, 1968): 47–53.
⁶⁰ Price, op. cit., pp. 145–46.
⁶¹ Caldwell, "The Urban Environment as an Ecological System", op. cit.
⁶² Ibid., p. 298; See also S. Marquis, "Ecosystems, Societies, and Cities," *American Behavioral Scientist* (July–August, 1968): 11–15; Lawrence J. R. Herson, "The Lost World of Municipal Government," in *Urban Government: A Reader in Politics and Administration* (1961).
⁶³ Bell and Held, op. cit., p. 176.

BIBLIOGRAPHY

Abrams, Charles, *The City Is the Frontier*. New York: Harper and Row, 1965; xii, 395.

Altshuler, Alan, *The City Planning Process: A Political Analysis*. Ithaca, New York: Cornell University Press, 1965; x, 466.

Bacon, Edmund N., "Urban Process," *Daedalus*, xcvii (Fall, 1968), 1165–78.

Bailey, James, "RFK's Favorite Ghetto," *Architectural Forum*, cxxviii (April, 1968), 46–52.

Banfield, Edward C., *Political Influence*. Glencoe, Illinois: Free Press, 1961; 354.

Banfield, Edward C. (ed.), *Urban Government: A Reader in Politics and Administration*. New York: Free Press of Glencoe, 1961; xii, 593.

Bell, Daniel, and Held, Virginia, "The Community Revolution," *The Public Interest*, XVI (Summer, 1969), 142–179.

Boulding, Kenneth, *The Meaning of the Twentieth Century: The Great Transition*. New York: Harper and Row, 1964; xvi, 199.

Caldwell, Lynton K., *Man and His Environment: Policy and Administration*. New York: Harper and Row, Publishers, 1975.

Caldwell, Lynton K., "Managing the Scientific Super-Culture: The Task of Educational Preparation," *Public Administration Review*, XXVII (June, 1967), 128–33.

Caldwell, Lynton K., "The Urban Environment as an Ecological System." *Indiana Legal Forum*, I (Spring, 1968), 298–309.

Carovillano, Robert L., and Skehan, James W. (eds.), *Science and the Future of Man*. Cambridge, Mass.: The MIT Press, 1970.

Churchman, C. West, "The Use of Science and Urban Affairs," *Governing Urban Society: New Scientific Approaches*. Monograph 7. Philadelphia: American Academy of Political and Social Science, May, 1967; 29–48.

Daland, Robert T., "Political Science and the Study of Urbanism," *American Political Science Review*, LI (June, 1957), 491–509.

Editorial. "Lowering the Cost of Housing: The Labor Union's View," *Progressive Architect*, XLIX (June, 1968), 100.

Erber, Ernest (ed.), *Urban Planning in Transition*. New York, Groseman Publishers, 1970.

Gardner, John W., "The Keynote," *Science and Technology and the Cities*, Compilation of Papers Presented for the Tenth Meeting of Panel on Science and Technology, 1969. Washington, D.C.: U.S. Government Printing Office, 1969; 1–8.

George, Alexander L., "Political Leadership and Social Change in American Cities," *Daedalus*, XCVII (Fall, 1968), 1194–217.

Goldberg, Edward M., "Urban Information Systems and Invasions of Privacy," *Urban Affairs Quarterly*, V (March, 1970), 249–64.

Golembiewski, Robert, *The Trenton Milk Contract*. The Inter-University Case Program No. 50. University, Alabama: University of Alabama Press, 1959; 19.

Gottlieb, Daniel W. (ed.), *Technology and the Cities*. Washington, D.C.: The Natural Science Foundation. 1974.

Gordon, Kenneth and Halm, Walter (eds.), *Assessing the Future and Policy Planning*. New York: Gordon and Breach Science Publishers, 1973.

Greer, Scott, *The Emerging City: Myth and Reality*. New York: Free Press of Glencoe, 1962; 232.

Harris, Britton, "Commentary on Relevance of Science and Technology to Urban Problems," *Governing Urban Society: New Scientific Approaches.* Monograph 7. Philadelphia: American Academy of Political and Social Science, May, 1967; 63–69.

Herson, Lawrence J. R., "The Lost World of Municipal Government," *Urban Government: A Reader in Politics and Administration.* New York: Free Press of Glencoe, 1961; 3–18.

Kaufman, Herbert, *The New York City Health Centers.* The Inter-University Case Program No. 9. University of Alabama: University of Alabama Press, Revised 1959; 18.

Kovacevic, Zivorad, "Summary Views and Comments," *Science and Technology and the Cities.* Compilation of Papers Presented for the Tenth Meeting of Panel on Science and Technology, 1969. Washington: U.S. Government Printing Office, 1969; 119–24.

Lessing, Lawrence E., "Systems Engineering Invades the City," *Political Power and the Urban Crisis.* Boston: Hollbrood Press, Inc., 1969; 513–26.

March, James G. and Simon, Herbert A., *Organizations.* New York: John Wiley & Sons, Inc., 1958; xi, 262.

Merton, Robert K., "Bureaucratic Structure and Personality," *Reader in Bureaucracy.* New York: The Free Press, 1952, 361–71.

Merton, Robert K., Gray, Ailsa P., Hockey, Barbara, and Selvin, Hanan C., (eds.), *Reader in Bureaucracy.* New York: The Free Press, 1952; 464.

Michael, Donald N., "On Coping With Complexity: Planning and Politics," *Daedalus,* xcvii (Fall, 1968), 1179–93.

Muir, William K., Jr., *Defending "the Hill" Against Metal Houses.* The Inter-University Case Program No. 26. University, Alabama: University of Alabama Press. 1955; 35.

National Committee on Urban Growth Policy. *The New City* (Donald Canty, ed.). New York: Frederick Praeger, 1969; 180.

Price, Don K., "Commentary on Adapting Government for Innovative Action," *Governing Urban Society: New Scientific Approaches.* Monograph 7. Philadelphia: American Academy of Political and Social Science, May 1967; 143–48.

Sapolsky, Harvey M., "Science Advice for State and Local Government," *Science,* clx (April 19, 1968), 280–84.

Scheiber, Walter A., "Commentary on the Relevance of Science and Technology to Urban Affairs," *Governing Urban Society: New Scientific Approaches.* Monograph 7. Philadelphia: American Academy of Political and Social Science, May, 1967; 70–73.

Shank, Alan (ed.), *Political Power and the Urban Crisis.* Boston: Holbrook Press, Inc., 1969; xii, 532.

Simm, Herbert A., *The Shape of Automation for Men and Management.* New York: Harper & Row, Publishers, 1965; xv, 111.

Sisson, Roger L., "Commentary on Impacts on Governmental Functions of Developments in Science and Technology," *Governing Urban Society: New Scientific Approaches.* Monograph 7. Philadelphia: American Academy of Political and Social Science, May, 1967; 101–9.

Smithsonian Institution. *Smithsonian Annual II: The Fitness of Man's Environment.* Papers delivered at the Smithsonian Institution Annual Symposium, February 16–18, 1967. Washington, D.C.: Smithsonian Institution Press, 1968; 250.

Spilhaus, Athelstan, "Technology, Living Cities, and Human Environment," *Science & Technology and the Cities.* Compilation of Papers Presented for the Tenth Meeting of Panel on Science and Technology, 1969. Washington: U.S. Government Printing Office, 1969; 33–43.

Starr, Roger, "Power and Powerlessness in a Regional City," *The Public Interest,* XVI (Summer, 1969), 3–24.

Stover, Carl F., "Industry, Technology, and Metropolitan Problems," *Public Administration Review,* XXVII (June, 1967), 112–17.

Sweeney, Stephen B. and Charlesworth, James C., (eds.), *Governing Urban Society: New Scientific Approaches.* Monograph 7. Philadelphia: American Academy of Political and Social Science, May, 1967; xiii, 254.

Thompson, James D., *Organizations in Action: Social Science Bases of Administrative Theory.* New York: McGraw-Hill Book Co., 1967; 192.

Tugwell, Franklin (ed.), *Search for Alternatives: Public Policy and the Study of the Future.* Cambridge, Mass.: Winthrop Publishers, Inc., 1973.

U.S. Congress, House. Committee on Science and Astronautics. *Science & Technology and the Cities*. Compilation of Papers Presented for Tenth Meeting of Panel on Science and Technology, 1969. Washington, D.C.: U.S. Government Printing Office, 1969; vii, 126.

Webber, Melvin M., "The Post-City Age," *Daedalus*, xcvii (Fall, 1968), 1091–110.

Willbern, York, "Professionalization in the Public Service: Too Little or Too Much?" *Public Administration Review*, xiv (Winter, 1954), 13–21.

Wood, Robert C., "Science and the City," *Smithsonian Annual II: The Fitness of Man's Environment*. Papers delivered at the Smithsonian Institution Annual Symposium, February 16–18, 1967. Washington, D.C.: Smithsonian Institution Press, 1968; 173–87.

MOTHERS AND DAUGHTERS
IN A BLUE-COLLAR NEIGHBORHOOD
IN URBAN AMERICA

Gina Oboler and Leon Oboler

In 1974 and 1975 a team of Temple University researchers executed a major demographic, social, and cultural survey of a working-class, largely (80 percent) Catholic neighborhood of Philadelphia.[1] One of the goals of this survey, and the core of this paper, was the testing of the hypothesis that working-class families in industrialized, urban western countries have a matrilateral bias to kinship, as has been discovered by Bott, Young and Wilmott, Coult and Habenstein, Komarovsky, and Anspach and Rosenbert.[2]

Manayunk (not a pseudonym) is a fascinating community. It is old by American standards, having already celebrated its bicentennial. Originally a mill town on the outskirts of Philadelphia, it was not incorporated into the city until 1854. Despite the incorporation, Manayunkers (as they call themselves) seem to be most proud of the independent identity they have maintained.

Manayunk is predominantly white (10 percent black) self-consciously ethnic, with a very substantial Polish population. It is a community, par excellence. People identify with it, and grown children realize that the life their parents have created in Manayunk is a viable and valuable one, even though it may not fit the outlines of the American Dream they learn about at their (Uitlander) high school. Manayunkers care about kinship; they care about religion; they care about having a good time. They conflate the ideas of "relative" and "friend" because many of their friends are relatives; and relatives are readily converted into friends—one has only to repose a good deal of trust in them and the conversion is carried out.[3]

Manayunk is self-consciously working class even though the disparity of incomes is perhaps greater than we would associate with a homogeneous working-class community. Homes are homes, not houses; and they are small, well-kept, and sources of great pride to their owners. Philadelphia has one of the highest proportions of home-owners in the country,[4] and Manayunk shares in this distinction.

Physically Manayunk is a stable community. It has maintained its integrity in the face of the attempts of developers who wished to change its waterfront by building high-rise apartments along it. It is changing ethnically, but there is no large-scale suburban flight. In fact, interviews reveal that there is a cyclicity of out-migration and in-migration according to the domestic cycle. Young couples move out after marriage but often attempt to move back in when they have large numbers of children. This is remarkable for two reasons: Couples with children are rejecting the green, open-space (suburban) option for their children in favor of an urban milieu; second, houses in Manayunk are very small. They do not readily accommodate large families in the roomy, middle-class style. Manayunkers seem not to notice. Rather, they prefer that families be close, not just emotionally, but physically as well. Nonetheless, it is important not to overstate the stability of the area, for a majority of children leave Manayunk and its environs.

Manayunk seems to be similar to Bethnal Green, the area of London studied so intensively by Wilmott, Young, and their collaborators.[5] Unlike Bethnal Green, however, there has been no governmental pressure to move the inhabitants—pressure that well might have created, or at least solidified, the matrilateral ties that Wilmott and Young found so important in organizing kinship interaction. We felt that Manayunk, then, would be an ideal test for the matrilateral bias hypothesis in a more natural setting than was afforded Wilmott and Young and that it would provide comparative data on family organization.

Initially, fieldwork began with a demographic, door-to-door survey of Manayunk. The questionnaire used was constructed to gather detailed demographic and economic data and to be compatible with the 1960 and 1970 U.S. censuses. This survey was to be the data base from which all members of a team of researchers could draw information and against which they could check the representativeness of various subsamples of the population they were dealing with.[6] In addition, the compatibility of the questionnaire with material gathered by the U.S. census would permit the drawing of detailed inferences that are not possible when aggregated data have no known population base.

In administering the questionnaire, the research team knocked on every door in Manayunk (roughly Census Tract 214 of the Philadelphia sector), and almost 400 responses (30 percent response rate) were obtained. Checking critical variables of the sample with census data, we concluded that this population constituted a representative profile of Manayunk. The data on the questionnaire broke down into six categories: personal data on the respondent and his or her spouse, composition and type of household, data on children no longer living in the home, other relatives, friends, and data on organizations the interviewee belonged to.

Of the total sample, a subsample of 212 was obtained for the present analysis. These 212 provided sufficient data to be included in this paper. A total of 119 cases provided enough data on residential history for both of a pair of spouses to be useful in testing hypotheses relating to the matrilateral bias theory.[7] Twenty of the total subsample of 212 questionnaires were discarded as providing insufficient data for present purposes, or unclear data, leaving a net subsample size of 192 for the analysis of household structure.

GENERAL HOUSEHOLD PATTERNS IN MANAYUNK

It is often taken as axiomatic that the American middle class places supreme value on the nuclear family, a unit comprising a married pair and their minor offspring, which is supposed to be an independent and self-sufficient economic and residential unit. This value system, however, is confined to the middle class. As David M. Schneider and Raymond T. Smith, writing on kinship and class, put it: "The normative structure of lower-class American kinship does not stress the independence and integrity of the unit of husband, wife, and children. . . . The composition of lower-class households can be more diverse without being considered unusual."[8] Schneider and Smith furthermore stress that the lower class places primary emphasis on solidarity between mother and children rather than husband and wife and that this contributes to the lowered importance of the nuclear family. In their schema, "working-class" is a transitional stage between "lower-class" and "middle-class," characterized by stable jobs and higher earnings on the part of men coupled with basically lower-class cultural orientations, including orientations towards kinship and residence patterns.[9]

The Manayunk residential data support this conclusion (see Table 1). Of 192 households, only 99 conform to what might be considered "classic" nuclear family types. Of these, 68 are cases of married couples with all or some of their nonadult children (ranging from 1 to 8 in number) living with them, and 31 are married couples living by themselves (elderly parents whose children have left home, young marrieds who have not yet started families, and a few couples who never had children). The remaining 93 households cannot be characterized as "classic" nuclear family arrangements, although some of them are not too divergent from the norm when considered in terms of the normal processes in the developmental cycle of domestic groups in American society. Thus, the 3 cases of single children over 30 living with their parents (Table 1, C-4) are simply abnormally long extensions of the nuclear family pattern. Twenty-four more cases (Table 1, A-3 and B-2) are ascribable to death and widowhood. Eight cases, those of widowed parents living with single children over 30 (Table 1, D-1) could possibly be viewed as the result of the combination of the two previously discussed processes. These cases seem to be a little different, however, since interview data reveal a tendency in cases of premature widowhood for one child to remain with the widowed parent rather than marrying. A disproportionately high number of never-married persons seem to come from such situations, although the total number of never-married persons is not great enough to make statistical analysis worthwhile. Finally, there is one case in which

TABLE 1

NUCLEAR AND NON-NUCLEAR
FAMILY HOUSEHOLD TYPES

I.	**"Classic" Nuclear Family Households**	**99**
	A. Parents and children	*68*
	1. Families with all children still living at home	43
	2. Families with some but not all children still at home	25
	B. Married couples only	*31*
	1. Elderly couples (children living elsewhere)	20
	2. Young marrieds (pre-childrearing)	6
	3. Long-married, childless couples	5
II.	**Other Than "Classic" Nuclear Family Households**	**93**
	A. Single-person households	*22*
	1. Never married (2 men, 1 woman)	3
	2. Divorced, separated (3 men, 1 woman)	4
	3. Widowed (4 men, 11 women)	15
	B. Single parents with children under 30	*22*
	1. Divorced, separated (4 men, 9 women)	13
	2. Widowed (1 man, 8 women)	9
	C. Nuclear families with adjunct members	*20*
	1. Married couple and separated, divorced, or widowed son/daughter and children of the latter (1 son, 7 daughters) (2 cases including other children of household head, one with foster children, as well)	8
	2. Married couple (in 4 cases, with children) and parent of one spouse (parent of wife, 3, parent of husband, 2)	5
	3. Husband and wife (in one case, with a son still at home) and sibling of wife	2
	4. Husband and wife with never-married children over 30	3
	5. Other	2
	a. Husband and wife, and foster child	
	b. Husband and wife, with son and daughter of husband's sister	

D. Other   29
   1. Widowed parents with single children over 30
     (3 men, 7 women)   10
   2. Adult siblings co-residing (2 cases include
     children of one sibling, and 1 includes
     boarders)   9
   3. Non-nuclear, three-generation households   4
   4. Households containing unrelated individuals
     (with some relatives as well in some cases)   6

TOTAL	**192**

nuclear family structure is approximated, except that foster children have been substituted for own children (Table 1, C-5a). Perhaps this group might have been counted as a "classic" nuclear family case.

Thirty-eight of 93 cases of non-nuclear family structure have been explained as the result of nuclear families having been modified by the actions of more-or-less normal processes of the developmental cycle. There still remain 55 non-nuclear family cases. Twenty-five of these cases are attributable mainly to divorce or separation (Table 1, A-2, B-1, and C-1), which, however statistically common it may be, is nevertheless not normatively viewed by Manayunkers or other American informants as a "normal" process.[10] Granting a special status to such cases, this still leaves 30 definitely unorthodox households, or 15 percent. Although comparative data are lacking, this is probably a high rate by middle-class standards. Of these cases, categories D-2, D-3, and D-4, as well as 2 cases from D-1, call for special comment. The composition of the households in these categories displays a tremendous range of diversity. The two cases from D-1 are situations in which a widower is living with adult unmarried children, but in one case the household also includes his sister-in-law, and in the other, a widowed daughter. The cases of adult siblings co-residing include the following permutations: cases in which both siblings never married, cases where one never married and one is widowed, and a case where four are widowed: two sisters (two cases), a sister and brother (five cases), and one sister living with three brothers (one case). These households also include the children of one of the siblings in two cases, and three boarders in one of the brother-sister cases. The non-nuclear, three-generation households include: a woman with four children, including a teenage daughter who also has a child; a man and wife living with his sister's son and wife and their child; a separated man living with his son and the latter's wife and child; and a widower living with two single children, a separated son, and the two children of the latter. The households containing unrelated individuals include: three cases of two same-sex friends living together (in two cases women, and in one, elderly men); a divorced woman with her two children, her two younger sisters, and an unrelated teenage male identified as her ward; a widow with an elderly woman described as a boarder and a teenage girl described as her "step-granddaughter"; two divorced women with the children of one and a 16-year-old male "friend" living with them because he cannot get along with his family.

Also from Table 1, all widowed persons living alone are over 60 years of age (9 of the 11 women in this category are over 70). The age range of single parents with children is 17 to 60. (In the case of one separated 17-year-old male with an infant son, his mother and sister are living around the corner and apparently giving him a considerable amount of supportive services.) The age range of never-married persons living alone is 27 to 73. The age range of divorced and separated persons living alone is 30 to 50+, and it is interesting to note that in this predominantly Catholic neighborhood, none of these persons is Catholic. However, the number of such persons is too small to be amenable to statistical analysis.

RESIDENTIAL CONTINUITY AND COMMUNITY STABILITY

One of the original reasons for choosing Manayunk as the area of study was that it appeared to be an exceedingly stable community—especially for an urban neighborhood. This is reflected in the ideology, quite prevalent among informants, that members of the community are highly interrelated by kinship ties and that Manayunk natives, more so than natives of other neighborhoods, are permanently attached to the community. This ideology is made clear in such popular aphorisms as: "If you throw a stone in Manayunk, you're likely to hit a relative," and "You can take a boy out of Yunk, but you can't take Yunk out of the boy." If this ideology reflects actual social patterns, one would expect Manayunk to be characterized by a high rate of community endogamy and residential stability of families in the community over several generations. Manayunkers should marry other Manayunkers, and the children of Manayunkers should continue to reside in Manayunk as married adults. To what extent do these patterns actually occur?

Of the 119 cases in which there are some residential history data for two spouses in a married couple, there are 114 cases with complete data on "Place Born" and "Place Raised" for both spouses. These may be divided as follows: both spouses raised in Census Tract 214, 25; one spouse raised in Census Tract 214, 40; and both spouses raised elsewhere, 49. Thus, among 228 married persons in the sample, 90 were raised in Tract 214, while 138 were not. Most of Manayunk's adult population is therefore not indigenous, nor is community endogamy the statistical norm (24 individuals raised outside Tract 214 came from the same community as their spouses). Including both cases where both spouses were raised in Manayunk and cases where both spouses were raised in the same community other than Manayunk, 33 percent of persons in our sample were raised in the same community as their spouses.

When Census Tract 214, Roxborough, Wissahickon, Belmont Hills (West Manayunk), Shawmont, and Miquon (i.e., Tract 214 and the most closely surrounding named communities) are taken as a unit, the tendency to endogamous marriage is slightly increased: both spouses raised in area, 44; one spouse, but not both, raised in area, 40; and both spouses raised elsewhere, 30. The rate of indigenous versus nonindigenous persons is also somewhat raised—128 persons in the sample were born in the area, 40 married in, and 60 were neither born in nor married in. Twenty-four of these latter persons did come from the same community as their spouses. So if Manayunk and surrounding named areas are treated as one community, we are now dealing with a 49 percent rate of community endogamy within our sample. It is clear, however, that even if Tract 214 and surrounding neighborhoods are taken as comprising the endogamous unit, the population of 214 still includes a considerable number of "outsiders"—persons who are not natives of this larger area. This would appear to contradict the folk ideology which holds that most of the people in Manayunk are interrelated.

What is not known, however, is how the incidence of community endogamy compares with that of other urban neighborhoods or that of small towns. One study of residential propinquity in marriage choices found that among 5,000 Philadelphia married couples, 17 percent had lived within two blocks of each other prior to marriage, 34 percent within five blocks, and 52 percent within a mile.[11] The 52 percent figure is considerably higher than our original community endogamy rate of 33 percent, and in order to get a figure approaching it (49 percent area endogamy), we have had to make the unit of study one which includes points much more than a mile distant from one another or from Manayunk. How, then, are the community endogamy rate, considerably lower than Bossard's rate for Philadelphia as a whole, and the discrepancy between the folk-model and actual marriage choices to be explained? Bossard's study was done in 1932, and in the intervening period certain developments in American society (e.g., the advent of the family car) may have made a general change in courtship and marriage patterns. Indeed, it is probably the case that Philadelphians in general are less endogamous in the present, and it may be that Manayunkers were more endogamous in the past.

One important change which is known to have occurred within the last generation could definitely contribute to an increased rate of marriage outside the community. There used to be a Catholic high school in Manayunk, but consolidation of the Catholic school system caused it to be closed. It is now necessary for Manayunk parents who wish their children to have a Catholic education to send them to school outside the community in central Philadelphia. Perhaps much stress should not be given to this factor, since the schools these students attend are sexually segregated. Nevertheless, they do meet friends from other neighborhoods and are likely to meet non-Manayunkers of their age and opposite sex when they travel outside the community to visit these friends. Thus, taking into account the time difference between Bossard's study and ours, it may be the case that community endogamy is decreasing. We still do not know, however, how Manayunk compares with other communities at the present time. Thus, it is not clear whether it is more reasonable to invoke Manayunk-specific factors or more general factors to explain this hypothesized change.

It should further be stressed that insofar as there does exist a unit which tends to be endogamous, this is not Census Tract 214 or the named community "Manayunk" (the two are not exactly congruent), but a larger area.

The same unit seems to figure in a discernible patterning of residential choices among children of couples in our sample. Of the children, at least one of whose parents was raised in Manayunk or the surrounding area (as previously defined), 72.3 percent have continued to live in this area as adults. This result is statistically significant ($\chi^2 = 13.77$, $P < .01$):

Children Living:

	In Area	Elsewhere	
Parents Raised:	63.67	37.33	
In Area	73	28	101
	23.33	13.67	
Elsewhere	14	23	37
	87	51	138

It must be noted that there is no statistically significant tendency for adult children to remain in the community in which parents were raised when the unit concerned is Manayunk or Census Tract 214.

Thus, there does indeed seem to be residential continuity of families within a restricted area over a number of generations, but the area characterized by this familial continuity is not Manayunk. High rates of endogamy and residential continuity of families within a larger area of which Manayunk is a part could, however, result in a large proportion of the residents of Manayunk being interrelated, although it is to be expected that all these people will have relatives in other parts of this larger area as well. Thus, the assertion that "if you throw a stone in Manayunk you're liable to hit a relative" may have a basis in fact, though Manayunkers do not appear to realize its corollary: "If you throw a stone across the river into Belmont Hills, you're liable to hit a relative, too." Cognitively, Manayunkers take Manayunk as their first point of reference and see it as a distinct, bounded unit.

FACTORS CONTRIBUTING TO
NON-NEOLOCAL RESIDENCE

Of the 119 cases which provided enough data on the residential history of both of a pair of spouses to be useful for any part of the present analysis, 65 couples responded positively to the question, "Since you have been married, have you ever lived with any persons other than your spouse and children?" Thirty-two responded negatively, and in 20 cases, data are missing. In addition, there are two cases where, while there is technically no history of non-neolocal residence, exceptionally close ties have been maintained with the wife's parents. These are cases where the couple is living in a house either next door to or two doors away from the wife's parents, in a house that is either owned by the latter, or was previously owned by them and has now been given to the daughter and her husband. These seem to be marginal cases of non-neolocal residence. Of the 92 couples in the sample of 119 who are currently residing neolocally, 39 have a history of previous non-neolocal residence (41 if the two cases cited above are counted as instances of non-neolocal residence).

Schneider and Smith[12] are not alone in asserting that non-neolocal residence is more prevalent in the lower socioeconomic classes. This is a common assumption about American kinship and residence patterns. We felt it reasonable to assume that more than one socioeconomic class is represented in Manayunk since our data reveal a very wide range in terms of income, occupation, and education. Consequently, we attempted to ascertain whether either income or education, as indices of class status, have any effect upon the occurrence of non-neolocal residence.[13] The educational level of either husband or wife at either the high-school-graduate versus non-high-school-graduate or the more-than-high-school level versus the less-than-high-school level was not significantly related to the couple's ever having resided non-neolocally. Using lower educational levels as the break-point for data analysis yielded even less significant results.

Wife's employment outside the home had a random relationship with past history of non-neolocal residence; and husband's income (using household income only for cases of neolocal residence where the wife's occupation is housewife), while it is not completely random, does not have a truly high level of significance ($\chi^2 = 1.68$, $P < .20$):

	Residence Pattern:		
	Non-Neolocal	Neolocal	
Husband's Income:	14.98	8.02	
≥ $10,000	17	6	23
	13.02	6.98	
< $10,000	11	9	20
	28	15	43

It therefore seems that in Manayunk there is no significant relationship between several variables that might be expected to provide an index of socioeconomic class and history of non-neolocal residence. We may therefore conclude that either (1) there is no relationship between class and non-neolocal residence in Manayunk, or (2) social class, as Schneider and Smith claim, is really a matter of cultural orientation and not socioeconomic factors, and perhaps the vast majority of people in our sample and in Manayunk share a single-class orientation in spite of differences in income, education, and so on.

Norms relative to the structure of families and households derived from differing cultural traditions might also be thought to be a factor which could affect the occurrence of non-neolocal residence. For this reason, we decided to see if residence history varies with respondents' stated ethnic identities. Table 2 gives the total ethnic-identity breakdown, for both spouses in cases where married-couple data are available, for household head in other cases (including some cases where there are two adult household heads) and for household head and spouse, where given, in nuclear family cases where a child of the household was interviewed. "Polish" is cited as the ethnic identity in about twice as many cases as any other category and accounts for slightly more than one-quarter of the total cases. Furthermore, it is usually cited as a "pure" ethnic identity and not in combination with anything else. "Irish" is the next most common, cited about half as often as Polish, followed by German, Irish-German combination, black, and Italian.[14]

TABLE 2

ETHNICITY

GROUP	MEN	WOMEN	TOTAL
Polish	36	49	85
Irish	21	22	43
German	14	14	28
Irish/German or German/Irish	13	13	26
Black	9	17	26
Italian	9	10	19
Irish/English	7	6	13
English	3	7	10
"American"-Anglo Saxon/WASP	4	3	7
Italian/German or German/Italian	4	1	5
English/German or German/English	3	2	5
Scotch-Irish	3	1	4
Lithuanian	3	1	4
Irish/Polish or Polish/Irish	1	3	4
Irish/French	–	3	3
Irish/Italian or Italian/Irish	1	2	3
Swedish	1	1	2
Irish/American Indian	1	1	2
Italian/Polish	2	–	2
Pennsylvania Dutch/German	1	1	2
"Mixed"	–	2	2
All Other (mentioned once each)*	15	12	27

*"Other" includes: Slovak, Croat, Scottish, Ukranian, French, French Canadian, Roumanian, Jewish, English/Polish, Scottish/Dutch, Polish/German, Danish/German, Slavic/German, German/Hungarian, German/French, French/Pennsylvania Dutch, Spanish/French, WASP/Polish, Welsh/Irish, Norwegian/Irish, Lithuanian/Irish, Slovak/Hungarian, Hungarian/Italian, French Canadian/American Indian, German/Irish/Polish, Mexican/Slovak/Italian, French/English, Irish/Dutch.

No significant relationships appear to obtain between non-neolocal residence history and ethnicity, taken as either (a) ethnicity of the husband, (b) ethnicity of the wife, or (c) cases where both husband and wife have the same ethnicity. In all cases, upon original survey of the data, Polish ethnicity seemed most likely to yield significant results, but upon analysis, no significance was revealed.

One factor did, however, reveal a significant correlation with past history of non-neolocal residence. This factor was the year in which the couple was married. It seems that most cases of past non-neolocal residence were cases where the couple resided with the parents of one spouse immediately after marriage until they were financially or otherwise able to move into neolocal residence. Couples who were married either during the 1930s, when times were difficult economically, or during the 1940s, when there was a nationwide housing shortage, are significantly more likely to have resided non-neolocally than couples who were married during other periods (significant: $\chi^2 = 8.13$, P $< .01$). For those cases where complete data are available, the breakdown is given in Table 3 and the following:

	Lived Non-Neolocally:			
	Yes		No	
Married:	14.28		9.72	
30s or 40s		20	4	24
	32.72		22.28	
Other		27	28	55
		47	32	79

Cases of couples married during the 1930s and 1940s, then, account for almost half of all cases of previous non-neolocal residence. This was the period in recent history when economic and other hardships made it most difficult for a young married couple to get started on their own. This factor must have been important for some couples during other periods as well, and it seems likely that financial, housing, and other similar difficulties during the early years of marriage are the most important single factor contributing to past history of non-neolocal residence. Let us turn now to the question of which

spouse's relatives are most likely to be called upon to help the couple
through such periods of hardship.

TABLE 3

PREVIOUS NON-NEOLOCAL RESIDENCE

Married	Now Residing Neolocally	
	Yes	No
pre–1920	0	2 (1)
1920–1929	2 (2)*	5
1930–1939	3 (1)	0
1940–1949	12 (1)	4
1950–1959	8 (1)	8
1960–1969	8 (2)	7
post–1969	4	5
	40 (7)	31 (1)

*Numbers in parentheses indicate deceased, divorced, or separated spouse cases.

SEX BIAS IN RESIDENTIAL PATTERNS

A number of studies in the past two decades have revealed that the
supposedly bilateral kinship systems of Western European and Western European-derived societies in fact show a marked asymmetry.
Especially in the working class, the kinship network in which a married couple participates tends to be skewed on the basis of sex: Wives
have closer ties with their relatives than either they or their husbands
have with the husband's kin, and husbands are drawn into interaction
with the wife's kin.[15] In their study of an East London neighborhood,
for example, Young and Wilmott found that married women are more
likely to live in close proximity to their parents' residence than are
married men and that married couples live more frequently near the
wife's parents than the husband's. Married women see their parents
and siblings more often than do married men, their mothers more often
than their fathers, and sisters more often than brothers. Married men
also see their mothers and sisters more often than their fathers and
brothers, but not as often as do women. Furthermore, married men

have more frequent contact with their mothers-in-law than they do with their own mothers, while women's contact with their mothers-in-law is much less frequent. Mothers provide various forms of aid (help at childbirth and in times of crisis, help in finding a house, child care services, loans, emotional support) to their daughters, who if they live near enough—and they frequently do—spend a large portion of each day in their mothers' homes, where their sisters are likely to be as well. Mothers thus become the central focus of solidarity in extended family groups of related women which consist of "the families of marriage of the daughters and their common family of origin." [16]

Elizabeth Bott also points up this matrilateral bias in the kinship system of the British working class: "Wherever there are no particular economic advantages to be gained by affiliation with paternal relatives, and whenever two or preferably three generations of mothers and daughters are living in the same place at the same time, a bilateral kinship system is likely to develop a matrilateral stress, and groups composed of sets of mothers and daughters may form within networks of kin." [17] Bott relates this bias to conjugal role segregation which allocates all domestic responsibilities entirely to the wife. The father is important as a financial support to the family, but he spends much of his time away from the domestic sphere and is deeply involved in an outside all-male peer group. His sons begin to follow his example at an early age, leaving mother and daughters to form bonds of solidarity as co-operating participants in the domestic sphere.

Schneider and Smith [18] have extended these observations of matrilaterality in the British working class to the explication of class differences in kinship noted in a survey of American kinship patterns in the Chicago area. And Komarovsky, [19] writing of the American middle class but making observations that could easily be extended to the working class, related sex bias in affective relations with kin (degree of attachment to parents, tendency to act in accord with parents' wishes, and so on) to differences in sex-role socialization. Due to the relative emphasis on greater independence training for boys than for girls, men achieve independence of their families of orientation while women remain close to their families and dependent upon them for support and approval throughout their lives.

Anspach and Rosenberg in their study of Philadelphia working-class couples confirm the hypothesis that wives tend to contact members of their kindred more frequently than do husbands, and that husbands tend to have more frequent contact with the spouse's kindred than do wives. However, they reject the idea that this difference is due to any sort of cultural value on "matricentricity" or the tendency of more solidary bonds to exist among female kin. Instead, they attribute the difference to age differences between spouses: "To a considerable extent, then, so-called matricentric bias is not a function of kinship (and hence the term matricentric is misleading) but rather is an artifact of the age differences in the conjugal pair." [20]

According to their interpretation, each spouse is responsible for any contact the couple has with her or his own kindred. Both men and women are almost equally likely to contact their kin, but the tendency to do so decreases with advancing age for both sexes. If wives seem to contact their kin more frequently than do husbands, then, it is because they are generally younger than their husbands. Anspach and Rosenberg point out that when husband and wife are nearly the same age, the tendency for wives to have more contact with their kin is reduced. Differences in frequency of contact with the spouse's kindred are also partly accounted for by differences in the spouse's age. Nevertheless, as Anspach and Rosenberg themselves point out, despite the fact that differences between husbands and wives are greatly reduced when age is held constant, they are not entirely eliminated. Age differences alone do not entirely account for matrilateral bias in patterns of contact with kin.[21]

With these discussions of matrilateral bias as background data, we have attempted to determine in the present research whether there is any sexual bias in patterns of kinship and especially residence in Manayunk. That such a bias might exist was suggested by such informant statements as: "Yes, I expect my sons will live around here . . . if they marry a girl from the neighborhood, that is. . . . You know, nine out of ten girls want to live near their mothers." Specifically, we hypothesized the following: (a) A couple who had resided non-neolocally would be more likely to have resided with kin of the wife than with kin of the husband. (b) Among married couples where only one spouse was a native of Manayunk, wives would be more likely to be natives of the community and to have brought their spouses there to live than would husbands. (c) Daughters of couples residing in the Manayunk area would be more likely to reside there also than would sons. And, (d) daughters living away from their parents' home would contact their parents more frequently than would sons living away from home. Though most studies of sexual bias in kinship have dealt with differences between husband and wife in the frequency with which they contact kin, we avoided comparisons involving contact except in the case of children, since in most instances we were able to interview only one of a pair of spouses.

Our first hypothesis, that couples who have resided non-neolocally are more likely to have resided with wife's than husband's relatives, received confirmation. Table 4 gives the responses to the questions, "Since your marriage, have you ever lived with anybody other than your spouse and children, and if so, whose relatives were they?" Note

TABLE 4

RESIDENCE WITH RELATIVES

Question and Answer	No.	Percent
Yes	65	(55.6)
Wife's Relatives	36	(30.8)
Husband's Relatives	14	(12.0)
Relatives of Both	11	(9.4)
Others	4	(3.4)
No	32	(27.3)
Missing	20	(17.1)

that these data do not include the two cases of couples living next to and in housing provided by the wife's parents. For couples who are now residing neolocally, but who previously resided non-neolocally (again, not including the two cases mentioned above), Table 5 gives the responses. It is clear that relatives of the wife have been considerably favored in both cases. Of our sample couples, 30.8 percent have lived with relatives of the wife at some time or other, while only 12.0 percent

TABLE 5

RESIDENCE WITH RELATIVES

Question and Answer	No.	Percent
Yes	39	(43.4)
Wife's Relatives	26	(29.0)
Husband's Relatives	7	(7.8)
Relatives of Both	4	(4.4)
Others	2	(2.2)
No	32	(34.4)
Missing	20	(22.2)

have lived with relatives of the husband. The result is statistically significant ($\chi^2 = 9.68, P < .01$).

We next sought to determine whether there is any set of conditions under which this bias in favor of residence with relatives of the wife is particularly emphasized or nullified.

ETHNICITY

For the majority of ethnic groups, no clear pattern of differentiation in terms of sex bias in residence emerged. For all groups, residence with the wife's family was more likely than residence with the husband's family. This remained the case whether the data were grouped by (1) husband's ethnicity, (b) wife's ethnicity, (c) ethnicity of both marital partners in cases where it was the same; and whether the data were grouped by (d) "pure" ethnicity only, or (3) ethnic combinations, grouped according to the ethnicity first mentioned in the combination. (For a breakdown of ethnic composition of the total sample, see Table 2).

Only one factor having to do with ethnicity—Polish ethnic identity of the wife—significantly increased the likelihood of a couple having resided with relatives of the wife. However, it seemed that the Polish ethnic identity of either partner to the marriage somewhat increased the probability of residence with the wife's family, although this was not statistically significant in either cases where the husband is Polish or cases where both spouses are Polish. Residence at some time with relatives of the wife has occurred in 32.2 percent of all marriages, 35.7 percent of all marriages in which the husband is Polish, 40.0 percent of marriages in which both spouses are Polish, and 43.0 percent of marriages in which the wife is Polish. A significant result ($\chi^2 =$ 6.63, P $<$ .01) is obtained for residence with the wife's as opposed to residence with the husband's relatives if the wife is Polish:

	Ethnicity of Wife		
	Polish	Not Polish	
Couple Lived With:	12.96	15.84	
Wife's Kin	15	21	36
	5.04	6.16	
Husband's Kin	3	11	14
	18	32	50

Thus, while residence with relatives of the wife is more likely than residence with relatives of the husband no matter what the ethnicity of either spouse, it is much more likely in cases where the wife is Polish.

AGE

Age is a significant variable in this analysis because it has been introduced into the discussion of sex bias in kinship patterns by Anspach and Rosenberg. The data discussed here, of course, concern residence patterns rather than the frequency of contact with members of the couple's kinship network. But if it is true, as Anspach and Rosenberg's data imply, that contact with kin (and perhaps as a corollary, closeness to them) decreases with age for both sexes, it might be argued that the reason a married couple is more likely to live with the wife's than with the husband's relatives is that a wife, being younger than her husband, will generally have a closer relationship with her relatives than he has with his at any time during their marriage. If this is the case, the greater the age difference between husband and wife, the greater should be the tendency for them to live with the wife's rather than the husband's kin. In fact, the data do not bear this out.

Age Difference Between Husband and Wife

	Less Than 1 Year	Between 1 and 2 Years	2 Years	More Than 2 Years	
Couple Lived With:					
Wife's Kin	7	10	12	5	34
Husband's Kin	4	3	5	2	14
	11	13	17	7	48

The results are not significant. As between age differences of one year or less as opposed to an age difference of greater than one year, there appears to be a slight tendency in the expected direction, but this difference is still far from the level of statistical significance ($\chi^2 = .50$, $P < .50$). It should be noted that because we were missing so much data on age, the number of cases is quite small. It may well be that with a larger number of cases these data would show greater statistical significance. But as far as can now be determined, age difference between husband and wife has no effect on the likelihood of their having lived with the relatives of one as opposed to the other.

EDUCATION

Forty-three percent of the husbands and 46 percent of the wives in our sample are at least high school graduates, while 15 percent of the husbands and 11 percent of the wives have more than a high school education. Though differences in education do not make a truly significant difference in the tendency of a couple to live with wife's or husband's relatives, there are some interesting nonsignificant tendencies. Thus, there is a slight tendency for the incidence of residence with the husband's family to be higher among couples in which the husbands have attained an educational level of high school graduation or more. In 53 percent of couples who have resided with the husband's relatives, the husband is a high school graduate; in 23 percent of such cases he has education beyond the high school level (as compared with figures of 43 percent and 15 percent, respectively, for all husbands). Conversely, there is a slight tendency for the incidence of residence with the wife's relatives to be higher among couples in which the wives have high school or higher level educations. The wife is a high school graduate in 59 percent of cases in which the couple has resided with her relatives, and has a higher level of education in 14 percent of such cases (compared with 46 percent and 11 percent for all wives). None of these results, however, reaches a high level of statistical significance. The closest to statistically significant results are achieved in the case of wife's education ($\chi^2 = 1.85$, $0.10 < P < .20$):

	Wife's Education:		
	H.S. Graduate	Not H.S. Graduate	
Couple Lived With:	18.96	18.04	
Wife's Kin	22	15	37
Husband's Kin or	22.04	20.96	
Only Neolocally	19	24	43
	41	39	80

Table 6 shows that there is also no significant correlation between which spouse has achieved the greater level of education and whether the couple has resided with the relatives of the husband or wife. Since none of these results is statistically significant, it may be concluded that the level of education of either spouse, or differences between them, is irrelevant for determining which spouse's relatives the couple has lived with in cases of non-neolocal residence.

INCOME

Husband's income, in cases where the husband is working and the wife is not also working, is not significantly related to past residential history, as seen in Table 7. Neither does any significant correlation show up in Table 8 between the wife's employment outside the home and residential patterns.

To summarize the data on sex bias in residential patterns presented so far, over the entire sample there is a significant preference for residence with the wife's kin over residence with the husband's kin in cases of non-neolocal residence. This preference is somewhat accentuated among people of Polish ancestry and is accentuated to a statistically significant degree among couples in which the wife is Polish.

TABLE 6

EDUCATION AND RESIDENTIAL HISTORY

| | Couple Lived With: | | | | | |
Education	Husband's Relatives	Wife's Relatives	Both Spouses' Kin	Non Relatives	No One Else	Missing Data
Husband's Education Greater Than Wife's	4	6	2	0	9	5
Both Have Same Education	7	18	6	2	11	10
Wife's Education Greater Than Husband's	2	7	1	2	6	6
Missing Data	1	5	1	0	6	0
	14	36	10	4	32	21

There does not appear to be a significant association of differences in non-neolocal residence patterns with any other factor (i.e., age, education, or income) which might be taken to be an indicator of social class, though there is a tendency toward an association between residence with the wife's kin and the wife having attained a high level of education. There is also a statistically nonsignificant tendency for a greater than one-year difference in age between the husband and wife to be correlated with residence with the wife's kin. A larger sample size with adequate data on age for both spouses would probably enhance the statistical significance of this result. Such an association between large age differences and residence with the wife's kin would be in keeping with the findings of Anspach and Rosenberg. However, contrary to their findings, age cannot come close to explaining away residential sex bias for our data.

TABLE 7

INCOME AND RESIDENTIAL HISTORY

Hus-band's Income	Hus-band's Rela-tives	Wife's Rela-tives	Both Spouses' Kin	Non Rela-tives	No One Else	Miss-ing Data	Total
			Couple Lived With:				
$ 5,000	0	0	0	0	0	3	3
$ 6,000	0	0	0	1	2	0	3
$ 7,000	1	1	2	0	3	0	7
$ 8,000	0	1	1	2	1	0	5
$ 9,000	0	1	0	0	3	0	4
$10,000	2	6	3	0	3	3	17
$11,000	1	3	0	0	3	2	9
$12,000	1	1	0	0	0	0	2
	5	13	6	3	15	8	50

TABLE 8

WIFE'S OCCUPATION AND RESIDENTIAL HISTORY

Couple Lived With:	Wife's Occupation		
	Housewife	Other	Total
Husband's Kin	12	2	14
Wife's Kin	29	5	34
Both Spouses' Kin	7	3	10
Non-Relatives	2	2	4
No One Else	22	7	29
Missing Data	13	7	20
	85	26	111

"MARRYING-IN"

Unlike household residence patterns, community residence patterns do not show any statistically significant tendency toward a sexual bias. It was originally hypothesized that if, as our informants stated, daughters try insofar as possible to live near their mothers, we could expect to find that among couples where one spouse, but not both, was a native of the Manayunk community, it would be the wife who more frequently had brought her husband to the community. In fact, there are only slightly more cases where the wife, but not the husband, was raised in Census Tract 214, or in 214 and the surrounding area (Roxborough, Wissahickon, East Falls, Belmont Hills, Shawmont, and Miquon), than vice versa. The difference is not large enough to be statistically significant in either case. For Tract 214 the figures are 22 versus 18; for the larger area, 24 versus 16. These results could not be improved upon by controlling for age. Other controlling factors, such as ethnicity and education, were not tried.

CHILDREN'S RESIDENTIAL CHOICES AND FREQUENCY OF CONTACT

It was hypothesized that a matrilateral bias in kinship relations, and especially affect toward kin as discussed by Komarovsky, would yield sex differences among the children of Manayunk residents in residence and frequency of contact. Female children should live closer to their parents than do male children and should contact them more frequently.

None of our tests for sex bias in children's residence or frequency of contact revealed any bias whatsoever. In fact, all comparative figures for male and female children come almost ridiculously close to absolute symmetry. The residential breakdown for the total aggregate of all 154 children living away from their parents' home on whom there are data is given in Table 9. (Male children away in the service are not counted in these figures.)

Nor did any sex bias show up in the residential choices of children within single families. It was thought that, whether living in Manayunk and the surrounding area or not, female children of a family might be

TABLE 9

CHILDREN LIVING AWAY FROM PARENTS' HOME

Living In:	Males	Females	Total
Manayunk	21	19	40
Surrounding Area	31	22	53
Elsewhere in Philadelphia	10	12	22
Other Suburbs and New Jersey	5	6	11
Pennsylvania and New York	5	3	8
Other U.S.A. and World	11	9	20
Total	83	71	154

located closer to their parents' home than their brothers. In an attempt to determine if this was the case, we recorded, for each family, the sex of the child living closest to the parents' residence. There were 48 families in which this could not be done because either only one child was living away from home, or all children living away from home were of the same sex. For those cases that could be used, there were 8 where the closest child was a male, 9 where it was a female, and 11 where a male and a female child were living equally close to the parents.

Similar results were found in frequency of contact, as shown in Table 10.

TABLE 10

CONTACT WITH PARENTS

Frequency	Children		Total
	Male	Female	
Once a day	6	6	12
Once a week	15	15	30
Once a month	4	4	8
Once a year	0	0	0
Less than once a year	0	5	5
Holidays only	1	0	1
Total	26	30	56

In short, there is no reason to believe that there is any sex bias whatsoever in residential choices of children and frequency of contact with their parents. But clearly the data are too sparse, N's are too small, and as a result, projections about the future of Manayunk would be premature.

Equally clearly, there is a matrilateral bias in kinship interaction in Manayunk. So far as we can tell from these data, gathered in a long-established, integrated community in the northeastern United States, this pattern is long standing and characteristic of industrialized urban life. It is not a creation of pressures toward fragmentation coming from outside the community, but rather a truly cultural feature of urban working-class life itself.

Although limited by the paucity of comparative data and by the number of respondents, our study of Manayunk suggests confirmation and rejection of some standard interpretations. Apparently, as the literature suggests, working-class ethnics tend to live in a matrilateral society and in families which do not conform to the nuclear ideal. Nonetheless, they do move away from home, possibly more now than in the past, and possibly because prosperity has afforded them a neo-local residence.

NOTES

[1] This study was carried out as a part of the National Science Foundation SOS Project GY 11456, entitled "Revitalization in an Ethnically Diverse Urban Community," conducted May 1974 through April 1975 under the auspices of Temple University. Our sincere thanks are extended to both these institutions for making this research possible.

[2] Elizabeth Bott, *Family and Social Network* (1957; reprinted, New York: Macmillan Co., The Free Press, 1971); Michael Young and Peter Wilmott, *Family and Kinship in East London* (London: Routledge and Kegan Paul, 1957); Alan D. Coult and Robert W. Habenstein, "The Study of Extended Kinship in Urban Society," *Sociological Quarterly* 3 (1962): 141–45; Mirra Kimarovsky, *Blue Collar Marriage* (New York: Vintage Books, 1962); Donald Anspach and George S. Rosenberg, "Working-Class Matricentricity," *Journal of Marriage and the Family* 34 (1972): 437–42; Donald Anspach and George S. Rosenberg, *Working-Class Kinship* (Lexington, Mass.: Lexington Books, D. C. Heath and Co., 1973).

[3] Alan Holden and Ann Malanchuk, 1975. "Perceptual Identities and

the Analysis of Social Relations in a Peripheral Urban Environment," in *Man Does Not Live in the Giant City*, Arthur D. Murphy ed., (Final Technical Report for National Science Foundation SOS Grant GY 11456, 1975).

[4] Sam Bass Warner, Jr., *The Private City* (Philadelphia: University of Pennsylvania Press, 1968).

[5] Young and Wilmott, *Family and Kinship in East London*.

[6] We are most grateful to Manuel de Alba, Juanita Gibson, Alan Holden, Bruce Johnson, Stefan Krotz, Ann Malanchuk, Arthur D. Murphy, Elaine Rosenstein, Bill Thompson, Veronica Veerkamp, John Wasilchick, Wayne Zachary, and Darrell Zimmerman.

[7] Only 92 of these cases came from spouses currently residing in "classic" nuclear family situations. There were 7 cases of nuclear family residence in which the respondent was a child of the household head. Because of the structure of the survey questionnaire, this resulted in usable data for one of the parents of the respondent only. An additional 17 from the total of 119 cases came from nuclear families with adjunct members, and 10 from cases where a widowed, divorced, or separated person was interviewed, but where residential history data adequate for the analysis were provided for the spouse as well as for the interviewee (meaning, of course, that data for a few now-deceased individuals enter into the analysis).

[8] David M. Schneider and Raymond T. Smith, *Class Differences and Sex Roles in American Kinship and Family Structure* (Englewood Cliffs: Prentice-Hall, Inc., 1973), p. 53.

[9] Schneider and Smith, *Class Differences and Sex Roles*, p. 84.

[10] David Schneider, *American Kinship* (Englewood Cliffs: Prentice-Hall, 1968).

[11] James H. S. Bossard, "Residential Propinquity as a Factor in Marriage Selection," *American Journal of Sociology* 38 (1932): 219–24.

[12] Schneider and Smith, *Class Differences and Sex Roles*.

[13] We decided not to use occupation as a variable because it turned out to be too difficult to divide into meaningful categories.

[14] Where data are available for both husband and wife, each is counted. In single-person households and those with an adult head and dependent only the household head is counted. In the cases of adult, co-resident siblings, all are counted.

[15] Young and Wilmott, *Family and Kinship in East London*; Komarovsky, *Blue Collar Marriage*; Anspach and Rosenberg, "Working Class Matricentricity."

[16] Young and Wilmott, *Family and Kinship in East London*, pp. 21–58.

[17] Bott, *Family and Social Network*, pp. 137–38.

[18] Schneider and Smith, *Class Differences and Sex Roles*.

[19] Mirra Komarovsky, "Functional Analysis of Sex Roles," *American Sociological Review* 15 (1950): 508–16.

[20] Anspach and Rosenberg, *Working-Class Matricentricity*, p. 441.

[21] Anspach and Rosenberg, *Working-Class Kinship*, p. 104.

SOCIOGEOGRAPHIC BOUNDARIES
AND PERSONAL MOVEMENT IN THE
MANAYUNK AREA OF PHILADELPHIA

Wayne W. Zachary and Irvin Lichtenstein

The ambitious goals of legislators and urban planners in the 1960s to revitalize the American city and include maximum community participation in social change have largely met with controversy and failure. A significant contributing factor to this failure has been the inability of peoples with diverse backgrounds but with common interests, such as blue-collar groups of varying racial and ethnic origin, to live together in stable and cohesive units. Recent community studies have shown that race and ethnicity are often the primary organizational features in blue-collar communities, making the formation of mixed neighborhoods with any solidarity difficult or impossible.[1] The Manayunk area of Philadelphia, Pennsylvania, has successfully established, quietly and independently, a stable environment for its racially and ethnically mixed population, and has maintained this environment for over two generations without conflict or signs of imminent breakdown. This unusual solution to the problems of urban heterogeneity and change led us to study Manayunk.[2]

RESEARCH CONDUCTED IN MANAYUNK

The research reported here is drawn from a larger study of the social organization of Manayunk. This larger study sought to employ a wide range of methodological and analytic techniques through the use of a team approach, with fifteen field workers ultimately involved in the project.[3] The data collection was divided into two phases. First, a detailed questionnaire, designed to elicit demographic and primary-link network data, was administered to a large sample of the community.[4] The questionnaire data were then computerized to facilitate use by field workers in conjunction with collection of ethnographic data in the second phase of the study. During the second phase, the team members dispersed into the community to carry out individual studies with diverse foci. When viewed together, the results of these studies were to provide a picture of the "Manayunk solution" to the problems facing cohesion in working-class urban neighborhoods. Our study focused on the way in which personal movements in geographical space, when statistically examined, acted to define the boundary of the community. The interest in personal movement was motivated by the findings of other team members.[5]

Several purely ethnographic investigations were conducted on single blocks, among single effective networks, and within single parishes (Manayunk is predominantly Catholic). Focusing on the role of effective and instrumental networks in the maintainence of community cohesion, ethnographers found that intense exchange of goods and services within narrow locales, most often blocks, created small tightly-knit units which had little interaction with other communities or even other nearby blocks. For most households, the social and material needs were met through the networks on the block, and there was little necessity or time for interaction elsewhere. Although historically each block contained members of one ethnic group only, high mobility within Manayunk over the last two generations has created mixed blocks, and the patterns of strong solidarity within the blocks have remained unchanged.

A semantic analysis of the labels for social roles used by Manayunk natives ("relative," "friend," "neighbor," and "acquaintance") found a strong similarity between "neighbor," and "friend"—both are territorial labels in Manayunk—but with a trust/not trust dimension clearly distinguishing the two. A friend was the type of person that was most trusted, but paradoxically, informants claimed that their "friends" were their "neighbors" and vice versa. It appeared that while the individual referred to remained the same, the label applied to the social relationship was changed with the type of behavior and context encountered. This suggested an overlap of genealogical, affective, and instrumental networks on the ground, precisely what was found by the previously mentioned network studies.

The block also played an important role in the labeling of deviants. While most residents agreed on criteria for labeling deviants, particularly improper public behavior on the block, actual application of labels occurred only within the block: a deviant was labeled on his/ her block, but not on adjacent blocks. Moreover, there were no deviants identified by the whole community, but one entire block was agreed upon as deviant. Together, these studies show Manayunk to be an aggregation of small units, blocks, each socially self-contained, and organized around a principle of "we take care of our own."[6]

Missing from this picture is the very real manner in which Manayunkers identify this "aggregation of blocks" as a named community and identify themselves with it (especially when outside Manayunk). Natives claim that a dense and generations-deep system of kinship ties and endogamy transcend the block networks and bring Manayunk together as a community. Oboler and Oboler dispell this myth and show that the opposite is in fact the case. A majority of adults have migrated into Manayunk from surrounding communities, and a majority of children leave at adulthood.[7]

PERSONAL MOVEMENT AND THE
PROCESS OF BOUNDARY DEFINITION

In our research we assumed that since this native explanation for community cohesion was invalid, the explanation must be found in patterns of interaction which were not observable to one on the "inside" but which nonetheless existed within Manayunk and would be observable to one on the "outside." We planned to interpret these observations through the social processualist theory of social structure.[8] The processualists view the structure of society as the "statistical outcome" of the processes of social transaction and interaction occurring within the society at any given time. "Outcome" must be interpreted here as any patterned result or consequence. These patterns and consequences are recognized and encoded at the cultural level into descriptive or explanatory cultural constructs.[9] Individuals within the culture may be aware of features of the social structure through their manipulation of these constructs without being cognizant of the patterns of transaction which gave rise to them.

We sought a variable which would allow us to examine and compare patterns of transaction encompassing the entire Manayunk area and to distinguish activities which habitually bound Manayunkers to interaction on their block or to interaction within the Manayunk area from those which led them outside of Manayunk. This would allow us to identify those patterns of activity by which the boundary of Manayunk was defined and maintained. The variable chosen was the movement of Manayunkers in their daily activities inside, out of, or through Manayunk. We felt that movement, especially over long distances, or difficult terrain, provides a fairly accurate reflection of the types of, and importance of, the interactions engaged in by individuals since significant investments of time and/or energy are involved. Manayunkers are clearly willing and able to travel over relatively large distances (twenty miles or more to work), and since the community is essentially located on a cliff, even travel within Manayunk involves considerable difficulties.

GEOGRAPHY OF MANAYUNK

The unique geography of Manayunk and the community's relation to other parts of Philadelphia are basic to any understanding of the patterns of movement by its inhabitants. Manayunk is located on the northeast bank of the Schuylkill River, in the southernmost part of northwest Philadelphia. The community begins at the river's edge, climbs the steep rise away from the river to the ridge about one and a half miles away, and spills over onto the plateau at the top of the ridge.

Further back on the plateau is the community of Roxborough, but there is no sharp demarcation point between the two. Many informants give the 50-foot cliff which lies immediately below the top of the ridge (the informants also use the term "ridge" to mean the area on the plateau) as the boundary between Manayunk and Roxborough on the north although this would place Manayunk Avenue in Roxborough. Moreover, many residents on the plateau consider themselves to live in Manayunk.

Roxborough also bounds Manayunk on the west, although, again, there is no definite line of demarcation. To the east of Manayunk is the community of Wissahickon, again with no recognized boundary.

While Ridge Avenue is considered by many Manayunkers as the northernmost limit of their community, Manayunk Avenue is more commonly given; and for that reason the project set Manayunk Avenue as the northern boundary for the initial demographic survey. The river provides a natural boundary on the south, and Roxborough Avenue and Leverington Street were chosen as the eastern and western boundaries respectively, so that the area under study would correspond to the United States Census Tract 214. Thus, "Manayunk" will be used to refer to the area within these boundaries, and "Manayunk/Roxborough," to the area with the same east/west boundaries, but extending to Ridge Avenue on the north. This includes all Manayunk, as well as lower Roxborough. The basic geography is shown in Figure 1. This map contains the boundaries of the demographic survey, given by the dotted line. The dashed line represents the cliff separating Manayunk from lower Roxborough. Where the dashed line crosses marked streets, the streets are actually stairways climbing the cliff, becoming roads again only at the top. Only Green Lane, Leverington Avenue, Carson Street, Lyceum Street, and Shurs Lane actually climb the cliff as roads. (Source: City of Philadelphia City Plans Division, Bureau of Surveys, 1974).

Across the river from Manayunk is the suburb of Belmont Hills. This community used to be called West Manayunk and was considered by the residents to be part of Manayunk. Within the last twenty years, however, it has been politically severed from Philadelphia and has taken the name of Belmont Hills. It is no longer thought of by Manayunkers as part of their community.

The main traffic expressway in the area lies just across the river from Manayunk and is used by many residents for access to the industrial parks in King of Prussia to the west and to the downtown (Center City) area of Philadelphia to the east. The Pennsylvania and Reading Railroads maintain stations in or near Manayunk, providing access to commuter rail lines and long distance rail lines which connect to the locals.

While Manayunk possesses no clear-cut political boundaries with

FIGURE I. Geography of the Manayunk Area (*Source: City of Philadelphia City Plans Division, Bureau of Surveys, 1974*).

its neighboring communities, it is a well-defined spatial and social construct in the minds of its inhabitants. We looked at individual movements to determine a pattern within these movements which had as an outcome at the systemic level the labeling of Manayunk as a distinct community. We found that public activities, such as going to work or to school, were conducted outside the area labeled Manayunk, while private or personal activities such as visiting friends, relatives, clubs, or churches were all conducted within the area labeled Manayunk. Shopping and health-care visits, defined as personal by Manayunkers, were conducted in an area Manayunkers defined ambiguously as being neither inside nor outside the community.

METHODOLOGY

One method of investigating movements patterns is the study of networks. Clearly networks are well suited for processual analysis since they are merely a shorthand way of aggregating the individual social interactions from which the social process is constructed. Because the collection of enough network data to represent accurately a community of five thousand was a near-impossible task, we chose an alternative method, the statistical analysis of survey data. To the extent that individuals make valid assessments of their own movement and that the questions asked correspond to the significant categories of the informant, the survey technique can be used, in a much shorter time period, to collect essentially the same data as a network study would provide.

We wished to determine the relationships between the two ways a trip can be categorized: in terms of the cultural category of activity to which the person is traveling (i.e., visiting, shopping, going to church, etc.), and in terms of the geographical destination. Our hypothesis was that the types of activity had patterned geographical destination (that the two methods of categorizing were strongly related), and that the specific relationships between them would explain the cultural definition of the community of Manayunk.

To test this hypothesis we needed data on the types and frequency of activities Manayunkers engaged in (hereafter referred to as trip-types) and on the geographical locations of the activities. For our data on movements we relied on a survey of users of public transportation in the Manayunk area. The decision to consider only travel done on public transportation was motivated by two factors. First, we were able to gain the cooperation of the Southeast Pennsylvania Transportation Authority (SEPTA) in the collection of data on SEPTA vehicles, thus assuring a large and exhaustive sample of movements made on public transportation. A comparable sample of trips made on foot or by car would have been much more difficult to obtain. Second, since Manayunk is located on such rugged terrain individuals could be reasonably expected to take public transportation to locations usually considered within walking distance.

The use of data from travel on public transportation placed only two restrictions on our overall results. First, we accepted *a priori* that no data could be collected about activities that did not take Manayunkers off their block, leaving us to consider only the differences between activities conducted inside Manayunk and those conducted outside Manayunk. Since the ethnographic data concerning interaction on the blocks were of such volume and high quality, this constraint was acceptable. Second, we found *a posteriori* that contrary to our expectations, Manayunkers used public transportation primarily to leave the community. Thus the data presented a picture biased toward those trips taken outside the community, even though Manayunkers move about within Manayunk more frequently than they leave it. However, there were sufficient data concerning trips within Manayunk to assess them vis-à-vis those taken outside Manayunk.

In the SEPTA survey, we asked informants to list the frequency with which they made various trip-types on SEPTA vehicles. Geographical destinations were assigned to each category of trip from data on the demographic survey, which contained extensive data on where (geographically) persons or activities important to each respondent were located. With these two kinds of data we felt we could determine where the resources defined by Manayunkers as being physically and socially important were located and how Manayunkers allocated their movements within their social networks to achieve their needs with regard to these resources.

The SEPTA survey contained fifty questions, grouped under nine headings. Ten questions dealt with types of trips taken and with their frequency, eleven with evaluations of the trip conditions, four with type of fare paid, three with evaluations of SEPTA employees, four with evaluations of other passengers, four with changes based on possible shorter waiting time, four with changes based on possible shorter travel time, seven with socioeconomic indicators, and three with details of the interview. The evaluative questions utilized a three-point likert scale with strongly positive, neutral, and strongly negative values. We placed the socioeconomic indicators on the SEPTA questionnaire to provide a basis for comparing the SEPTA sample with the demographic survey sample, since our methodology was based on the assumption that the two samples would be comparable on a basic socioeconomic profile. The questions used in the SEPTA survey, along with mnemonic variable names are given in Table 1. For the SEPTA sample, we had an N of 280. The survey was taken on three separate days, during the interval from 6:00 A.M. to 10:00 P.M., by professional polltakers employed by SEPTA.

TABLE 1

THE SEPTA SURVEY

QUESTIONS ASKED	VARIABLE NAME
Frequency of Use	
Number of trips taken each week to:	
Work	WORK
Shopping	SHOP
Sporting Events	SPORTS
School	SCHOOL
Libraries or Museums	LIBRARY
Doctor or Clinic	MEDICAL
Friends or Relations	FRIENDS
Church	CHURCH
Clubs or Associations	CLUBS
Social Security, Welfare, or Government Offices	GOV'T

QUESTIONS ASKED			VARIABLE NAME

Evaluation of SEPTA Service and Equipment

In your experience, SEPTA service and equipment is usually:

Clean	Neutral	Dirty	CLEAN
Fast	Neutral	Slow	FAST
Cheap	Neutral	Expensive	CHEAP
Unfrightening	Neutral	Frightening	SCARY
Safe	Neutral	Dangerous	SAFE
Easy	Neutral	Difficult	EASY
Quiet	Neutral	Noisy	QUIET
Convenient	Neutral	Inconvenient	CONVT
Comfortable	Neutral	Uncomfortable	COMFORT
Uncomplicated	Neutral	Complicated	COMPLICAT
Restful	Neutral	Tiring	RESTFUL

Evaluation of SEPTA Passengers

SEPTA Passengers are usually:

Orderly	Neutral	Disorderly	ORDERLY
Friendly	Neutral	Unfriendly	FRIENDLY
Courteous	Neutral	Rude	COURTEOUS
Helpful	Neutral	Unhelpful	HELPFUL

Evaluation of SEPTA Employees

SEPTA employees are usually:

Friendly	Neutral	Unfriendly	FRIEND
Courteous	Neutral	Rude	POLITE
Helpful	Neutral	Unhelpful	HELPS

Reduced Waiting Time

How long do you usually have to wait for
SEPTA? WAIT

How many more trips per week would you
take if waiting time were cut by:

Fifteen minutes	WLESS 15
Ten minutes	WLESS 10
Five minutes	WLESS 5

Reduced Travel Time

How long do you usually spend traveling on
SEPTA?   TRAVEL
How many more trips per week would you
take if travel time were cut by:
Fifteen minutes   TRLESS 15
Ten minutes   TRLESS 10
Five minutes   TRLESS 5

Socio-Economic Indicators

How many persons are in your family?   FAMILY
If married, have you lived in Manayunk since
your marriage?   YUNK
Do you usually have a car available for your
use?   CAR
Sex   SEX
Occupation   JOB
Education (highest finished)   ED
Approximate Family Income   INC

Details of the Interview (completed by interviewer)

Location of the Interview   PLACE
Time of the Interview   TIME
Interviewer Number   INTERVIEWER

Fare Paid

Type of fare paid:
Full   FULLFARE
School   SCHLFARE
Senior Citizen   OLDFARE
Railroad   RAILFARE

The demographic survey to be linked to the SEPTA study, contained
310 questions, grouped into six sections: (1) personal histories of
the interviewee and his/her spouse, (2) socioeconomic questions on
other members of the household, (3) location, employment, and personal histories of children no longer living in the home, (4) location,

employment, and personal histories of other relatives in the area, (5) location, employment, and personal histories of friends of the interviewee, and (6) locations and types of clubs and organizations belonged to by the interviewee and/or the spouse. This survey had an N of 383 households, or approximately one-third of all households in Manayunk.[10]

ANALYSIS

As a first step in the analysis, we used our indicator variables to test for statistical discrepancies between the samples drawn in the SEPTA survey and in the demographic survey. Six socioeconomic questions—sex, income, education, size of family, occupation, and availability of a car—were placed on the SEPTA questionnaire to permit statistical comparisons with the demographic survey results, which represent an unbiased sample of the Manayunk community as a whole. An additional question asking whether the respondent had lived in Manayunk since her/his marriage was motivated by an analysis of the demographic data, which showed that the strongest predictor of several kinship variables, such as family size, dispersal of relatives, and ethnic heritage, was whether the individual had remained inside Manayunk since marrying. This provided a further basis for comparison and inference between the two data sets.

Comparisons were made between the demographic data and the SEPTA data using a chi-square statistic, assuming that the demographic survey data represented the (population) expected values for each cell in the contingency table. The results showed only the variable sex as having any significant difference between the two data sets.

Thus, more women were interviewed as users of public transportation than one would expect from an unbiased sample. A second chi-square test was conducted on sex and the availability of a car. This test showed that significantly fewer women had access to cars than would be expected by chance (chi-square $= 6.87813$, 1 df, p $= 0.0087$). Since the female bias in the SEPTA sample was significant but not overwhelming, the lack of availability of a car seems sufficient to account for the increased female ridership. More statistical analysis is needed, however, to further specify this relationship and validate our deduction.

It is important to note that there was no significant difference between the two data sets with regard to income, educational level, or residence in Manayunk since married. Thus, while the frequency and type of use of public transportation may vary with these variables, they do not contribute to the "use/don't-use" differential. As a final statistical preliminary, we developed one-way breakdowns for each variable in the data set (forty-seven factors in all) to be sure there were no variables with zero variance. None were found, allowing us to proceed with our main analysis technique—factor analysis.

Factor analysis is a statistical technique which simultaneously assesses the relationships among a large number of variables. It does this by constructing "regression" lines through the data in succession, each of which accounts for the maximum percent of the variance not accounted for by the last line drawn. By aggregating all variables close to a constructed line, those variables which behave similarly are determined. This is precisely what was desired for the SEPTA data set.

We conducted an initial factor analysis of forty-seven variables on the SEPTA survey. From the results of the factoring, we were able to eliminate variables under the headings of reduced travel time, reduced waiting time, and interview conditions, and aggregate the evaluative (likert-type) questions and frequency of trip variable into ten linear combinations. The linear combinations are given in Table 2, which gives the linear combinations used in the second factoring. PASSENGER is taken to represent the overall evaluation of the public transit passengers. EMPLOYEE represents the overall evaluation of public transit employees. SERVICE is an evaluation of the service on the transit system, and EASY is an evaluation of its convenience. FEAR is an assessment of the amount of anxiety associated with riding public transportation. SHOPPING through TOTAL are combinations of various categories of trips. SHOPPING combines retail shopping and medical services. RECREATION combines trips to sporting events, libraries and museums. It is a measure of recreational use.

TABLE 2

LINEAR COMBINATIONS BASED ON THE FIRST FACTORING

NEW VARIABLE	LINEAR COMBINATION
PASSENGER	= ORDERLY + FRIENDLY + COURTEOUS + HELPFUL
EMPLOYEE	= FRIEND + POLITE + HELPS
SERVICE	= CLEAN + FAST + QUIET + RESTFUL
EASY	= EASY + CONVENIENT + COMPLICAT
FEAR	= CHEAP + SCARY + SAFE + COMFORT
SHOPPING	= SHOP + MEDICAL
RECREATION	= LIBRARY + SPORTS
LOCAL	= FRIENDS + CHURCH + CLUBS
MARGINAL	= GOV'T + SHOP + LIBRARY + SPORTS
COMMUTE	= SCHOOL + WORK
TOTAL	= SCHOOL + WORK + SHOP + SPORTS + LIBRARY + MEDICAL + CHURCH + CLUBS + GOV'T + FRIENDS

LOCAL combines trips to friends, relatives, church, and clubs and associations. It is a measure of community-level activities. COMMUTE measures essential use, combining trips to work with trips to school. MARGINAL measures elastic or marginal use by combining those trip-types which are non-essential and may be made by alternate means of transportation. These are trips to government offices, shopping, libraries, museums, and sporting events. TOTAL is a measure of all trips taken. These combinations are all based on the results of the first factoring, with the exception of TOTAL.

These ten linear combinations along with the six socioeconomic indicators were used as input for a second factor analysis. This second factoring produced seven factors. From these factors, we constructed the associations given in Table 3. A variable is considered to be associated with a factor if it "loads" highly (i.e., if it is located near the regression line which that factor represents) without regard to sign.

TABLE 3

VARIABLES ASSOCIATED TOGETHER IN THE
SECOND FACTORING

Factor 1	Factor 2	Factor 3	Factor 4	Factor 5	Factor 6	Factor 7
Shop-ing Mar-ginal Local –Com-mute	Recrea-tion –Sex	Total Com-mute	Service Conve-nience	Educ Income	Car Com-mute	Passen-ger Fear

Note: The variables associated together are listed under the appropriate factor
and are given in order of decreasing magnitude of the factor loading; negative
loadings are given by a minus sign.

Variables with negative loadings are interpreted to be in complementary distribution with those with positive loadings (i.e., they are inversely related). The details of the factor analyses, including the interpretations of each of the factors, are given in Appendix I.

The next step in the analysis was to place these associations, where possible, in the context of the geography of the social networks of Manayunkers as taken from the demographic survey data. Only Factors 1, 2, and 3 were used in this part of the analysis. Factor 5 was discarded because it contained no movement variables (COMMUTE, SHOPPING, RECREATION, MARGINAL, or LOCAL) but rather seemed to document an already established relationship, viz., that educational level and income level are related. Factor 4 was eliminated because it dealt only with perceptions of the attractiveness of the transit system. While this factor was extremely important to SEPTA, it is not related to the structure of movement by Manayunkers except with regard to whether they use public or private transportation. The same is true for Factors 6 and 7.

The data used to assign geographical destinations to the activities represented by the variables used in the second factoring are given in

Appendix II. Only the results derived are presented here. We found that friends and relatives are usually located within the Manayunk area. Clubs and associations are also usually located within the Manayunk area and almost all churches attended are located within Manayunk. Shopping and medical facilities are generally located in the Ridge Avenue area designated here as Manayunk/Roxborough. Manayunkers differ as to whether this area is part of Manayunk or Roxborough. Libraries are located within Manayunk, while there are insufficient data to identify where Manayunkers would usually be going when they identify their destination as "government facilities."

Schools above the elementary level are located outside the Manayunk/Roxborough area. Elementary schools are located within Manayunk but are traveled to entirely on foot. The locations of the jobs of Manayunkers are generally outside the Manayunk/Roxborough area, and often far outside the area. Museums, as well as recreational and sporting events, are generally found outside the Manayunk/Roxborough area also.

With the above information on the geographical destinations of various trip-types, it is possible to view the associations in Table 3 with regard to a geographical grid. We can then try to discern some features of movement which account for the culturally defined geographical boundaries of Manayunk as a statistical outcome of these features of movement. In doing this, we will consider only the associations on Factors 1, 2, and 3, as previously explained.

FACTOR 1

Factor 1 associates the variables SHOPPING, MARGINAL, and LOCAL, all in complementary distribution with COMMUTE. If we examine the destination points of the contributing variables to the first three, we see that they refer mainly to trips whose destination points lie within the Manayunk/Roxborough area.

SHOPPING is composed of trips to shopping and routine medical services, both located in the Ridge Avenue (Lower Roxborough) area. LOCAL is composed of trips to friends, relatives, churches, clubs, and associations. All refer to trips within Manayunk/Roxborough.

MARGINAL poses somewhat of a problem, because the destination pattern for its contributing variables is mixed. For trips to government agencies the destination cannot be determined. We are then left with trips to sporting events and museums, which are generally located outside Manayunk/Roxborough, and trips to shops and libraries which are mainly within the area.

COMMUTE, in complementary distribution with the other variables, definitely refers to trips taken to places outside the community, since travel to work and school implies destinations outside Manayunk/Roxborough.

Our conclusion, cautiously given because of the uncertainty of MARGINAL is that this factor represents a dimension which scales an inside-the-community/outside-the-community distinction on the destination of the trip. High loadings indicate variables which include trips that are strongly differentiable by their destinations. A negative loading refers to trips away from the area referred to as Manayunk/Roxborough, while a positive loading refers to trips within that area. It is possible that for MARGINAL, the relatively larger number of trips being made under SHOPPING is carrying that factor loading to its high positive value.

FACTOR 2

The relationship between the variables RECREATION and SEX was discussed above. Here we are interested only in the variable RECREATION, composed of trips to libraries, museums, and sporting events. Trips to sporting events definitely have destinations outside Manayunk/Roxborough, whereas trips to libraries and museums have destinations both inside and outside the community. The preponderance of destinations on this variable (RECREATION) are likely to be placed outside of Manayunk/Roxborough.

This dimension refers to trips taken outside the community, but not to all such trips, since COMMUTE does not load highly with RECREATION. In fact, COMMUTE can be seen to load moderately highly in the opposite direction. Our conclusion, then, is that this factor refers to trips only to destinations outside Manayunk/Roxborough, but scales them on a business/pleasure dimension.

FACTOR 3

Factor 3 associates TOTAL and COMMUTE, apparently acting as an indicator of intensity of travel. It is clear that the components of COMMUTE, trips to work and school, have destinations outside the community and that MARGINAL, RECREATION and SHOPPING, all composed of trips within the community, have slightly negative loadings (although the magnitude of the loadings makes them insignificant). However, LOCAL has the next highest loading on the factor after COMMUTE. Since LOCAL has the second highest mean of the frequency-of-use variables (i.e., it includes the second largest number of trips), we concluded that Factor 3 is in fact a potency dimension, scaling the number of trips taken. This will de facto place trips outside the community to work and school high on the scale.

UNDERSTANDING THE COMMUNITY BOUNDARY

We can now use these three dimensions of movement to assess what the label "Manayunk" represents. From Factor 1, there is a cluster of activities—shopping, attending churches, clubs, and associations, visiting friends and relatives—which all take place in some bounded area we have called Manayunk/Roxborough. These activities are clearly contrasted in Factor 1 with those of attending school and work, which take place outside this same area. The fact that natives label this space as their neighborhood ("Manayunk") is an indication that these patterns of interaction have been acknowledged and encoded at the cultural level.

From Factor 2, it appears that the pleasure/business distinction is not applicable to travel within the community, but is meaningful only with regard to travel outside the Manayunk/Roxborough area. The ethnographic evidence supports the conclusion that interaction within the Manayunk area is defined as primarily social and not economic. Activities such as shopping are as much social as economic in Manayunk, if not more so.

From Factor 3, travel within the geographical community is mainly by private automobile and by foot, as opposed to travel outside the community, which is oriented on a public/private transportation dimension. This is not to say that all travel outside Manayunk is done

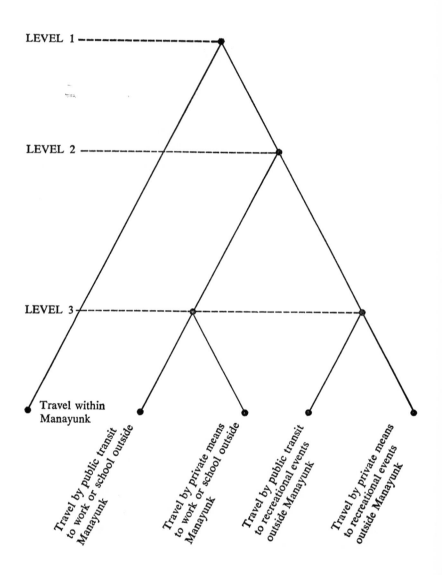

LEVEL 1

LEVEL 2

LEVEL 3

Travel within
Manayunk

Travel by public transit
to work or school outside
Manayunk

Travel by private means
to work or school outside
Manayunk

Travel by public transit
to recreational events
outside Manayunk

Travel by private means
to recreational events
outside Manayunk

FIGURE 2. Tree representation of the factor analysis results.

on public transit, but rather that nearly all travel within Manayunk is not done on public transit.

Figure 2 represents the results of the factor analysis as a binary tree. Each distinction drawn by a factor is placed in the tree on those branches to which it applies. The distinction of level 1 is taken from Factor 1, that at level 2 is taken from Factor 2, and those at level 3 are taken from Factor 3. The labels associated with each leaf in the tree represent the overall label applying to that leaf from the factor analysis. At the top level, the tree has two branches derived from Factor 1: travel "inside Manayunk" and travel "outside Manayunk." At level 2 the right branch is subdivided by Factor 2 into a "business" and a "pleasure" branch. Finally, at level 3 both of those branches are subdivided into "public transportation" and "private transportation" branches. The important feature of this representation is the absence of further branches on the left-most branch, that representing travel within Manayunk. From this analysis of the factors, movement by Manayunkers is divisible into at least five distinct types, but four of these refer to travel outside the community. From the point of a "statistical outcome" one aggregation of activities—private social behavior—takes Manayunkers inside a single geographical area (this is marked by the topmost branching, or Factor 1) and is not differentiable any further. In this way the factor analysis identifies the relationships by which movement distinguishes the area labeled "Manayunk" from the remainder of the world of Manayunkers.

The ambiguous way the area between the ridge and Ridge Avenue is defined can give us some insight into the way these patterns of movement can result in a negotiability of neighborhood boundaries. All activities associated with variables loading positively on Factor 1 are conducted within Manayunk proper (below the ridge), except those identified by the variable SHOPPING (shopping and medical facilities) which are located on the plateau above the ridge. These facilities were located on Main Street in Manayunk until the previous generation when the Great Depression forced them to be moved to the Ridge Avenue area. Evidence from the recollections of older residents indicates that the area above the ridge was "redefined" after the businesses of Main Street moved there in great numbers. As Manayunkers, accustomed to conducting their commercial activities in Manayunk, were forced to conduct them on Ridge Avenue, this area became less and less "Roxborough" to them. People living in lower Roxborough, however, began to refer to the area more as "Roxborough" since they no longer needed to travel into "Manayunk" for their commercial activities. At the present, the boundary of Manayunk and Roxborough seems to be negotiable depending on where one is standing, or more correctly, living. For individuals living below the ridge, the area on the plateau between Ridge Avenue and the ridge could be in Manayunk, since their shopping and other commercial activities regularly bring them into that area. For individuals living above the ridge but below Ridge Avenue, this area would be Roxborough since their commercial activities would not require them to travel into the area below the ridge. From the processualist viewpoint, Manayunk is culturally defined not as a geographically fixed area, but as a label for the area where individuals who identify themselves as Manayunkers can find closure on their everyday personal and commercial activities. If facilities or individuals necessary to those activities are moved, then the definition (geographically) of Manayunk can be extended or diminished to accommodate the changes.

The people who identify themselves as Manayunkers are those who have used the numerous crowded and dead-end streets on the cliff as a basis for forming self-sufficient blocks, which transcend the cultural barriers of race and ethnicity. They have divided the remainder of their social world into two parts, an inside (called "Manayunk") and an outside, which are distinguished by a boundary marking the limit Manayunkers must travel to fill those social and economic needs not met on the block—for shops, doctors, churches, clubs, and associations. At both levels, block and community, Manayunkers have shown an ability to negotiate their definition of Manayunk in order to accommodate changes in their social world and establish a new, stable closure. It is this ability to establish closure through the negotiability of their neighborhood boundary, and to establish stability through that closure, that is the Manayunk solution to problems of urban heterogeneity and change that we first set out to study and explain.

APPENDIX I

FACTOR ANALYTIC TECHNIQUES EMPLOYED

Factor analysis requires a strict interval property for all variables to be factored. We felt that all variables but three met this requirement, since they were all either (1) likert three-point scales which are normally assumed to be interval valued in psychometric research, (2) binary, making them automatically interval, or (3) naturally occurring interval scales, such as monetary units or cardinality (number of something). The only nominal variables, JOB, PLACE, and INTERVIEWER, were deleted from the list of variables when the factor analysis was conducted. Since we were seeking factors which would be independent, we used the standard principal-parts factor method with varimax rotation.[11] This insured the most independent, or orthogonal, factoring. The SPSS factor analysis program was used.[12]

In the first factoring, all forty-seven acceptable variables were considered. The factor analysis program constructed seventeen factors. In interpreting these factors, it became clear that for most, only variables from a single heading in the SEPTA questionnaire were loading highly. Remembering the warnings of D'Andrade, Schweder, and Holden that semantically similar questions would be answered alike on that basis alone, the questions which generated these variables were examined for semantic similarity.[13] For ten of the seventeen factors, there was a great deal of semantic similarity among the questions which generated the variables loading highly on the factor. The pairwise correlations for variables on a given factor were also high (larger than .7), and on these two bases, we decided to combine these ten factor groupings into ten single variables, one from each factor. The linear combinations involved are given in Table 2. A second factoring was then conducted using sixteen variables, the ten linear combined variables, and the six socioeconomic indicators from the original questionnaire.

This second factoring resulted in the construction of seven factors. The rotated factor matrix is given in Table 4. We used a loading of .5 or higher as high loadings. Factors 1 through 5 account for more than 88 percent of the variance when taken together, and each of the

TABLE 4

VARIMAX ROTATED MATRIX FOR SECOND FACTORING

Variable Name	Factor 1	Factor 2	Factor 3	Factor 4	Factor 5	Factor 6	Factor 7
PASSENGER	.0004	.0736	.0325	.1752	.0718	.0592	.5714
EMPLOYEE	−.0704	−.0550	.1292	.3888	.0282	.0884	.1863
SERVICE	−.1274	−.0636	.0261	.6250	.0297	−.0632	.0831
EASY	.0757	.1306	.0405	.5247	−.0065	.0833	.0895
FEAR	−.0806	−.1798	.0389	.3704	−.0762	−.1346	.3778
SHOPPING	.9198	−.0220	−.0875	−.1347	−.2274	−.0570	−.2776
COMMUTE	−.4130	−.3202	.6791	−.2098	−.1149	.4070	.1398
RECREATION	.2288	.9163	−.0541	.0660	.1978	−.0112	.1493
LOCAL	.4588	.3702	.2706	.1314	−.0319	.2713	.0863
MARGINAL	.8526	.1046	−.0023	−.2081	−.0066	.1270	.1241
SEX	.0002	−.5935	.0104	.0615	.0839	.1495	.0793
CAR	.0166	−.1100	.0485	.0842	−.0610	.6257	.0209
ED	−.0289	−.0782	−.0819	.1712	.6230	−.0213	−.0169
INC	−.1407	.2336	.1977	−.1613	.6920	−.0766	.1244
FAMSIZE	−.1367	−.0352	.3993	.3441	.2336	−.0987	−.0465
YUNK	−.1796	.3708	.1267	.4486	.1071	.0873	−.0088
TOTAL	.1628	.1008	.9610	.1348	.0152	.0344	.0599

This is the rotated factor matrix from the second factoring, using varimax orthogonal rotation. The variables are those given in Tables 1 and 2.

first four factors accounts for more than 10 percent of the overall variance. We offer tentative interpretations of the seven factors:

Factor 1 identifies the "marginal," or nonessential use of the transportation system. Travel to shopping or medical services (SHOPPING) loads quite highly (.91), along with all other nonrequired types of uses—trips to government facilities, libraries and museums, and sporting events (MARGINAL). The variable LOCAL, which includes trips to friends' and relatives' homes, trips to church, and trips to clubs and associations, also loads highly, although not so much so as MARGINAL and SHOPPING.

Factor 2 associates RECREATION, containing trips to sporting events and to libraries and museums, and SEX in complementary distribution. The interpretation is that the sample is disproportionately female, and females tend to travel to sporting events less frequently than males. Moreover, trips to sporting events comprise the major part of the variable RECREATION. Factor 2 merely notes the above relationship.

Factor 3 deals with the total number of trips taken. Both TOTAL, total frequency of use, and COMMUTE, trips to work or school (referred to as inelastic demand) load highly. Our interpretation is that inelastic use is numerically the most frequent type of use. It was noted earlier, however, that it also suggests that the significance of inelastic use is on a different dimension from the components of marginal use, which lie on Factor 1. COMMUTE loads moderately highly on Factor 1, but in complementary distribution with the other variables which load highly.

Factor 4 seems to be an evaluation of the attractiveness of the transportation system itself. Perceptions of the service level and the overall convenience of riding public transportation both load highly. The evaluation of public transit employees and of the anxiety level associated with using public transportation load moderately highly. Interestingly, YUNK, an indicator of cultural commitment to the Manayunk community also loads moderately highly. Our interpretation is that these evaluative statements are moderately associated with the cultural value system peculiar to Manayunk.

The fifth factor is clearly a socioeconomic factor, with educational level (ED) and income (INC) both loading highly. Factors 6 and 7 merely help clarify features of ridership on public transportation. In Factor 6 inelastic demand is associated with the availability of an automobile. Our interpretation is that the availability of an automobile influences the extent to which an individual uses public transit to work or school.

Factor 7 is another evaluative dimension concerning the public transit system itself. Here the evaluation of other passengers and of anxiety load moderately highly. This is conceivably a factor which associates an unfavorable evaluation of other passengers (perhaps with regard to race?) with increased anxiety about use of public transit.[14]

APPENDIX II

LOCATING THE CATEGORIES IN GEOGRAPHICAL SPACE

Appendix II details the procedure and data used in designating the probable destination of trips taken to activities represented by the variables which loaded highly on Factors 1, 2, and 3 of the second factor analysis. These variables were COMMUTE (trips to work or school), MARGINAL (trips to shop, visit friends, relatives, libraries, clubs, and associations), SHOPPING (trips to shopping and medical facilities), and RECREATION (trips to recreational activities). The destinations were assigned to these sociological categories from analysis of data in the demographic survey as well as from ethnographic data collected by other members of the project.

The demographic survey asked the respondent for the location of the residence of any children of the household not living at home, for up to four children. It asked the same for up to five other relatives and up to five friends. In addition, the location of up to three clubs and/or associations was sought. Finally, the respondent was asked to give the location of her or his job and that of her or his spouse and any other working members of the household, as well as the location of the church attended by respondent and spouse.

Table 5 gives a summary of the data concerning the location of children no longer living in the home, other relatives, and friends of respondents. "Within Manayunk" refers to the area defined by the demographic survey. "Within Roxborough" refers to the adjoining community of Roxborough. "Within Adjacent Communities" refers to Wissahickon, Belmont Hills, and East Falls. "Within Philadelphia Area" includes other parts of the city of Philadelphia, as well as adjoining counties—Bucks, Montgomery, and Delaware—and New Jersey. All other locations are included in "Outside Philadelphia Area." Clearly, Manayunkers find most of their friends within the boundary of Manayunk, as defined by the boundaries of the demographic survey. The same is true for relatives other than children, but not for children. It is interesting to note that when asked to name other relatives, there was a marked tendency among the respondents to name the geographically closest relative first, rather than the genealogically closest. The

TABLE 5

LOCATION OF CHILDREN NOT IN THE HOME,
OTHER RELATIVES, AND FRIENDS

PERSON	LOCATION OF RESIDENCE (%)				
	Within Manayunk	Within Roxborough	Within Adjacent Communities	Within Philadelphia Area	Outside Philadelphia Area
Child 1	22.8	21.0	10.6	32.4	13.2
Child 2	27.9	17.5	17.7	22.2	14.7
Child 3	26.3	7.9	18.4	29.0	18.4
Child 4	15.4	7.7	38.5	23.0	15.4
Relative 1	63.5	18.0	6.5	11.0	1.0
Relative 2	48.8	22.3	8.5	17.3	3.0
Relative 3	44.0	25.0	12.9	17.2	.9
Relative 4	50.0	26.8	9.0	11.6	2.6
Friend 1	75.3	15.3	4.7	4.2	.5
Friend 2	70.3	12.9	3.7	13.1	0.0
Friend 3	70.9	10.9	7.7	9.0	1.5
Friend 4	72.8	6.2	6.0	9.0	6.0
Friend 5	70.5	5.9	11.8	11.8	0.0

same is true, although less so, for friends. Children were named in the order of their birth by the guidelines of the survey.

Unlike friends and relatives, most children living outside the home do not live in Manayunk. This indicates, among other things, a high degree of emigration from Manayunk, a reasonable proposition considering the limited number of housing units available in Manayunk, the zero potential for the building of new units (there is no available vacant land), and the tendency toward large families (the mean number of children is greater than four).

The high emigration level means that most Manayunkers have many relatives outside Manayunk—in the case of native Manayunkers, emigrated collaterals, and in the case of immigrants, lineals in the native community. However, the data for relatives indicate that only those living within the community are thought of first. That is, when asked to name five relatives, over 70 percent of the time the respondent named only relatives living within Manayunk. It thus appears that when asked questions about family, the Manayunker will respond with respect to relatives living within Manayunk only. This type of order of serial recall has been used previously by Sanday.[15] By the same inferential procedure, the data for friends indicate that when asked questions about friends, the Manayunker will also respond with regard to friends living in the Manayunk area.

Table 6 gives the locations of the jobs of respondents, excluding housewives, and the locations of clubs or associations of which respondents were members. From the location-of-job column, it is apparent that relatively few Manayunkers work in Manayunk, and fewer still in Roxborough. In fact, nearly 65 percent of the Manayunkers

TABLE 6

LOCATIONS OF JOBS AND CLUBS/ASSOCIATIONS

LOCATION OF DESTINATION	TYPE OF DESTINATION (%)			
	Job	Club 1	Club 2	Club 3
Within Manayunk	27.6	59.1	62.7	57.2
Within Roxborough	7.6	24.3	18.6	19.1
Within Adjacent Communities	15.0	4.7	5.1	14.1
Within the Philadelphia Area	46.0	11.1	11.9	0.0
Outside the Philadelphia Area	3.8	.8	1.7	9.6
TOTALS	100.0	100.0	100.0	100.0

questioned worked outside the Manayunk/Roxborough area. Thus, when individuals are questioned about trips taken to work, it can be inferred that the majority listed are taken to destinations outside Manayunk/Roxborough.

The opposite is the case with data for the locations of clubs and associations. More than half the locations given are inside Manayunk itself, and another 18.6 to 24.3 percent are located within Roxborough for the first, second, and third club or association named. In all three clubs named, more than 75 percent of the locations given are within Manayunk/Roxborough. Unlike questions about trips to work, then, questions about trips to clubs and/or associations are likely to refer to trips made within Manayunk/Roxborough.

Regarding travel to school, all secondary public school students attend Roxborough High School, located in Roxborough. Parochial school students (overwhelmingly Catholic) attend any of several Catholic high schools located in nearby communities. There are many colleges and universities in Philadelphia; however, none are in or near Manayunk or Roxborough. All trips to secondary and above level schools are made outside Manayunk.

Elementary schools are, on the other hand, all located within Manayunk. The several Catholic primary schools associated within local parishes inside Manayunk are inaccessible by public transit and are attended by children who live within walking distance. The same is true for the two public elementary schools. Any trips made to school would be answered with regard to trips made to secondary and post-secondary schools located outside Manayunk.

Trips to churches are taken mainly within Manayunk, since over 83 percent of Manayunkers belong to churches located within the Manayunk/Roxborough area. The information for the locations where Manayunk residents shop and receive their medical services must be taken from the ethnographic data collected by other project members, since the demographic survey does not contain these data. Most shopping is done "up the ridge" in the business district of Ridge Avenue. Very little is done in Manayunk proper, or in downtown Philadelphia or suburban shopping areas.

In the preceding generation, the commercial activity now centered on Ridge Avenue was located in the Main Street area of Manayunk. There is a long tradition, informants say, of conducting most or all shopping within Manayunk; and with the Main Street shopping area now closed down residents prefer to shop as close to Manayunk as possible—on Ridge Avenue. It can then be assumed that the majority of travel for shopping is made to the Ridge Avenue shopping district inside the Manayunk/Roxborough area. Similarly, the commonplace medical services are also rendered in the same business district.

Libraries and museums pose a difficult problem. The museum district of Philadelphia is far removed from the Manayunk area, so that trips to any of the dozens of museums in the area would be to destinations outside Manayunk. There is a branch of the public library within lower Roxborough, however, suggesting that trips to the library would be made to this destination. In the absence of more data, no firm destination type can be assigned for trips to libraries and museums.

Data on the location of sporting events attended by Manayunk residents must also be drawn from ethnographic data of other project members. All professional sporting events attended would be located outside Manayunk, but there is also a tendency for Manayunkers to participate in organized nonprofessional sporting programs, such as softball leagues. The majority of these programs have their facilities in upper Roxborough, although only homegames are played there; other games are played elsewhere. The North Light Boys' Club, located in Manayunk, sponsors extensive athletic activities for school age residents. But with this exception, all trips to sporting events are made to destinations outside the Manayunk/Roxborough area.

There is insufficient data on the types of government institutions used by Manayunk residents to assess the likely destination of trips to government agencies.

NOTES

[1] W. Whyte, *Street Corner Society: Social Structure of an Italian Slum* (University of Chicago Press: Chicago, 1955); H. Gans, "Planning and Social Life: An Evaluation of Friendship and Neighbor Relations in Suburban Communities," *Journal of the American Institute of Planners* 27, (1961); 134–40; *The Urban Villagers* (Free Press: New York, 1962);

U. Hannerz, "Gossip, Networks, and Culture in a Black American Ghetto," *Ethos*, I (1967): 134–40; F. Barth, *Ethnic Groups and Boundaries* (Little, Brown and Co.: Boston, 1969); W. Kornblum, *Blue Collar Community* (University of Chicago Press: Chicago, 1974).

[2] We would like to thank the National Science Foundation, (the Experimental Programs Division in particular) who funded the research reported here with grant GY11456. Our thanks also go to Arlene Sternfeld and the Southeast Pennsylvania Transportation Authority who supervised the collection of the SEPTA data set, and to Whitney Thompson, Arthur Murphy, and Henry Selby of Temple University who provided valuable comments on our work while it was in progress and on this manuscript.

[3] Alan Holden, Bruce Johnson, Ann Malanchuk, Gina Oboler, Leon Oboler, Elaine Rosenstein, William Thompson, John Wasilchick, and Darryl Zimmerman; and Manuel de Alba, Stefan Krotz, and Veronica Veerkamp (and the authors). William Schwab of Temple University acted as administrative head of the project.

[4] J. A. Barnes, "Networks and Political Process" in *Local-Level Politics*, M. Swartz, Ed. (Aldine, Chicago: 1968); A. Wolfe, "On Structural Comparison of Networks," *Canadian Review of Sociology and Anthropology*, 7 (1970): 226–44.

[5] For a full report of these findings, see A. Murphy, *Man Does Not Live in the Giant City*, Final Technical Report, NSF Grant SOS11456, (1975).

[6] J. Wasilchick and W. Thompson, *We Take Care of Our Own*, In *Man Does Not Live in the Giant City*, A. Murphy, ed., Final Technical Report NSF Grant GY11456 (1975).

[7] G. Oboler and L. Oboler, "Mothers and Daughters in a Blue-Collar Neighborhood in Urban America," *South Atlantic Urban Studies* I, (1977).

[8] M. Swartz, V. Turner and A. Tuden, *Political Anthropology* (Aldine: Chicago, 1966), Introduction; M. Swartz, *Local Level Politics* (Aldine: Chicago, 1968), Introduction; F. Barth, *Ethnic Groups and Boundaries* (Little, Brown & Co.: Boston, 1969).

[9] Two examples from Manayunk are "if you throw a stone in Manayunk you're likely to hit a relative," and "you can take a boy out of Yunk, but you can't take Yunk out of the boy."

[10] See G. Oboler and L. Oboler, "Mothers and Daughters" for further details of the demographic survey methodology.

[11] H. Harman, *Modern Factor Analysis* (University of Chicago Press: Chicago, 1967).

[12] N. Nie, D. Bent and H. Hull, *Statistical Package for the Social Sciences* (McGraw-Hill, New York: 1972).

[13] R. D'Andrade, "Trait Psychology and Componential Analysis," *American Anthropologist*, 67, (1965): 215–28; R. Schweder, "Illusory Correlation, and Personality Theory" (Paper prepared for the Mathematical Social Science Board Conference, Quail Roost, May 2–4, 1974); A. Holden, "Kith and Kin: The Semantic Correlates of Social Cohesion," (M.A. Thesis, Department of Anthropology, Temple University, 1976).

[14] Although Manayunkers still utilize racial and ethnic stereotypes and prejudices when dealing with non-Manayunkers, and are strong supporters of the conservative city government, they have not chosen to structure their community on either of these parts of their ideology. The fact that they exist in the ideology is underscored by Factor 7.

[15] P. Sanday, "The 'Psychological Reality' of American-English Kinship Terms: An Information 'Processing Approach'," *American Anthropologist* 70 (1968): 508–23; "Analysis of the Psychological Reality of American English Kinship Terms in an Urban Poverty Environment," *American Anthropologist*, 72 (1971): 555–70.

THE SUBURBAN WILDERNESS:

A Historical Approach

to Metropolitan Decentralization

Donald E. Bain, Jr.

In the preface to his seminal study of Boston, Sam Bass Warner, Jr., suggests that "If the city is ever to become susceptible to rational planning there must come to be a common understanding of how the city is built."[1] Scholars have been slow to develop theoretical or methodological approaches to the city-building process. With a few notable exceptions, they have scarcely touched the suburban aspects of this phenomenon. Most of the literature on suburbs—narrowly focused and limited to the period since 1945—has failed to place the suburb within the history of national urban growth.[2]

The popular view usually sees suburbanization as essentially a development of the years since World War II. It is not. While the actual *number* of people moving into urban ring areas has been greatest since 1950, the *rates* of suburban population increase peaked much earlier. Current efforts indicate that the basic patterns of land use, institutional functions, and political organization were established long before a majority of the metropolitan population lived beyond the city's edge, and it was on this foundation that subsequent suburban communities expanded. Moreover, suburbia has been approached by most social scientists as merely an empirical abstraction for viewing trends in American electoral or social behavior. Structurally it is rarely seen as anything more than an appendage of the city. Present research suggests however that at least some suburbs possess a developmental cycle of their own—a history—which is more than a by-product of a nearby expanding metropolis. What follows is an attempt to sketch the growth of one such community from a rural township to a thriving middle-class suburb of Buffalo, New York. Hopefully, an examination of one local case will shed light on the larger process of change occurring throughout metropolitan America during these crucial years.

The early twentieth century saw a crisis in American cities. Political corruption, social unrest, and fiscal collapse all evidenced a decaying urban environment. These problems were not new. What sets this era apart from earlier decades was rather the fact that for the first time much of the urban population began acting on the situation. A new middle class was emerging. Aggressive, affluent, and vocationally bound to the city, this group was determined to make urban existence conform to their standards of order and efficiency. As Robert Wiebe has stated in his study of America in transition: "A change in the quality of perceptions, not in the quantity of unique evils, produced a broad reappraisal of the cities around 1900."[3]

The resulting middle-class attempts to reorder their surroundings aimed at making city life more congenial. These efforts went in two directions. The first, urban "progressivism", sought the reform of government and society. Progressives believed that cities were salvable, that they must be made fit for work and residence. Yet, while this well-publicized group of reformers was trying to save the city, an increasing percentage of their middle-class brethren took a second direction and quietly abandoned it. Anticipating the spirit of this exodus, Adna Weber in 1899 concluded his seminal work, *The Growth of Cities in the Nineteenth Century*, with the observation, "The rise of suburbs . . . furnishes the solid basis of hope that the evils of city life . . . may be in large part removed."[4]

Statistics cannot portray the nature of this migration but do suggest its magnitude. Between 1900 and 1910, for instance, central city populations in the United States grew 37.1 percent while the population of ring areas increased by 25.6 percent. This trend assumed particular significance after 1920 when fringe areas began to grow more rapidly than central cities. Thus during the 1920s cities grew 24.2 percent, but the suburban population was swollen by 33.2 percent. During the 1940–50 decennium suburban growth had climbed slightly to 34.2 percent, while population increase in core areas sank to 13.8 percent.[5] The most conspicuous consequence of this trend has been the tendency of metropolitan areas to decentralize and expand outward in concentric rings of diminishing population density. In human terms, these rapid changes in populations meant a massive relocation of people from both rural and urban areas into the land adjacent to American cities.

Developments in the city of Buffalo mirror these trends. Dominating the economic base of western New York, Buffalo in the nineteenth century served as a critical entrepot in the movement of western beef and cereals to the eastern seaboard. By the 1880s the city was a leading railway center and at the turn of the century was the seventh largest industrial metropolis in the nation.[6] Growth continued into the twentieth century when two world wars and an expanding transportation industry stimulated local manufacturing. While metropolitan growth has continued over the past century, decentralization in Buffalo has paralleled national developments. Thus in 1910, 80.1 percent of the Erie County population lived within the municipal boundaries of the city. In 1930 the city was still growing but at a decreasing rate, and by 1950 growth had almost stopped (Table 1). The composition of the city's population also changed. Although the percentage of foreign born declined slightly, the total nonwhite population increased 148 percent from 1910 to 1920 and 200 percent over the next decade. Similarly the 1940–50 period saw a 106.2 percent rise in nonwhites.[7] In contrast growth rates of the white population have steadily declined. In 1910 the white sector had increased 22 percent over the previous decade. This dropped rapidly during the next twenty years and by 1940 Buffalo was losing more white residents than it was gaining. This is not to say that the white population of the entire metropolitan area declined for it maintained a fairly even rate

TABLE 1

DECENNIAL INCREASES IN POPULATION FOR ERIE
COUNTY AND CITY OF BUFFALO

AREA	YEAR				
	1910 %	1920 %	1930 %	1940 %	1950 %
County	22	20	20	5	13
City	20	20	13	1	1

of growth. But obviously white families were increasingly settling outside the city.

The degree of decentralization is reflected in the growth rates of the
six townships adjacent to the city. Forming an arc around the core
area, Lackawanna, Tonawanda, Hamburg, West Seneca, Cheekto-
waga, and Amherst encompass the city leaving the western edge exposed to Lake Erie (see Figure 1). The total population of the six
townships had an average growth rate of 25.6 percent in the first ten
years of this century. By 1920 this average growth rate had risen to
64 percent and the six fringe areas accounted for almost a tenth of the
county's entire population (Table 2).[8] The 1920–30 decade was the

TABLE 2

INCREASES IN POPULATION OF SIX ADJACENT
TOWNSHIPS

TOWNSHIP	1910 %	1920 %	1930 %	1940 %	1950 %
Amherst	10	36	110	20	74
Lackawanna	N.A.	23	34	3	12
Cheektowaga	48	56	75	20	81
Tonawanda	80	153	356	29	72
West Seneca	−14	53	47	22	37
Hamburg	30	43	51	6	9
Decennial Average	25.6	64	117	20.0	47.5

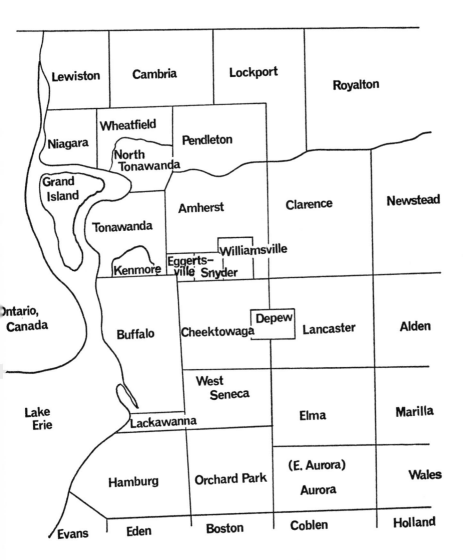

FIGURE I. Erie County, New York.

period of most rapid development in the suburbs as the townships' average growth rate increased to 117 percent, accounting for 14 percent of the county's residents. By 1950 expansion had slowed to a 50 percent decennial increase, but by then nearly a quarter of Erie County lived in these six townships.

Geography and transportation facilities initially determined the economic character of the towns. Lackawanna and Tonawanda, bordering Lake Erie, were by the turn of the twentieth century well developed industrial satellites of Buffalo. Both of these townships had incorporated cities within their boundaries which helped accelerate growth. Because these cities were primarily manufacturing centers, local standards defined them as working class communities. By the late 1920s, however, Tonawanda had shed this image and was expanding as a middle-class suburb. The town's large area made this possible. While the Niagara river side of Tonawanda was heavily industrialized, ample land in the eastern section allowed for residential development. Lackawanna, much smaller in size, was by 1900 almost totally overrun by graineries and steel mills. Today it remains a symbol of industrial blight.

Prior to World War I, the four remaining adjacent townships had little more connection with the city than other nearby farming areas. State highways leading into Buffalo did, however, help to reinforce the physical continuity between the city and these outlying districts. During the last years of the nineteenth century, streetcar lines also began operating into Buffalo. While these early railways drew the towns both physically and psychologically closer to the city, they were generally not built with suburban communities in mind. Rather, they ran to incorporated villages—basically independent of Buffalo—within the townships' boundaries. Unlike the intracity lines of the nineteenth century these railways played only a minor role in the shaping of local economies or population concentrations. Despite the exuberance of one local newspaper editor—"Let the eagle scream and the rooster crow, Williamsville is to be connected with Buffalo by a first class Electric Railroad"—the high tide of growth did not come until after the World War I. Then, it was the automobile which spawned expansion.[9]

Like the other townships, Amherst was a town in name only during the nineteenth century. In fact, so scant was its history that the emergence of the town as a consciously perceived suburb during the 1920s has tended to obscure its earlier past. Yet circumstances predating this transition—such as the physical form of the town, its network of public services, and the traditions of interaction between local government and the business community—largely shaped its suburban development. An examination of the dynamics of this change must therefore begin by laying bare the foundation upon which the suburb grew.

Like all other townships in western New York, the Amherst boundaries were first drawn in the eighteenth century by the famous Holland Land Company.[10] In Spring 1798, the company commissioned Joseph Ellicott to survey the 3.3 million acres which today comprise the eight western counties of New York State. Ellicott was to divide this territory into townships six miles square and subdivide these into 320-acre farm lots. A stockholder in the company, Ellicott sought to provide access to this land for prospective buyers. To this end he employed a Seneca Indian to widen an old trail which stretched the fifty miles from Batavia to Buffalo. This road ran in a due westerly direction from Batavia until it reached the southwestern corner of Amherst Township whence it veered sharply to the south into Buffalo. In 1799 two of the land company surveyors purchased 320 acres of Amherst from their own company and erected a sawmill. The sawmill was not put into operation, however, until 1805 when Jonas Williams and David Evans, both land company employees, bought the building and land. Evans apparently was satisfied to be an investor and returned to Batavia, but Williams stayed on to manage the mill and eventually to open a tannery. Though records of these years are sparse, one local historian left his impression of the town:

> The forest to the north of the ridge rising up from their lowlands and swamps; the forest on the south stretching to the Indian Territory of Elma and Big Tree; a mud road not very wide nor very good, filled with ruts as usual, dipping into a little stream . . . an unpainted primitive mill with its usual debris; and perhaps a footbridge. Here and there a few log cabins stood apart. A little

noise perhaps but not much. Three or four miles to the northward the trapper in the swamps and evening stillness could hear distinctly the muffled roar of Niagara Falls in the distance.[11]

The growth of the town during the next forty years can be understood in terms of two population trends occurring in the United States: migration to the west and movement to towns and cities.[12] Thus by midcentury the city of Buffalo had grown into an important entrepot for the shuffling of settlers to the west and raw materials to the east. One of the major overland routes in this movement was the turnpike running from Albany to Buffalo. This road, following as it did Ellicott's original Indian trail, ran across the full width of Amherst's southern tier and was the corridor around which the town's population became concentrated.

As the oldest settlement, the village of Williamsville developed as the social and economic center of the township.[13] By 1850 six local businessmen, convinced of the advantages in fiscal consolidation, applied for incorporation to the State Legislature. Of the 119 eligible voters within the square mile of proposed village boundaries, 67 voted for and 50 voted against such a move.[14] Although the remaining 3,500 inhabitants of the town were not measurably affected by incorporation of the village, this event had an impact on the town as it began developing into a suburb of Buffalo some sixty years later. By that time tradition was hardened into permanence as the social, political, and economic organization of the township centered on the village. It was here that local farmers looked for representatives to sit in county and state assemblies. This practice endured throughout the period of suburbanization for it was the village business community which had the time and experience to enter politics.[15] This meant that the local community elites not only were able to control both village and town government but they could do so without hindrance from the larger town population which relied on municipal services located in Williamsville.

The removal of this dependency came with the creation of public facilities in areas outside the village yet within the township.[16] The most significant of these developments occurred from 1890–1910 in the two unincorporated hamlets which had grown around the main road leading into Buffalo when the first handful of suburban commuters built homes in Amherst. Situated in the southwest corner of the township, Eggertsville was, in 1900, a cluster of homes lining the crossroads of Main Street and Eggert Avenue. Immediately to the east was the hamlet of Snyder consisting of about 35 families. Although the construction of a trolley line through the center of these two areas in 1891 did not add enormously to their populations, it did serve to integrate them with other sections of the township.[17] Also, by the second decade of the century these two hamlets had built their own fire companies, schools, churches, and postal services, thus reducing their dependence on the village.

By 1900 the commercial and residential section of the town was organized around the two hamlets and village which spread across the south of Amherst. The mere presence of these places did not, however, ensure future growth. Why then did they become the nexus around which the later suburban community would develop? Answers to this can be found in the complex of factors which contributed not only to the growth of Amherst but were also central to the nature of twentieth-century suburbanization. First, the turnpike running from Batavia to Buffalo gave the southern part of the town constant exposure to travelers and was a natural stopping point before the final leg of a journey into the city.[18] In Amherst this road was of particular importance because even local traffic moving between Williamsville and Buffalo had to pass through the entire breadth of the town. In addition, each of these three communities formed at the junction of Main Street and at least one other road. The direction of growth which emerged in the twentieth century was determined in large part by the access, beyond Main Street, that this network of roads gave to developers. Whether using a buggy or an automobile, it was simply more convenient to live near the main thoroughfare. Another reason for the suburban development of Amherst was that Eggertsville, Snyder, and Williamsville all had by 1900 at least rudimentary forms of public services. This is significant for the availability of these facilities weighed heavily in the decisions of speculators to subdivide and develop residential sites.[19] Perhaps just seeing the faint outline of a community such as that found in Snyder or Eggertsville, gave investors a glimpse of potential business tangible enough to inspire confidence in their speculations.[20] Finally, the physical presence of these institutions and the accessibility to the city afforded by a system of roads provided prospective home buyers with sufficient amenities to leave the city. For, while Americans were in the first decades of the century eulogizing the rustic simplicity of rural life, they were not prepared to abandon totally the security of urban existence.

In 1910 Amherst was still a rural township. Of the 4,600 inhabitants, a quarter lived in the village of Williamsville and about 40 families were residing in each of the two hamlets.[21] The rest were farmers. The next ten years saw the town grow by 36 percent, and the 110 percent increase from 1920 to 1930 marked that period as one of suburbanization.[22] But these changes came gradually, and the years immediately preceding World War I found Amherst comfortable in the security of a small rural community. The four-mile walk from Williamsville to the city line showed little change from what preceding generations had seen. The land was very flat and well cleared, occasionally interrupted by a small patch of woods purposely left to brace a barn or house against the southwestern weather that came rolling across Lake Erie. There were not many people and life was quietly predictable. Few things existed in Amherst to invade a sense of good order.

Yet just to the south, Buffalo was churning with the problems of political corruption, ethnic conflict, and fiscal decay. The most pressing issue revolved around progressive attempts to recharter the city.[23] The old charter allowed sweeping mayoral powers. Appointments could be made without common council approval and the mayor was allowed to place twenty-two of the thirty-three department heads and commissioners.[24] Dissatisfaction with the resultant system of spoils and misgovernment led to the formation of the Buffalo branch of the National Municipal League.[25] The League was supported by prominent Buffalo citizens including Dean Carlos Alden of the University of Buffalo Law School; a local producer of automobile parts, William Crosby; and the area's Democratic state senator, Malone. Agitation for reform was given the most impetus, however, by the publicity it received from William Connors, owner of the city's two largest newspapers, the *Courier* and the *Inquirer*.[26] Conner's role is of first importance, for not only did he champion reform, but he also exposed the battle between city hall and the Progressives. For the first time, Buffalo was afforded detailed information on the mismanagement in city administration. Although the charter supported by these men was adopted in January, 1916, it fell short of expectations and was eventually replaced by another in 1927.[27] But doubts now surrounding the operation of city administration proved lethal to the image of municipal government in particular and city life in general. This darkened perception of the city was emerging on a national scale. It combined with the dislocations of World War I and increasing automobile ownership to create a situation in the early 1920s where the middle-class population, especially, was looking outward to the city's rim for a less turbulent environment.

In sharp relief to Buffalo, the town of Amherst was a model of concord. By this time subtle suburban features were emerging in the form of tasteful housing developments built expressly for affluent commuters.[28] There are no building permits to use as indices for home construction, but the 4,600 to 6,200 jump in population from 1910 to 1920 suggests the extent of growth. This occurred, however, without disrupting the function of town government, primarily because the village and hamlets had sufficient municipal services to absorb these moderate increases.

The concord was soon to be fractured. Following a postwar recession, accelerated mortgage programs and a relaxation of price controls contributed heavily to a real estate boom. This, coupled with improved transportation facilities, available capital, and the confidence of Coolidge prosperity stimulated the suburban property market.[29] The revival of residential construction is reflected in the increased numbers of suburban dwellers. In Buffalo, by 1920, 9.1 percent of the county's population lived in the six townships adjacent to the city; by 1930 this had risen to 20 percent.[30] In the 1920s evidence of this could be seen as new schools were built, banks opened, old farms subdivided, and historic town landmarks razed. While the northern part of Amherst remained in semirural detachment, the southern section received the full impact of this growth, expanding 110 percent from 1920 to 1930 (see Table 2). Thus within a few years the physical organization of Amherst was rearranged around a community, 50 percent of whom had not lived in the town in the previous decade.[31]

The new arrivals were a fairly homogeneous lot. Judging from the cost of houses they bought, most were middle class. All depended on the city for employment, and most affiliated with the Republican Party.[32] The number and speed at which churches were built in the town after 1920 suggests they were religious people. By 1926 there were over a dozen places of worship serving eight different groups and a third Catholic church was under construction.[33] Equally remarkable was the willingness of new residents to spend seemingly unlimited tax funds on the schooling of their young. Local government initially responded to this attitude by modifying existing nineteenth-century structures and utilities. As other old town services, such as fire protection, police, sewage and water, were outstripped by the sheer number of new residents, it became apparent to local leaders that modern facilities were required if growth was to be sustained. What resulted was a commitment by the business community elites to develop the town as an attractive, prosperous suburb. In 1928 the sole, and official, town newspaper, *The Amherst Bee*, proclaimed on its masthead, "A Home Here Offers Health, Wealth and Culture."

The town board was responsible for implementing the fiscal, administrative, and structural reordering of Amherst. Composed of one supervisor and four councilmen, all chosen by popular election, board members were inevitably loyal, representative members of the town's business establishment. The goals of these men, defined as they were by a national tradition of political capitalism, moved throughout the decade beyond the narrow limits of individual profits to embrace the larger context of commercial expansion in the entire town. To this end new bridges were constructed, water drainage was provided, and fire protection was updated. In an effort to attract the urban bourgeoisie with metropolitan amenities, the town board awarded franchises to install electric, telephone, and gas service.[34] As other, more costly, provisions were made, the most debated issues raised in the town centered on the financing of schools, roads, and sewers. Thus, the basis of what is today understood as the suburban continent had as its beginning the establishment of these primary services, and it was upon this foundation that the successes and failures of future development depended.

These changes, duplicated in other suburban communities, were in many ways part of a larger process of fiscal and public works reforms being carried out on a state level in New York during the 1920s.[35] Under the direction of Governor Alfred E. Smith the state's revenue program was reorganized. The main source of funds had been the property tax, but under Smith this was steadily minimized and by 1928 it was only one-half mill per dollar of assessed valuation.[36] To offset these losses other revenues were created. Mortgage taxes, liquor taxes, a franchise tax for banks, trust companies and financial corporations, and a personal income tax were all used to raise money. The use of bond issues for long-range improvements in parks and roads was perhaps Smith's most innovative fiscal measure, because it distributed the expense of capital improvements over a long period of time and subsequently distributed the cost among a greater number of taxpayers.[37] Yet this method of financing new development was important in another way in that it set an example that smaller civil divisions were to follow. The minutes from the Amherst town board show no indication of a bond being floated until 1924.[38] In the seven years following this date however, under the impulse of rapid growth and the precedent established by the state legislature, the town passed sixteen major bond issues.[39]

Other fiscal policies initiated in Albany also proved helpful to suburban communities like Amherst. The sharing of state revenue with local government began in 1896 when the Raines Liquor Tax Law was passed. From this point on, local governments were assigned increasing amounts of the state's tax receipts. In addition, this revenue-sharing plan was applied to newly fashioned sources of income such as the fees for motor vehicle registration, income tax, and the 1926 franchise on financial institutions. From 1919 to 1928 the amount of money raised by taxes in New York, assigned to local government, rose from $9,318,000 to $62,381,000.[40] The significance of these subventions was that they gave political autonomy to local governments like the one operating in Amherst, while freeing them from the fiscal machinery of the city which they adjoined. This was of great impor-

tance, for unlike nineteenth-century streetcar suburbs, which were located within municipal boundaries and were dependent on central
city administrative decisions, the responsibility for shaping new suburban communities was left in the hands of local forces.[41]

In Amherst the business community elite tied this responsibility to
their traditional aims. These men came to believe that the function of
the town was to provide investment opportunity for local entrepreneurs so that they might earn a profit. Nowhere were these goals more
clearly stated than in the *Amherst Bee*. The owner of the paper,
George Measer, was a native of the town whose fortunes were considerably dependent on local development. In 1922, commenting in an
editorial on the easing of the post-World War I recession, he suggested
that this, ". . . should induce businessmen here to endeavor to raise
the plane of their business to as high a level as possible. Always striving for something better and keeping everlasting at it are the best
earmarks of success."[42] This advice was directed to the village merchants of Williamsville. But Measer and his colleagues looked beyond
the village and envisioned bigger things for Amherst: "There is a
persistent rumor that several large real estate deals in this town are
shortly to be consummated. They involve large acreage which will be
utilized in public and private ways."[43] This was not unusual news
coming from a man who lunched daily with fellow merchants and town
officers. Nor was it surprising that he should punctuate his editorial
on "The Future of the Town," with the observation that "As a rule it
is the business life which defines the community."[44]

There is, of course, no official record of the casual relations between
the brokers, bankers, and merchants of Amherst. What can be inferred
from interviews and social interaction, however, is that there was a
union of interest among these groups. An inarticulate dimension of
this can be found in the tone of advertisements, town board meetings,
and editorials which create the impression that collectively the community elites were anticipating a boom. More specifically, each time a
large parcel of land was sold, the *Bee* would deliberately attempt to
rouse the town into excitement. When in October 1922 a Buffalo
realtor bought a 136-acre farm, Measer gave the news front-page
coverage. Still elated over the sale, he discussed the implications of it

in the editorial column. Here, with rather heady expectations, he suggested what a continuation of such speculation would bring the town in terms of "revenues, publicity and growth." The article concluded by predicting that as a result of such transactions, "The community will then be stirred to [even] more activity bringing increased business and valuation."[45]

In one sense, this enthusiasm was a reflection of the rapidly expanding national economy.[46] The United States had emerged from the war as a creditor nation. Real income was increasing; the building industry experienced a revival after 1922; and corporate investments increased from $11 billion in 1921 to $19 billion five years later.[47] But if the effects of the Harding-Coolidge prosperity were encouraging on a national level, the people of Amherst were able to draw on another source of confidence to bolster their provincial aspirations. What gave credence to Measer's optimism and at the same time heartened his fellow entrepreneurs were the facts of growth when measured by increasing town property valuations. No investor in the New York Stock Exchange followed Dow Jones' average or the *New York Times* financial page more closely than Amherst's leadership watched the county assessor's yearly valuation returns. This was their index of growth. Thus in 1922 the town's worth of $13,149,980 was nearly double that of 1915.[48] By 1925 this had grown to $16.5 million, and the last year of the decade saw a $31.7 million valuation. So sensitive was the town to this as a barometer for gauging success that by 1925 it had become a matter of civic pride to weigh Amherst's gains against adjoining townships.

This attitude was not limited to the town's leadership.[49] Through refined marketing methods employed by private builders, prospective home owners were educated to think of their purchase as a capital investment.[50] Procuring land in the town was, according to some developers, tantamount to placing money in a blue chip stock. As one advertisement suggested, when buying in Amherst, "A handsome return on your investment is assured."[51] The psychology was contagious. By the end of the decade a number of civic organizations had been created, all of which included in their purpose the "boosting and betterment" of the area. In 1925 alone, a Rotary Club, a Chamber of Commerce, and two citizen groups were formed. One of the more active of these was the United Snyder Association which adopted as its slogan a phrase that captured the spirit of the time—"Watch Snyder Grow."[52]

Viewing themselves as the custodians of local growth, community elites throughout the decade actively pressed for public improvements. When in 1922 for instance it became apparent that the village water system was hopelessly inadequate, twenty-three town fathers staged a rigorous campaign to educate and persuade taxpayers of the need for a new system. In one article, "Fact versus Camouflage," supporters of the improvements reminded the readers that, among other things, "The growth of the Village depends on soft water."[53] In the same issue, Measer, himself a signer of the article, made an appeal to the residents by asking, "Why should you hesitate in doing your bit towards the development and betterment of the community in which you live? Are you going to help increase real estate and home values of your local community and the opportunities for investment, business and employment there?" And in what was perhaps the most succinct expression of how community elites defined the town, he answered his own question by stating: "The good, loyal citizens of your home town are striving constantly to increase the money making possibilities there."[54]

What was happening here can be understood in terms of local leadership trying to instill in residents the notion that they personally had a stake in the growth of the town. This may not have taken much convincing for perhaps the new suburbanites came to Amherst with this understanding. If there were any doubts, however, they would be challenged by the social order which defined local life: "Only by taking a personal interest in the welfare of the community can you ever hope to be honored and respected here."[55] Community. Honor. Respect. These were the very marrow of middle-class virtue and represented values increasingly absent from city life. In Amherst the result was the emergence of a "growth ethic" defined by local leadership and cultivated among residents, civic associations, and government. In their efforts to create a private corporate community of capital investors, the native elites established a central theme for town growth.

The time, energy, and cooperation required to create new municipal services gave a sharp focus to local life. Many of the new residents,

having left the city precisely because they felt it was becoming un-
manageable, undoubtedly perceived developments in Amherst as a
refreshing change from their previous surroundings. Lacking other
levels of social interaction and perhaps feeling a need to define their
lives in relation to their new environment, many of the arrivals accepted the commitment to growth as the basis of local life. Thus at
the intersection of "old town" priorities and "new town" hopes was
a sense of community established in suburban Amherst.

Yet these changes did not come without considerable cost. To
finance municipal operations, the town weighed liabilities incurred
against anticipated increases in tax returns. Furthermore, bonded indebtedness was allowed to more than quadruple.[56] As a result, the
depression of the 1930s weighed heavily on Amherst. The town was
haunted by the enormous public debt accrued during the previous
decade. This was somewhat reduced by a State Court of Appeals decision to award the town $205,000 in back taxes held by the county.[57]
But Amherst was still in trouble as suggested by the $35,000 in prop-
erty tax owed in 1933 to the town by unemployed residents.[58] The
immediate cause of these problems could be found to a large extent
in the bankrupt national economy.[59]

Compounding this problem was the inability of local government,
such as the one operating in Amherst, to manage the manifold responsibilities of growth during the 1920s. Before World War I, when development was proceeding at a manageable rate, traditional methods
of coping with problems were sufficient. For example, the town board
would vote on proposals to build a new highway and, if approved,
would post bonds, receive bids, and supervise construction.[60] Following the war, the backlog of prospective buyers wishing to build homes
in Amherst exceeded the town's supply of access roads into the subdivided lots. Anxious to fill this demand, the town board transferred
responsibility of road construction to commercial developers. Although the board continued to award franchises to gas, water, and
electric companies, the location of trunk lines was determined by
speculative builders. They were also given free license in the conversion of land. Bolstered by the enthusiasm of growth and eager for
the tax returns of swollen property values, the board indiscriminately

approved 73 major land subdivisions from 1923 to 1930.[61] Thus, what had been a measured process of decision making by the town planning committee prior to World War I now shifted to the opportunism of private developers. It is tempting to picture local officials swamped with paperwork and decisions they were unequipped to cope with, obliviously allowing these forces to shape the community. For it was in this crucial period of transition from a rural township into a suburb that planning and control were most vitally needed. Yet not until 1936, after the southern third of the town was subdivided, did the board institute zoning and building ordinances.

The tangible results of this were already apparent in the form of gas stations located next to churches and clusters of cheap, landless houses. The most offensive impact would have to wait until after World War II when the metropolis spread into the suburb and compounded past mistakes. To suggest that Amherst and similar suburbs were unplanned sprawls is a misnomer; growth merely lacked government regulation.

The depression awakened residents to the need to reverse this trend. In debt for nearly a million dollars worth of public expenditures and fearing higher taxes as a result of increasing property foreclosures, the citizens looked to local government as the agency that was at once the cause and possible cure of their plight. Thus, homeowner groups like the United Snyder Association and the Eggertsville Citizens' Association pressed the town board into acting on problems with a firmer hand. Measer, dimly beginning to realize what was happening, summarized such sentiment when he called for, "new town laws to create a more businesslike and effective method of handling the town affairs."[62] The budget was trimmed and federal relief was received, but it was too little and too late. Taxes were raised and houses were repossessed.[63]

Hard times also ushered in a period of self-examination for the town. The anxiety of unemployment, relief rolls, and food rations expressed itself in a number of ways. First, people asked how a prosperous community could find itself in fiscal ruin? Curiously, many of the native leaders pointed to the rampant public spending required to sustain the commuting suburbanites, as the cause of Amherst's problems. These feelings were countered by Buffalo residents claiming that their tax dollars were now paying for the "orgy of spending" in Amherst during good times.[64] To this the local newspaper replied that had former Buffalonians now living in the town, remained in the city, those that were left would not be paying their bills. Even the local state assemblyman, Arthur Swartz, blamed "city people because they move to suburbs and demand all the services they had been accustomed to."[65]

These skirmishes reached their height in 1933 when town supervisor A. F. Beiter created a local paranoia by announcing: "Several movements have been on foot to make the large municipalities the central governing force and take from the towns many of the rights they now hold."[66] To combat this, Beiter went off to a conference of small town officials in Mineola, Long Island, the purpose of which was to "build up a protective wall against encroachment on home rule within towns."[67]

These antagonisms, revealing as they are of latent hostilities and fears between town and city, were only a veneer covering deeper problems. For, by the mid-1930s the town was still in fiscal distress, and new forces were emerging which demanded more effective results from the town government. The most notable of these was the Amherst Brokers and Builders Association and the newly formed United Citizens Association, both of which began acting on issues rather than discussing them in editorials. Largely through the efforts of these organizations, traditional community institutions, which had managed or mismanaged government, were challenged. Thus it was with popular support that Jack Belinson, sewer committee chairman of the Builders Association, demanded that the town take over a disposal plant shared until then with the village. Belinson argued that the Eggertsville-Snyder area could be afforded proper service only if the village was denied use of the facilities.[68] The power of the "New Town" on local politics is demonstrated in the successful exclusion of the village from using the plant. The impulse for mobilizing on such issues was generated by the impotence of government in the early depression years and was symptomatic of the need and demand for more effective, responsive leadership. Ironically, it had been the very lack of local control which, whether consciously perceived or not, was a primary reason for people leaving the inner city originally and moving to a place like Amherst.

The results of these changes in the town were twofold. First, the depression helped sharpen the local sense of community. Before 1929 a substantial part of the town had little to bind it together as a conscious social unit except geographic proximity and a manufactured commitment to growth. Faced with the adversity of the depression, they were pressed into association by the common purpose of actually having to struggle for economic solvency. This association was significant because patterns of organization and the traditions of interaction established during this time became the basis upon which suburbanization commenced after World War II. Second, the town board, awakened to the needs of a larger and more complex population, was stirred into readjusting the structure of town government.[69] Clearer lines were drawn between the municipal responsibilities of village and township, zoning laws were adopted, annual financial reports were published, and by 1938 a planning committee was in operation.[70] In 1940 local politics was still the ward of older community elites, but they were now responsible for controlling growth and providing management acceptable to the residents.

Although the timing and pace of growth may vary, a study of other American cities might well reveal patterns of development similar to the one found in Amherst. From 1900 onward, the emerging middle class sought to cope with metropolitan existence by building communities that provided access to the central city, but which offered sufficient social and fiscal autonomy to avoid the problems these centers were experiencing. This movement was encouraged and at times generated by private and public forces favoring metropolitan decentralization. Eventually business elites of older fringe communities such as Amherst joined in the effort to expand the economic base of their suburban bailiwicks. In the process, the actual shape of metropolitan America was rearranged as were the conditions which gave character to suburban life.

NOTES

[1] Sam Warner, Jr., *Streetcar Suburbs* (Harvard University Press, 1962), p. viii.

[2] In addition to Warner's work exceptions include H. J. Dyos, *Victorian Suburb* (Leicester University Press, 1961), and Jean Bastie, *La Croissance de la Banlieue Parisienne* (Presses Universitaires de France: Paris, 1964). For a general review of research in the social and behavioral sciences see Scott Donaldson, *The Suburban Myth*, (Columbia University Press, 1969).

[3] Robert Wiebe, *The Search for Order* (New York, 1967), p. 167.

[4] Adna Weber, *The Growth of Cities in the Nineteenth Century* (Cornell University Press, 1967), p. 475. Originally published in 1899 by Columbia University as Volume XI of *Studies in History, Economics and Public Law*.

[5] See Amos Hawley, *The Changing Shape of Metropolitan America: Deconcentration Since 1920* (Glencoe: The Free Press, 1956), and Donald Bogue, *Metropolitan Decentralization: A Study in Differential Growth* (Oxford, Ohio: Scripts Foundation in Research, 1951). For attempts at controlling this see, "Planners in the Changing American City, 1900–1940" by John Hancock, *Journal of the American Institute of Planners*, September 1967, pp. 290–304.

[6] See J. T. Horton, *A History of Northwestern New York* (New York, 1947).

[7] C. A. Yeracaris and Elwin H. Powell, "Population Patterns and Social Organization on the Niagara Frontier," *Urban Characteristics of the Niagara Frontier*, published by the Committee on Urban Studies, State University of New York at Buffalo and the University of Buffalo Foundation, 1964, pp. 81–83.

[8] Ibid., p. 77. The entire county had twenty-six townships. For a discussion of their relationships to each other, see "The Geographic Portrait of Western New York," by Harding Jones and Reginald Pegrum in *Urban Characteristics of the Niagara Frontier*. See also *History of Erie County*, edited by Walter S. Dunn, Jr., Buffalo and Erie County Historical Society, 1972.

[9] *The Amherst Bee*, October 20, 1892, p. 1. (Hereafter cited as *A.B.*)

[10] See Truman White, *Erie County*, Vol. I (Boston: Boston History Company, 1898), p. 497.

[11] Quoted in *A.B.*, March 10, 1938, p. 1.

[12] For general coverage of this see Richard Wade, *The Urban Frontier* (Harvard, 1959). On a local level Michael Frisch, *Town into City*, (Harvard, 1972).

[13] There are no usable histories of the village. Pedestrian coverage of leaders and happenings can be found in the Chamber of Commerce publication, *History of the Town of Amherst*, by Sue Young, 1965.

[14] *Town Board Minutes*, (hereafter cited as *Minutes*) Vol. I, 1850.

[15] On this point see *Minutes*, June 25, 1914, and August 3, 1914, where election districts are divided and rearranged.

[16] See *Minutes*, August 14, 1901, p. 127; May 15, 1902, p. 152; March 3, 1903, p. 166; May 6, 1905, p. 242; for examples of new franchises awarded for placement of utilities in these two areas.

[17] On this point see Horton, Chapter V.

[18] There were many toll gates on this route, one of which was located in Amherst on Main Street near Getzville Road. This was constructed in 1837 and not abandoned until 1899. See Young, *History of the Town*, p. 191.

[19] See *The Commercial Advertiser*, September 30, 1910, p. 10.

[20] For nineteenth-century applications of this see Warner, *Streetcar Suburb*, pp. 117–18.

[21] United States Bureau of Census, *United States Census of Population: 1910* (Washington: Government Printing Office, 1910). See also the special *New York State Census* for 1905, 1915, and 1925.

[22] Yeracaris and Powell, p. 79. Also see Table 2.

[23] See "Like the Fingers of the Hand: The Family and Community Life of First Generation Italian-Americans in Buffalo, 1880–1930," Virginia McLaughlin, Unpublished Ph.D. dissertation, State University of New York at Buffalo, also Elwin Powell, *The Design of Discord* (Oxford, 1970), for Buffalo problems during the Progressive period.

[24] Buffalo City Charter, Art. 2, Sec. 1, 1892.

[25] Horton, p. 363, on this last point see Frank Stewart, *A Half Century of Municipal Reform* (University of California Press, 1950).

[26] Horton, pp. 363–64.

[27] What further complicated this process was that before 1923 all changes in municipal laws had to be approved by the state legislature. On this point see *The Constitution of the State of New York* (1894 as amended and in force January 1936). See also, *Proceedings of the Common Council of the City of Buffalo*, 1928, pp. 392–97, and Horton, op. cit., p. 406.

[28] Manuscript Section, Buffalo and Erie County Historical Society, "Amherst Estates: An Investment in Contentment," 25ZC A51.

[29] For general coverage see George Soule, *Prosperity Decade* (New York, 1947). On property values see Marion Clawson, *Suburban Land Conversion in the U. S.* (Baltimore, 1971).

[30] Yeracaris and Powell, p. 77. These percentages were computed from the author's data.

[31] From 1920 to 1930 the entire town population increased from 6,286 to 13,181. United States Census for 1920 and 1930.

[32] Erie County Board of Elections: 1900–1960. Results, Towns, Cities, on microfilm in Lockwood Library, State University of New York at Buffalo.

[33] See Young, *History*.

[34] See *Minutes*, March 30, 1918, p. 58; April 22, 1919, p. 84; May 5, 1917, p. 15.

[35] For general coverage see Ellis et al., *A History of New York State* (Ithaca, 1967).

[36] Ellis, p. 405. On Alfred E. Smith see Oscar Handlin, *Al Smith and*

His America (New York: 1958), and Smith's autobiography, *Up to Now: An Autobiography* (New York: 1929).

[37] Ellis, p. 405.

[38] Perhaps the thought simply had not occurred to the government or perhaps there was no need for such elaborate financing.

[39] See *Minutes*, March 5, 1924, p. 23; April 6, 1926, p. 165; June 23, 1925, p. 223; November 16, 1925, p. 256; March 7, 1927, p. 353; January 28, 1938, p. 159; February 6, 1928, p. 104; February 6, 1928, p. 105; March 5, 1928, p. 196; January 7, 1929, p. 275; January 21, 1929, p. 293; October 28, 1929, p. 485; November 11, 1929, p. 504; June 22, 1931, p. 198; July 16, 1931, p. 222.

[40] Ellis, p. 406.

[41] For example, see Sam Warner, Jr., *Streetcar Suburbs* (New York: 1962), and H. J. Dyos, *Victorian Suburb* (Leicester: 1961).

[42] *A.B.*, June 22, 1922, p. 2.

[43] Ibid., p. 2.

[44] Ibid., p. 2.

[45] *A.B.*, October 12, 1922, p. 2.

[46] See *The Growth of the American Economy*, by B. F. Williamson (New York, 1951), Jonathan Daniels, *The Time Between the Wars* (New York, 1966), and the standard economic history of the period George Soule, *Prosperity Decade* (New York, 1947).

[47] Soule, pp. 147–60.

[48] *A.B.*, September 25, 1924, p. 1.

[49] *A.B.*, August 29, 1929, p. 1.

[50] See for example, the *Buffalo Commercial Advertiser*, also *A.B.*, July 5, 1923, p. 3; July 12, 1923, p. 5; August 9, 1923, p. 1; July 15, 1926, p. 3.

[51] *A.B.*, April 19, 1925, p. 12.

[52] *A.B.*, May 19, 1927, p. 1. Only two weeks prior to this, the same group had rigorously worked to ensure the passage of a $130,000 proposal for additional school facilities. See *A.B.*, May 5, 1927, p. 1.

[53] *A.B.*, August 24, 1922, p. 5.

[54] *A.B.*, August 24, 1922, p. 2.

[55] Ibid., p. 2.

[56] See *Proceedings of the Board of Supervisors of Erie County*, 1920 and 1930 for complete financial statement of Amherst. Also see *A.B.*, March 16, 1933, p. 1 for a review of indebtedness.

[57] *A.B.*, January 19, 1933, p. 2.

[58] *A.B.*, February 9, 1933, p. 1.

[59] See Broadus Mitchell, *Depression Decade* (New York: Holt, Rinehart and Winston, 1953), for national coverage.

[60] See *Minutes*, April 5, 1909, p. 172; December 9, 1910, p. 244; October 5, 1914, p. 384, February 5, 1917, p. 3.

[61] *Minutes*, February 5, 1923, p. 256; July 7, 1924, p. 66; January 3, 1925, p. 122; April 6, 1925, p. 166; May 21, 1925, p. 191; September 9, 1925, p. 238; May 12, 1925, p. 260; April 12, 1926, p. 363; November 14,

1927, p. 78; February 20, 1928, p. 182; February 27, 1928, p. 184; July 23, 1928, p. 89.

[62] *A.B.*, February 16, 1933, p. 5.

[63] *Minutes*, 1931, 1932, also see *A.B.*, January 5, 1933, p. 2.

[64] *A.B.*, January 19, 1933, p. 2.

[65] Ibid., p. 2.

[66] *A.B.*, January 26, 1933, p. 1.

[67] Ibid., p. 1.

[68] On this point see the *A.B.*, February 24, 1938, p. 1.

[69] A token start came in 1933 when the board was expanded, see *A.B.*, January 12, 1933, p. 2.

[70] *A.B.*, March 10, 1938, p. 1.

URBANIZATION AND THE CHANGING SOUTH:

A Review of Literature

James C. Cobb

In 1928 U. B. Phillips cited the struggle to maintain white supremacy as the "central theme" of Southern history. In subsequent
years scholars offered several alternatives to Phillips' interpretation.
C. Vann Woodward suggested that consciousness of its tragic past
made the region stand apart, and David Potter believed that there was
a peculiar "folk culture" which distinguished the South. More recently
Howard Zinn described the South as America's "mirror image," a
regional embodiment of the nation's most undesirable qualities. Although these critics raised some serious questions about the adequacy
of Phillips' hypothesis, none of them offered a broader, more convincing explanation of the South's unique role in American history.[1]
In spite of their failure to agree on an explanation for Southern distinctiveness, most scholars felt that the region's peculiar social and
political traditions would face a serious challenge as urbanization and
industrialization weakened old thought and behavior patterns.

Several recent studies have demonstrated that the South is losing
its physical and demographic peculiarity. Between 1945 and 1960 its
farm population fell from one-third of the total to just over 20 percent.
Between 1948 and 1968 personal income rose from two-thirds to
three-fourths of the national average and in the same period the per-

centage of the South's population residing in metropolitan areas increased from 41 to 54 percent. John C. McKinney and Linda Bourque presented data predicting that the region's median educational level would approach that of the non-South by 1980.[2] Such evidence made it clear that if physical modification was to bring about a metamorphosis then the process should now be easily observable, especially in urban areas.

Urbanization as an agent of change had been the subject of a famous essay in which Louis Wirth argued that an urban environment could remake or alter human behavior. For Wirth population heterogeneity distinguished the city: "The personal traits, the occupations, the cultural life, and the ideas of the members of an urban community may therefore be expected to range between more widely separated poles than those of rural inhabitants."[3] Population diversity provided opportunities for a variety of experiences, while the city's faster paced, more economically oriented exchange of goods and services not only led to impersonality but also freed residents from the strict social conventions of rural life. Wirth asserted that class barriers disintegrated in the cities because of unavoidable contact with those of different origin, political persuasion, and social standing. The diverse masses of people in need of services created a leveling influence that forced urbanites to subordinate some of their individual preferences for the benefit of the "average citizen."

Wirth further surmised that the urbanite was more anonymous than his rural counterpart and consequently more likely to turn to voluntary organizations and group activity. The urban situation tended to produce a heterogeneous political environment in the midst of an already variegated personal one, especially since the city's population contained more persons in the prime of life than the population as a whole. Even the family, the chief instrument for inculcation of time-honored customs, declined in the city because mothers tended to work outside the home, and persons not actually members of the immediate family were likely to be a part of the household. Finally, in urban areas the white collar class comprised a more substantial segment of the population than it did in the countryside. Wirth felt that all these factors could only mean heightened receptivity to change.

Students of southern politics embraced Wirth's conceptual description in part, no doubt, because it agreed with the assumptions of Progressive historians and conformed to the "New Deal" model for the study of political behavior. This explanation credited the New Deal with vindicating the Populists by forging a new voting coalition of blacks and working-class whites which provided support for economic liberalism and social welfare legislation. The new coalition offered a politics based on "real" economic class considerations rather than moribund traditionalism and racism. Wirth's appraisal made the city seem a promising environment for the growth and maturation of the New Deal coalition; greater likelihood of interracial contact would presumably mitigate animosity, and anonymity would encourage whites to associate with blacks more frequently. At the same time freedom from customary restraints presented blacks with broader opportunity for political activity. These developments seemed to promise the liberalization of southern politics.

Scholars who utilized the New Deal model expected urbanization to play a central role in making the region's politics more rational and interest oriented. In the classic expression of this approach V. O. Key, who identified southern political backwardness with the success that tradition bound black belt whites had enjoyed in providing leadership at crucial periods, suggested that urbanization contained the seeds of a political revolution in the South.[4] Charles O. Lerche in *The Uncertain South* optimistically concluded that the South's growing urban population had at last given it a new "center of gravity."[5] One contributor to John C. McKinney and Edgar T. Thompson's *The South in Continuity and Change* stressed the role of urbanization in disrupting the unity that had long characterized the region and another credited the urban environment with spawning a new, more politically rational southerner.[6] James Vander Zanden in *Race Relations in Transition* equated urbanization with the status ambiguities and disorientations which promoted change. Like Wirth, Vander Zanden argued that the impersonality of the urban environment gave blacks the opportunity to break out of the caste system and to progress according to their own ability and effort.[7] Other scholars optimistically predicted that segregation could not survive in an urbanized South.[8]

McKinney and Bourque, who accepted Wirth's premise in their discussion of the "nationalization" of the South, argued that "the social structure, characteristic of the older feudal and agrarian South is being rapidly dismantled and left behind in response to the demands of urban living."[9] Seeing the region caught up in the social movements of the 1960s which they felt were urban phenomena, McKinney and Bourque presented evidence of increased physical similarity between the South and the rest of the nation, but their discussion of the accompanying social change rested solely on the validity of Wirth's thesis.

De jure racial segregation was a cardinal feature of "the southern way of life" and the achievement of black equality often came to be synonymous with a loss of distinctiveness by the entire region. After the invalidation of the white primary the most likely agent of political progress for blacks seemed to be the ballot. The most impressive attempt to assess the effectiveness of black political participation was Donald R. Matthews and James W. Prothro's *Negroes and the New Southern Politics*. Although Matthews and Prothro accepted the Wirthian premise that the urban-industrial life was more "rational, impersonal, and less tradition-bound" than life in rural areas, their research suggested that scholars may have vastly overrated urbanization and industrialization as facilitators of black voter registration. So surprising were their findings that Matthews and Prothro retreated to the explanation that the census definition of "urban" referred to all areas with populations greater than 2,500. Such a categorization included many "cities" which were quite small and the authors suggested that another definition of "urban" might have resulted in different conclusions about the relationship between urbanization and black voter registration.[10] In sum, Matthews and Prothro felt that if they had examined only the region's larger and more industrialized cities their findings might have supported Wirth's thesis by showing a positive relationship between urbanization, industrialization, and change.

Several studies have offered differing evaluations of the significance of increased black political participation. In *The Impact of Negro Voting*, William R. Keech studied the effectiveness of the ballot in producing favorable political decisions for blacks in Durham, North

Carolina, and Tuskegee, Alabama. Keech concluded that blacks in
Durham had made more gains since becoming voters than had those
in Tuskegee and attributed the fact to Durham's being more industrialized and "modern" and thus more like Wirth's model than Tuskegee, which represented the "traditional" South. Although Durham
compared favorably to Tuskegee, its blacks had been unable to use
the vote to combat segregation and discrimination in housing and
employment.[11] Another work which emphasized the influence of environmental factors on black political fortunes was Everett C. Ladd's
Negro Political Leadership in the South. Ladd found that Winston-
Salem, North Carolina, was more favorable to black political activity
than Greenville, South Carolina. Winston-Salem was clearly the more
cosmopolitan area, but even there blacks had progressed very slowly
and had secured only those concessions which whites could make
relatively painlessly.[12]

In *The Politics of the Southern Negro,* another examination of black
politics which discussed the influence of urbanization, Harry Holloway
argued that traditionalism was strongest in the South's rural areas.
Holloway saw Atlanta as the prototype of the changing South, a city
too busy—or too profit-oriented—to hate. Atlanta's experience provided the only empirical basis for his conclusion that urban areas were
setting the pace for the South's transformation and he did not adequately explain why heavily industrialized and densely populated
Birmingham fiercely resisted change.[13] Similar explanations for Atlanta's receptivity to change came from Robert Crain and Morton
Inger's *The Politics of School Desegregation.* Crain and Inger lauded
Atlanta, crediting its moderation to the dominance of a profit-minded,
image-conscious business elite which influenced decisions made by
municipal and school board officials. When the authors looked at
New Orleans' agony over school desegregation, they placed the blame
on a wealthy, aristocratic elite not deeply concerned about the city's
image. Their explanation implied that vibrant, growing Atlanta seemed
more like the city that Wirth described than did stagnant New Orleans.[14]

The importance of urbanization to the New Deal model explains
the desire to study political behavior in cities, and it also explains why
those who wanted to test the model looked to the city. Numan V.

Bartley in *From Thurmond to Wallace* demonstrated that urban areas
in Georgia had exhibited distinctive voting patterns. Prior to 1964 the
cities had been a source of support for moderates in the Democratic
primaries as upper-class whites and blacks formed an unrecognized
coalition opposing racist demagogues and their lower-class white supporters. However, the Republican "southern strategy" allowed whites
to support respectable racially conservative candidates and they took
advantage of the opportunity. By 1968 support for liberal, change-
oriented candidates survived in urban areas only among blacks and
a sprinkling of white liberals. Key's predictions about the New Deal
coalition had not been correct, not even in the city where its prospects
were brightest.[15]

In *Biracial Politics* Chandler Davidson disagreed with Bartley's
assessment of the status of the New Deal coalition. Comparing findings
from his own study of Houston with data gathered from other cities,
Davidson saw bright prospects for racially moderate candidates who
could make an economically liberal appeal to blacks and lower-class
whites. Davidson demonstrated similar voting patterns on the part of
blacks and blue-collar whites, but failed to find an active coalition
triumphant over racial antipathy. Much of the evidence he presented
indicated that Houston remained a city locked in the grip of racism.
Only 12 percent of the city's blacks held white-collar jobs in 1960
as compared to 52 percent of whites. Residential segregation was extremely high and in the school year 1970–71 only 26 percent of
Houston's blacks were attending integrated schools.[16]

Other scholars have also demonstrated that southern cities have not
undergone the transformation which the New Deal model anticipated.
In *The Negro Leadership Class*, a study of New Orleans, Daniel C.
Thompson confirmed the failure of an urban environment to promote
change. Thompson pointed out that in 1960 median black income in
that city was 65 percent of median white income. This represented
only a 5 percent increase since 1940. Naturally, Thompson found no
blacks in the higher echelons of leadership in the city.[17] Karl and
Alma F. Taeuber's *Negroes in Cities* showed that urban areas were
hardly the melting pots which Wirth described. The Taeubers concluded that residential segregation remained a major obstacle to racial

equality and pointed out that southern cities had actually become increasingly segregated since the Civil War. They observed that the South was the only area where population growth and economic gains by urban blacks had not to some degree counteracted white efforts to maintain residential segregation.[18]

In *White Southerners,* Lewis Killian offered some similarly pessimistic observations. He noted that 86 percent of the socioeconomic scores of central city blacks in the South were below 50 as compared to the 78 percent figure for blacks nationwide. Killian stressed the 1960 census data showing that 83 percent of inner-city black families in the South had incomes below $3,000.[19] Carl F. Grindstaff conceded that urban blacks were better off than their rural counterparts in the South, but he also demonstrated statistically that the relative economic distance between blacks and whites in cities was greater than in rural areas.[20]

The works described here indicate that some cities have witnessed more social and political change than others. Analyses of the entire region show the effects of urbanization to be similarly uneven. The contributors to *The Changing Politics of the South* observed that the growth of cities has affected the political climate in Arkansas, Florida, North Carolina, Mississippi, and Virginia. In Arkansas and Virginia growing urban areas have become a source of support for progressives and moderates. In North Carolina and Florida cities seem to have encouraged the growth of conservative Republicanism, and in Mississippi the ramifications of urban growth are not yet recognizable.[21] These varying and inconclusive findings imply that there is little basis for generalizations about the political significance of southern urbanization.

The evidence which has emerged thus far does not indicate that urbanization has eroded traditionalism and racism in the South. Wirth's appraisal of the city might partially explain the experience of an Atlanta, Winston-Salem, or Durham, but these cities' accomplishments fail to obscure the shortcomings of the many urban areas where racial progress has been slight. Perry Howard and Joseph L. Brent have argued that urbanization is in itself no guarantee of receptivity to change. Howard and Brent theorized that the caste system can easily transplant itself to the urban environment where it provides the same limitations on conduct that it did in rural areas.[22]

Richard Dewey made a similar argument when he spoke of the likelihood of "bilateral" cultural movement between the city and open country.[23] Given the possibility of a thriving caste system in the city, it is likely that those who possess the desire and the resources to maintain positions of superiority will do so. Thus, as Grindstaff demonstrated, the relative socioeconomic distance between whites and blacks in a city could be as great or greater than in nonurban areas. The caste system does seem weaker in some cities than in others, but the same differences exist between rural areas. Thus, Dewey argues that the most logical conclusion is that the variations in the degree of change observed in southern cities may be the result of cultural factors at the local or subregional level.

Survey research data support Dewey's conclusions; several studies have shown that living in an urban environment is no guarantee that a white southerner's attitudes will be more "mainstream" than those of his rural counterparts. Norval D. Glenn and J. L. Simmons concluded that those who had expected urbanization to reduce cultural differences between the South and the rest of the nation were likely to have a long wait.[24] John S. Reed's examination of survey data led him to conclude that the people of the South's cities remain "distinctively southern." Like Dewey, Reed theorized that the region's peculiarity must be explained at the cultural or institutional level where the inordinate strength of the family and church has undermined the influence of education and the media and thereby impeded the "nationalization" of the South.[25] Even Alfred O. Hero, who proceeded from the Wirthian premise that "growing urbanization" had "attenuated agrarian values," discovered significant ideological variation between residents of different cities. Hero found demographic factors such as educational levels, white population heterogeneity, and the socioeconomic standing of city leadership to be crucial in predicting the attitudes of southern urbanites.[26]

The distinct possibility that portions—perhaps very substantial portions—of an urbanized South can retain many of the old customs and traditions suggests the need for a reassessment of the New Deal model in terms of its ability to explain southern political behavior in the postwar period. Racial prejudices remain an effective barrier to any coalition of "have-nots" and the liberalizing effect of black political participation has been negligible. Why did the New Deal model's optimistic predictions about the effects of urbanization fail to come true? In the first place scholars placed too much faith in the influence of the urban environment. During the postwar period the inner city, instead of being the scene of myriad human interactions, became a deteriorating eyesore. By the early 1960s, Wirth's vision described only selected districts within southern cities and had little application to the low-density metropolitan areas which were experiencing the most rapid population growth.

Critics of Wirth's theory have argued persuasively that economic condition, cultural characteristics, life cycle stage, and residential instability affect ways of life more directly than population size, density, or heterogeneity.[27] In *Metropolitan Political Analysis*, Oliver P. Williams described urbanism as the product of humans' desires to locate themselves according to desired interaction patterns with objects and people. Thus, urbanites are active participants pursuing locational strategies rather than passive acceptors of environmental influences.[28]

Even if environmental influences for change were present in the urban South, there were also powerful stabilizing forces. The briefest look at the region's past demonstrates that its traditions, customs, and prejudices have been remarkably resilient. To expect urbanization rapidly to alter a society which had refused to be conquered by the Civil War, Reconstruction, Populism, or the New Deal was to ignore the southern past. Furthermore, there was never any guarantee that those in positions of strength would not resist assaults on their supremacy. Rather than yield to the theoretical forces at work to unseat them, the prevailing elites were more likely to pyramid their resources, capitalize on inertia, and stave off all challenges. For blacks, political progress was largely dependent on numerical strength. Years of deprivation made blacks' needs distinctive; meeting these needs required the kind of "special interest" politics which was possible only if blacks were able to dominate decision making in their city. Finally, the black challenge to white supremacy in urban areas may have conservatized rather than liberalized politics because the threat of black control tended to polarize politics along racial lines.

If one recognizes the obsolescence of the "way of life" approach to urban study and accepts the apparent failure of urbanization to remake the South's old behavior and thought patterns, it does not follow that he should dismiss future efforts to analyze social and political developments in southern urban areas. On the contrary the South must now be understood as it is, an urban, or more accurately, a metropolitan region. However, reassessment of the impact of urbanization on the South will prove more profitable if assumptions about the psychological aspects of urban life are avoided, at least temporarily, in the interest of concentrating on some of the tangible, observable concomitants of southern urbanization.

One development which accompanied urban growth in the South and was identified by scholars as a positive influence on black-white relations was the heightened concern of boosters and business leaders with their city's reputation as a nice place "to work and live." This desire to project a "progressive" image led to the initial removal of discriminatory barriers in several urban areas. For many, the example of Atlanta seemed to predict that the southern city would be saved by its chamber of commerce. Skeptics refused to believe that meaningful changes in white racial attitudes could arise from economic motives and it would be helpful to know more about the long-term effects of business boosterism on race relations in the urban South.[29]

In spite of the failure of increased black voter participation to bring the expected rewards, urban areas, because they provided the best opportunity for political organization, are the logical starting point for an overall assessment of the significance of black voting in the decade since the 1965 Voting Rights Act. Keech's study of black voting could now be followed profitably by similar research in cities of varying sizes and types in the interest of formulating some assessment of the actual effect of black political participation on racial progress in diverse urban environments.

Often when blacks, usually by their superior numbers, won control of city politics, they found that the white exodus had left them more of a problem than a prize. Deserted or shunned by middle-class whites the South's cities lacked the financial and civic leadership resources essential to a solution of their problems, and whites who remained in such cities felt increasingly vulnerable as their numbers declined in the face of the black challenge. When white suburbanites blocked annexation or governmental consolidation in the interest of protecting life styles and lightly taxed pocket books they often thwarted both the city's self-improvement projects and its attempts to secure federal aid necessary to provide needed services and assistance to its citizens. Annexation attempts also posed a dilemma for urban blacks who on the one hand stood to benefit from increased revenues, but on the other realized that injection of a group of predominantly white voters into the electorate would dilute their political influence. This phenomenon was an urban rather than a southern one, but its impact on black political fortunes demands more critical assessment.

The broadening of the South's middle class accompanied urbanization in the postwar years and supplied disciples for a revival of the Republican Party.[30] It is now apparent, however, that two partyism did not bring liberalized politics. At the state and local level the conservatism of southern Republicans often meant that Democrats need not be fearful of a black alliance with the opposition. It would be valuable to know the mutual effect of political activity by blacks and Republicans. Did Republicans enjoy greater success when a sizable black electorate was well organized and threatened to take over the Democratic Party? Did blacks fare better if Republican strength was great or small? If Republicans offered a full or significant slate of candidates for local offices, how did their policy orientations differ from those of their Democratic opponents? The recent successes enjoyed by Republican presidential candidates in the South reflect the party's impact on attitudes toward national politics, but too little is known about whether two-partyism is attacking, reinforcing, or modifying the provincialism of local and state politics. The South's cities seem to be the logical place to begin further analyses of southern Republicanism.

It is doubtful that even if these questions and the many others raised by urbanization are answered, scholars will be able to produce a consensus as to whether the South has completely shed its distinctiveness. In reaching such a verdict too much depends on the standards of comparison and the degree of peculiarity the individual researcher feels is significant. Insofar as urban growth is concerned, however, if the South remains distinctive, it is becoming increasingly less so. By attempting to deal with the observable and in some cases measurable effects and concomitants of urbanization, students of the southern experience will be contributing to a more realistic appraisal of the region's past, one which will also provide insights into present problems and future prospects.

NOTES

[1] Ulrich Bonnell Phillips, "The Central Theme of Southern History," *American Historical Review* 34 (October 1928): 30–43; David M. Potter, "The Enigma of The South," *Yale Review* 51 (October 1961): 42–51; C. Vann Woodward, *The Burden of Southern History* (Baton Rouge, 1960); Howard Zinn, *The Southern Mystique* (New York, 1964).

[2] William C. Harvard, *The Changing Politics of the South* (Baton Rouge, 1972); John C. McKinney and Linda Brookover Bourque, "The Changing South: National Incorporation of a Region," *American Sociological Review* 35 (June 1971): 399–412.

[3] Louis Wirth, "Urbanism as a Way of Life," *American Journal of Sociology* 64 (July 1938): 1–24. Wirth was but one of the famous urban scholars at the University of Chicago, where urban sociology had its beginnings; see: William Diamond, "On the Dangers of an Urban Interpretation of History," in Eric F. Goldman, ed., *Historiography and Urbanization: Essays in American History in Honor of W. Stull Holt* (Baltimore, 1941), pp. 67–108.

[4] V. O. Key, Jr., *Southern Politics* (New York, 1949), p. ix.

[5] Charles O. Lerche, *The Uncertain South* (Chicago, 1964), p. 236.

[6] Leonard Reissman, "Urbanization in the South"; Edgar T. Thompson, "The South in Old and New Contexts," in John C. McKinney and Edgar T. Thompson, ed., *The South in Continuity and Change.* (Durham, N.C.), pp. 88, 478.

[7] James W. Vander Zanden, *Race Relations in Transition* (New York, 1965). See also: Arnold M. Rose, "The American Negro Problem in the Context of Social Change," *Annals of the American Academy of Political and Social Sciences*, No. 357, (January, 1965), pp. 2–3.

[8] J. Milton Yinger and George E. Simpson, "Can Segregation Survive in an Industrial Society?," *Antioch Review* 18 (Spring 1958): 15–24.

[9] McKinney and Bourque, "The Changing South," p. 402.

[10] Donald R. Matthews and James W. Prothro, *Negroes and the New Southern Politics* (New York, 1966), pp. 124–25.

[11] William R. Keech, *The Impact of Negro Voting: The Role of the Vote in the Quest for Equality* (Chicago, 1968).

[12] Everett C. Ladd, *Negro Political Leadership in the South* (Ithaca, New York, 1966).

[13] Harry L. Holloway, *The Politics of the Southern Negro* (New York, 1969).

[14] Robert Crain, et al., *The Politics of School Desegregation* (Chicago, 1969).

[15] Numan V. Bartley, *From Thurmond to Wallace: Political Tendencies in Georgia, 1948–1968* (Baltimore, 1970).

[16] Chandler Davidson, *Biracial Politics* (Baton Rouge, 1972), pp. 82, 115–36.

[17] Daniel C. Thompson, *The Negro Leadership Class* (Englewood Cliffs, New Jersey, 1963).

[18] Karl and Alma Taeuber, *Negroes in Cities* (Chicago, 1965).

[19] Lewis M. Killian, *White Southerners* (New York, 1970).

[20] Carl F. Grindstaff, "The Negro, Urbanization and Relative Deprivation in the Deep South," *Social Problems* 15 (Winter 1962): 352.

[21] Havard, *Changing Politics*, pp. 87, 281, 483–84, 359–96.

[22] Perry H. Howard and Joseph L. Brent, III, "Social Change, Urbanization and Types of Society," *Journal of Social Issues* 22 (January 1966): 73–84. In the same issue of the *Journal of Social Issues*, see: Lewis Killian and Charles Grigg, "Race Relations in an Urbanized South," 20–29. Recent research in Mississippi suggests that the caste system continues to be a restrictive influence on black political aspirants and voters. See: Lester M. Salamon, "Leadership and Modernization: The Emerging Black Political Elite in the South: *Journal of Politics* 35 (August 1973): 615–46; Lester M. Salamon and Stephen Van Evera, "Fear, Apathy and Discrimination: A Test of Three Explanations of Political Participation, *American Political Science Review* 67 (December 1973): 1288–1306.

[23] Richard Dewey, "The Rural-Urban Continuum: Real But Relatively Unimportant," *American Journal of Sociology* 66 (July 1960): 460–66.

[24] Norval D. Glenn and J. L. Simmons, "Are Regional Cultural Differences Diminishing?," *Public Opinion Quarterly* 31 (Summer 1967): 176–93.

[25] John S. Reed, *The Enduring South* (Lexington, Massachusetts, 1972), pp. 42, 84087.

[26] Alfred O. Hero, *The Southerner and World Affairs* (Baton Rouge, 1965), pp. 318–36.

[27] Herbert J. Gans, "Urbanism and Suburbanism as Ways of Life: A Re-evaluation of Definitions," in Arnold Rose, ed., *Human Behavior and Social Processes* (Boston, 1962), pp. 625–48.

[28] Oliver P. Williams, *Metropolitan Political Analysis* (New York, 1971).

[29] The author's own research in Augusta, Georgia, leads to the conclusion that the boosterism which opened lunch counters and theaters to blacks did little more that was positive and in the long run impeded further advancement because the overwhelming concern with appearances demanded that white officials direct attention away from racial and socio-economic problems lest a potential investor suspect that Augusta was not

an ideal location for a new industry. James C. Cobb, "Politics in a New South City: Augusta, Georgia, 1946–1971," (Ph.D. dissertation, University of Georgia, 1975).

[30] Alexander Heard, *A Two Party South* (Chapel Hill, 1952); Donald S. Strong, *Urban Republicanism in the South* (University of Alabama: Bureau of Public Administration, 1960); Donald R. Matthews and James W. Prothro, "Southern Images of Political Parties: An Analysis of White and Negro Attitudes," *Journal of Politics* 26 (February 1964): 32–111; Anthony M. Orum and Edward W. McRanie, "Class, Tradition and Partisan Alignments in a Southern Urban Electorate," *Journal of Politics* 32 (February 1970): 156–76; Jerry Perkins, "Bases of Partisan Cleavage in a Southern Urban County," *Journal of Politics* 36 (February 1974): 208–14.

RESEARCH NOTE

ON MOBILITY IN ATLANTA

William Harris

In 1968 Richard Hopkins published data on intragenerational mobility in Atlanta from 1870 to 1896.[1] In many respects his was a pioneering article, particularly in that it provided information for the first time on social mobility among blacks, and that it made several interesting comparisons of the black, native white, and immigrant populations in Atlanta. One of the most interesting, as well as surprising, results of Hopkins' research was his conclusion that geographical mobility was greater among whites than among blacks—contradicting the commonly held notions of unstable black communities in the last century, in constant flux. In the terms commonly used by social historians, the "persistence rate"—the proportion of a population which persists in the same place over a given number of years—was higher for blacks than for whites in Atlanta from 1870 to 1896.[2]

In the course of research on work and the family in Atlanta after the Civil War, I gathered data intended to provide complementary figures on intergenerational mobility among Atlanta's blacks.[3] I collected the names of all black males aged 11 to 19 listed in the 1870 census, together with the occupations of each father (or mother, if the mother was the household head), and the names of all black males aged 18 to 32 in the 1880 census, with the intention of comparing sons' occupations in 1880 with parents' occupations in 1870. To my surprise, I found such a low rate of persistence—about 10 percent of those on the 1870 list appeared on the 1880 list—that I abandoned the attempt. Since Hopkins had reported a fairly high rate of overall persistence of 47 percent from 1870 to 1880 for blacks, and since the rate was an equally high 46 percent for the 20 and under age group, I had expected to find considerably more of these young men in 1880 than I did find.

Since my exhaustive sample of young blacks showed such low persistence, I returned to Hopkins' article to see if I could find some explanation for the differing results. I believe that the difference lies largely in three difficulties in Hopkins' method. A minor one is perhaps the most obvious. Hopkins began with a sample of males from the 1870 census and looked for them in the 1880 Atlanta City Directory. He assumed that the directory would be at least somewhat inaccurate and would leave out some names, so he also checked the 1879 directory and the 1881 directory and if a person "was found in any of the three volumes" he was considered to have resided in the city in 1880.[4] The difficulty is that by counting someone who appears in the 1879 directory as an 1880 resident, Hopkins has in effect measured the nine-year persistence rate, and not the ten-year persistence rate, thus inflating his figures by an indeterminate, though probably small, amount. A more reasonable check for omissions would be to include all those who appear in both the 1879 and 1881 directories.

Two other problems are, I think, more important. Hopkins has apparently neglected the problem of name duplication. This is especially significant for the black population, which adopted last names en masse at emancipation and therefore show a large number of duplications.[5] We have no way of knowing for sure if an Edward Johnson in 1870 is the same Edward Johnson who is listed in 1880, unless his address is the same, or unless we can get additional information about such things as age or other family members, which is not available in directories.[6]

Finally, Hopkins' samples are too small. They include 226 blacks and 258 whites. With this size of sample, any percentage, such as the percentage of a sample which persists after 10 years, is an accurate description of the actual percentage in the population itself only within about ±7 percent. When the original sample is broken down into smaller categories—for example of age or of occupation—this likelihood of error (or "confidence interval") gets larger. The confidence interval for percentages of that part of his sample of blacks 20 years old or younger, which included 28 persons in 1870, is about ±18 percent. Therefore statements about small portions of his total sample are likely to be fairly meaningless.[7]

I think there are two conclusions to be drawn. The first, a general one, is that historians who work with and write about quantitative data should use, and report, relevant statistical measures of significance for their data. The second, more specific, is that the cumulative effects of the methodological errors discussed here are such that Hopkins has overestimated, perhaps substantially, the rates of persistence for Atlanta's population from 1870 to 1880. While the overall effects of sampling errors are quite unpredictable, the problem of name duplication would, I think, lead to a larger exaggeration of the persistence of blacks than of whites. Hopkins' conclusions in this area should be considered quite tentative until they are modified or confirmed by further research with a more valid methodology.

NOTES

[1] Richard Hopkins, "Occupational and Geographic Mobility in Atlanta, 1870–1896", *Journal of Southern History*, XXXIV (May, 1968), pp. 200–13.

[2] Ibid., p. 213.

[3] Some of the results of this research appeared as "Work and Family in Black Atlanta," *Journal of Social History*, 9 (Spring, 1976).

[4] Hopkins, "Occupational and Geographic Mobility", p. 201, fn. 5. Another essay by Hopkins, which extends his analysis to movement within the city, was published under the title "Status, Mobility, and the Dimensions of Change in a Southern City: Atlanta, 1870–1910," in Kenneth T. Jackson and Stanley K. Schultz, eds., *Cities in American History* (New York: Alfred A. Knopf, 1972). This latter essay incorporates data and conclusions from the 1968 essay, and the criticisms below apply equally to both.

[5] See for example Joel Williamson, *After Slavery: The Negro in South Carolina During Reconstruction, 1861–1877* (Chapel Hill: University of North Carolina Press, 1965), p. 311.

[6] For comments on this problem in connection with Irish immigrants,

see Stephen Thernstrom, *The Other Bostonians: Poverty and Progress in the American Metropolis, 1880–1970* (Cambridge, Mass.: Harvard University Press, 1973), pp. 273–74.

[7] The intervals are calculated using a *t* test for proportions, as described, for example, in Hubert Blalock, *Social Statistics* (New York: McGraw-Hill, 1972), pp. 211–12. The confidence level is 95, which means that the probability is less than .05 that the true proportion in the population is outside of the confidence interval. This confidence interval was calculated on the assumption that the proportion being estimated is about 50 percent; more extreme proportions in either direction will have smaller intervals at the same confidence level, and thus be estimated with greater accuracy.

Not all of Hopkins' conclusions are statistically questionable. Each case depends on the size of the samples on which the conclusions are based. He is, for example, quite unjustified in the conclusion that 47 percent overall black persistence from 1870–1880 is "significantly higher" than overall native white persistence of 45 percent in that period; (Hopkins, p. 212) such a difference would occur often in samples as large as his, even if the populations were identical in persistence. Similarly, the unskilled native whites did not leave the city at a "significantly higher rate" (p. 211) than unskilled immigrants; his samples of 34 natives and 42 whites would show differences as large as Hopkins found about one-fourth of the time, even if actual persistence were identical. On the other hand, he is on stronger foundation in asserting that unskilled native whites were less persistent than unskilled blacks. The point here is that statistical tests are required in each case if we are to draw reasonable conclusions from sample data.

PART III

BOOK REVIEWS

THE PEOPLE OF HAMILTON, CANADA WEST.
MICHAEL KATZ.
**Cambridge: Harvard University Press,
1975. Pp. xiii, 381. $17.50.**

The People of Hamilton, Canada West is less a social history of that
Canadian city than it is a report on an ongoing research project.
Michael Katz has used this opportunity to assess how far he and his
associates have come and where they are going. They have given much
intelligent thought to the categories and concepts used in social history
today, and Katz develops criticisms and refinements of these in his
analysis of the data on Hamilton. But, the study is more historical
sociology than social history, because of the limitations of the time
period, of the decade of the 1850s. Although there was not complete
stasis in Hamilton in that decade, major alterations of the basic components of social structure occur slowly, so that the book is more a
description of Hamilton at one point in time than an analysis of
significant change over time. Katz analyses two basic components of
social structure, social stratification and the institution of the family,
but he does not relate them conceptually so as to produce a unified
history of a people.

According to Katz, a stable system of social stratification existed in
Hamilton, because the persistence of structures of inequality was

tempered for the individual by widespread transiency. There were four major structures of inequality—the occupational structure, the distribution of wealth, the social and demographic (ethnic and religious) identity of the economic ranks, and the distance between social ranks. Hamilton's social structure was rigid, and Irish Catholics consistently formed an under class. While there was some correspondence between ethnic-religious divisions and the distribution of wealth, occupation was related only weakly to wealth. Katz argues convincingly that Stephen Thernstrom and others who have used occupation as a proxy for class and status have made unfounded assumptions about the social structure and thus have drawn incorrect conclusions about social mobility.

Although the four structures of inequality persisted during the 1850s, transiency in the form of geographical and economic mobility mitigated the effects of the system for the individual by creating vacancies at all levels. Katz uses more refined measures of mobility than others have; he charts occupation, wealth, property holding, and use of servants. There was almost as much downward economic mobility in Hamilton as upward. Unlike those who have been dazzled by the rags-to-riches myth, Katz understands that people perceived the downward movement and that it shaped their outlook on life too. He is sensitive to that feature of nineteenth-century life that is so foreign to us today—the lack of a typical or stable life pattern. The wealthy sometimes lost their positions, and men's fortunes varied frequently. Hamiltonians were often as anxious from the contemplation of failure as they were optimistic from the opportunity for success. While Katz also goes a step further than others have by showing the correlation between property ownership and age, he, like others, fails to consider the implications of the correlation of age with measures of mobility. Typically one's wealth increased through middle age, and it is questionable whether individuals would have perceived this as mobility or simply expected it as customary, defining "real" mobility as that which was out of the ordinary.

The People of Hamilton, Canada West also includes an examination of the family as an independent institution in society. Katz describes the family and household structures which were prevalent, contrasting them with those found elsewhere, and adds to the usual description with his concept of semi-autonomy for youth. Teenagers usually left home when they began to work, but until they married they lived as boarders under an adult's supervision. Katz reveals, as others have, that during the 1850s this period of semi-autonomy began to shrink as many more young men stayed at home with their parents rather than board elsewhere. Except for increased teenage unemployment caused by economic conditions in the 1850s, Katz cannot account for this change in the situation of youth. This is an example of the problems caused by the short time period covered, since this trend away from semi-autonomy toward the dependency we take for granted today has been long and continuous.

Katz develops several other themes of interest to social historians. One is the identification of the commercial city as a type separate from the preindustrial or industrial cities. Its economic and geographic structures underlay its special social structure. Katz also gives a fine description of the entrepreneurial class which dominated the commercial city with its anxious, competitive style and its foundations in the web of credit. He is quite sensitive to the problems of class analysis and seems rightly to have settled on a three class system—entrepreneurs, artisans, and laborers—to describe the major social divisions within Hamilton.

Although Katz makes valuable additions to the theoretical foundations of social history, the book is marred by its organization and style. It is full of interesting information and important themes, but too frequently the book reads like a series of rebuttals to other historians, and the connecting threads between sections are lost. This decreases the book's appeal to any but specialists in social mobility and family studies and often leads Katz into unproductive arguments. For instance, he spends several pages disagreeing with Peter Laslett's definition of the extended family only to create a new concept that does not aid our understanding of family life in Hamilton. In the decade in question, Katz describes Hamiltonians as living in nuclear families, which often took in boarders. His insistence on calling families with boarders "extended" is really irrelevant, since no change occurred in family structure to necessitate comparative terminology. Another stylistic problem is the use of the first chapter as a summation that is both too detailed to be a simple introduction of the main themes and not detailed enough to explain important points to the reader. Katz introduces several vital definitions, like that of economic ranks, which are unclear because of brevity.

Perhaps such organizational stylistic problems are endemic in a report on ongoing research, but they will cause the book to lose all but the dedicated enthusiast in the field. For this is indeed, as Katz suggests, a "mixture of hard data and rash speculation," and much of it is undigested, if fascinating.

Susan E. Hirsch
University of Virginia

THE URBAN ECONOMY:
PROBLEMS OF THE MODERN ECONOMY.
Ed. by HAROLD M. HOCHMAN.
**New York: W. W. Norton & Company, Inc., 1976. Pp. xxiv, 296.
$14.95**

This book is a collection of readings destined for supplementary use in urban economics courses. The obvious difficulty with a review of such a book is that one must not only assess the tone and cohesiveness of the overall collection, but also the utility and validity of the material in the individual selections as well. It is to this latter task we turn first.

The book is divided into five parts. Part I, Urban Structure and Functions, draws on a giant from sociology (Kingsley Davis) and a giant from economics (Robert Dorfman), although neither piece is likely to excite students. The most interesting and useful selection comes from an eminent, if less well-known scholar, Edwin Mills, who succinctly explains the difficulty in defining a city, provides good working definitions, and carefully offers reasons for the existence of urban areas.

The purpose of Part II, Urban Finance and Governance, is not well defined. It consists of general essays on the problems facing major cities as well as a specific essay on revenue sharing. The opening essay in this section by Dick Netzer does not provide the student with reasoned arguments or careful empirical investigation of the problems facing urban centers; it is a collection of half-truths and wishful ideology. He flatly states "poverty and race" to be the major problems facing cities and concludes that ". . . the national government is the proper source of support for the bulk of poverty-linked social services provided in urban areas." To reach this conclusion he argues that urban poverty is a national problem in an unusual way. He says the poor have immigrated to cities from everywhere because the housing, the unskilled jobs, and "the variety of social services they require tend to be available only in central cities." But if housing in cities is inadequate and if unemployment rates for the poor are higher on average in cities than elsewhere, then the availability of social services must be the marginal attraction. This would indicate that the problem is quite the opposite of Netzer's suggestion that such migration is in response to forces "essentially national" in character. In addition, he argues that the immigration of the poor has been uneven and a geographical accident in its impact on certain cities and states; to prove this point he cites New York state's geographical proximity to Puerto Rico. Needless to say, other major cities (certainly states) are much closer. In general, this selection is weak and certainly fails to fill Hochman's billing as "the best over-all summary of issues in the field of urban public finance."

The best of the essays in this section, in terms of validity and utility to students, is Wilbur Thompson's "The City as a Distorted Price System." Whether or not instructors ultimately agree with it, this selection offers a reasoned economic framework which can be used to analyze the sources of specific urban problems and to suggest alternative solutions. In essence, Thompson applies the body of theory found in the public finance area of economics to city problems by stressing that not all public services are alike—the nature of the goods and services provided vary from purely public to quasi-public to purely private and, hence, can best be allocated by applying varying degrees of an explicit price system.

In Part III, The Economy of the Central City, Chinitz does an excellent job detailing the economic consequences of several municipal social policies. Jay Forrester, on the other hand, makes the mistake of assuming an "inherent" conflict between the growth of national output and the quality of life. His logic suggests that falling output would lead to increasing quality of life, but few would be willing to take such a risk. However, his essay is so controversial that it will stimulate student discussion. The other selections in this part are quite adequate, although they overemphasize the conditions of poverty. (I wish you good luck in explaining to your students just what Kain and Meyer mean by their requirement that programs be "properly articulated and synthesized" to be effective.)

Part IV, The Future of the Inner City, is an attempt to provide an evaluation of present social policies aimed at shaping the future of urban ghetto residents. This may be the most interesting and rewarding section of the book to students. The essay on black capitalism by Andrew Brimmer and Henry Terrell is well written and presents arguments founded in economic theory which indicate that this policy may retard the economic advancement of blacks in the long run.

The book comes full circle in Part V, Urban Crisis and Urban Prospect, by returning to the question of what is the urban crisis. Banfield's material provides the target and the other writers take their shots. These selections are valuable to students as a sample of the range of thought concerning the origins of the urban crisis and the orientation for future social policies.

Taken as a whole, this book of readings rates an average grade for cohesiveness. It would be an asset to those who wish to teach a fairly general, not-too-economic, urban economics course. It would, however, be most beneficial to students taking other types of public policy courses (e.g., sociology and political science) where exposure to simple economic arguments would be helpful, but is usually lacking.

Rodney H. Mabry
Clemson University

THE REFORMATION IN THE CITIES: THE APPEAL OF PROTESTANTISM TO SIXTEENTH-CENTURY GERMANY AND SWITZERLAND.
Steven E. Ozment.
New Haven: Yale University Press, 1975. Pp. xi, 237, $12.50.

When Oscar Handlin and John Burchard wrote in the early 1960s that "the historical development of the city has received only sporadic attention," few scholars could foresee the development of a "new urban history" or the great proliferation of books on the history of cities that has taken place over the last fifteen years. Steven Ozment's *The Reformation in the Cities* is influenced by this movement, at least insofar as it prompts him to attempt to reconcile two trends in Reformation studies: one which concentrates on traditional intellectual history, another which concentrates on urban or regional affairs.

The author's specific purpose is to study changes in ideas and institutions in the sixteenth century, focusing on the manner in which the towns and cities of Germany and Switzerland reacted to the Protestant Reformation during the first half of that century. He first examines the religious attitudes of the lay population on the eve of the Reformation; second, the variety of forms whereby the Protestant message was transmitted; and finally, the general pattern of the Reformation from inception to consolidation.

Skillfully using the popular religious literature of the period— vernacular confessional manuals, lay catechisms, tracts, verse, and drama —Ozment develops the thesis that late medieval religion had become a terrible psychological burden for the laity. The complexity and frequency of religious rituals, coupled with the obligation to engage in lengthy self-examination and confession of sin, deepened the sense of guilt of the pious. By the fifteenth century efforts to create a viable lay piety included restrictions on clerical privileges and the lay promotion of preacherships, but while these were successful in curbing the abuses of the clergy, they did not deal with the root of the problem—the anguish created by the most basic beliefs and observances of the Church. According to Ozment, the main attraction of the Protestant message was the relief it offered from psychological tyranny. It also promised escape from episcopal bureaucracy and a new social ethic that invested secular life with unprecedented importance. Whereas the Church "measured lay by clerical life, the Reformation went a long way toward subjecting clerical to lay values" (p. 22). Moreover, the new social service ethic to be followed by clergy and laity alike was to be adopted without political revolution against established authority. Protestant leaders, being shrewd tacticians, repeatedly reassured local and territorial rulers that reform did not entail political revolution. Reformers were willing to pace the progress of the reform according to political exigency. More important, the Protestant belief in the priesthood of all believers allowed political leaders to play a flattering role as spiritual authorities. In many places the reform was adopted by staging disputations in which ministers interpreted Scripture and magistrates sat in judgment (invariably favorable) of their interpretations. Thus within a city the Reform movement would typically begin with evangelical preaching, spread with the formation of a wide popular following—especially among the lower and middle strata of burghers—and be consolidated by government sanction. It is little wonder then that "the full spectrum sixteenth-century urban society came to embrace the Protestant message" (p. 47). This message appealed to groups harboring anticlerical and antimercantile feelings, as well as to middle-strata burghers engaged in trade and to craftsmen working for them, to groups wanting to democratize society as well as those fearing political upheaval, to those seeking social mobility as well as to social conservatives. It appears that the Protestant message, described by Ozment as a seemingly inconsistent combination of religious radicalism and social conservatism, had in it something for everyone. Indeed, one wonders who was left out, and herein lies one of the fundamental problems with Ozment's book. If the reform message promised so much to so many, how can we explain the fact that so many towns and so many people chose not to be converted?

"The basic thing one needs to know in weighing the attraction of the Reformation," the author states, "is exactly what Protestants proposed to do to the religious life of cities and towns. How were communities to be altered . . . by the implementation of Protestant ideas?" (p. 47). Unfortunately this question is not adequately answered.

Ozment's thesis does not really focus on what is peculiar to the quality of *urban* life and culture, as opposed to late medieval society as a whole; thus he cannot tell us what made the Protestant message especially attractive to urban dwellers or that uniquely affected the content and outcome of the Reformation. If late medieval religion had become psychologically unbearable, was it more so for the city dweller than for the peasant? If political leaders stood to gain a new and flattering role, did not territorial princes and rural magnates stand to gain as much as city magistrates? Since the Protestant message often glorified farming and handicrafts in a manner that appears anachronistic in the developed mercantile economy of sixteenth-century German and Swiss cities, it is not clear why it should have appealed to urban groups more than to others.

That the Reformation was attractive to urban dwellers, among others, is without doubt; what remains to be seen is how the internal economic and social conditions of the cities, their political institutions, their organization of urban space, and their impact on the mentality of the city dweller affected the ideas of the Reformation. Conversely, would the cities of Germany and Switzerland have been significantly different had they not implemented Protestant ideas?

Ozment's bold challenge to Max Weber's characterization of Protestantism and its psychological effects will provide a stimulating basis for discussion among Reformation scholars, as will his introductory essay on trends in Reformation research. His thoughtful analysis of the Protestant message goes a long way toward explaining a great deal of difficult and frequently inconsistent material that has all too often been neglected by historians unwilling to examine popular culture. The book is therefore a welcome addition to the literature on the Reformation, especially for those interested in history "from the bottom up." Readers who want to know how urban life relates to cultural history in general, and to the Reformation in particular, will probably be stimulated by Ozment's discussion but not satisfied with his analysis of these crucial problems.

Judith C. Brown
The Johns Hopkins University

BUDGETING: A COMPARATIVE THEORY
OF BUDGETARY PROCESSES.
AARON WILDAVSKY
Boston: Little, Brown & Company, 1975. Pp. xvi, 432. $15.00.

The results of Aaron Wildavsky's research into the politics of governmental budgeting are well known to students of the public sector. The present volume, containing his last original research on contemporary budgetary processes, will be a welcome addition to the earlier literature for two reasons. First, it presents in similar terms descriptions of budgetary processes in different environments, thus enabling comparisons to be made and conclusions to be drawn regarding the importance of alternative environmental variables. Second, much of the previously published material of Wildavsky and his collaborators, together with some unpublished material of Wildavsky's students, is brought together here in summary form. Thus, the book is valuable as an overview of the existing literature on budgeting. To this end, complete citations to the earlier material are given and an ample bibliography of the budgeting literature is included.

The opening chapter lays the foundation for developing a theory of budgetary processes. Budgeting is defined as the allocation of financial resources through political processes to serve differing human purposes. This is, of course, quite close to an economist's conception of the role of the entire public sector, not just the budgetary process alone. Wildavsky asserts that the best way to obtain knowledge about budgeting is to examine the roles played by the participants under a variety of environmental conditions. In particular, the focus must be on those participants who act as expenditure advocates and on those who act as guardians of the public purse. The budgetary process is then perceived to be a means of conflict resolution among the advocates and between advocates and guardians. The most important environmental variables are wealth and certainty, where certainty appears to be in all essentials identical to political stability.

Part II of the book describes the actual budgetary experience in differing environments. Two chapters are devoted to budgeting in the United States, which is classified as rich and certain. The various spending agencies of the Executive Branch play the role of advocates, while the Appropriations Subcommittees of the House of Representatives are cast as guardians. Given this conceptualization, a mathematical model is presented, familiar from Wildavsky's earlier joint work with Otto Davis and Michael Dempster. Here budgetary requests and Congressional appropriations are expressed as simple linear functions of past experience and as a host of exogenous variables. Although the explanatory power of the model is weak, it is believed to be a better predictor than any known alternative. While it is convenient to those seeking an overview of the state of research on budgetary processes to have this material included, the attempt to quantify and predict outcomes seems curiously out of place in a study otherwise devoted to description.

Following this analysis of budgetary processes in the United States, prediction is put aside, and attention is concentrated on a description of budgeting in Great Britain, France, and Japan. These three countries are classified as the rich and certain. Unfortunately, the author does not comment on the absence of any role for the legislative body in these countries as compared with the United States and the assignment of the guardian role to an agency of the Executive. The absence of a role for the legislature attributed elsewhere to the poor and uncertain also characterizes municipal budgeting in the United States. Wildavsky notes, moreover, that municipal councils tend to become more active in the budgetary process when partisanship characterizes municipal elections. This seems to demand more attention to the impact of partisan conflict in budgeting than the author gives.

The poor and the uncertain, as the less-developed countries are called, are examined in Chapter 7. Here, budgeting is perpetual—what might be called "budgeting as you go"—and one wonders in what sort of relevant sense this could be called a budgeting process at all. Wildavsky then turns to state governments in the United States and asserts that the critical issues for these entities is deficit financing: a deficit implies poverty and certainty; a surplus, wealth and certainty. Unfortunately, the author fails to note that the existence of a deficit or surplus may itself be determined by the budgeting process, thus lending an air of circularity to the discussion. Finally, he describes a few deviant cases where either the advocates or the guardians or both are absent.

Part III compares the budgeting processes examined in Part II and finds a universal existence of role players and, except in the poor and uncertain, a reliance on incremental budgeting. The differences appear to be primarily institutional. Among the rich and certain countries, it is asserted that differences exist in the norms which are used for conflict resolution—legal arbitration in France, interpersonal trust in Britain, proportional balance in Japan. Finally, Wildavsky attempts to quantify the "economic pressures" and the "political pressures" which confront budgeters in the rich and certain countries, thus permitting a classification of these countries on the basis of their "economic surplus" (or "deficit") and their "political surplus" (or "deficit"). While one should certainly place more reliance on Wildavsky's seat-of-the-pants judgments regarding budgeting than on those of almost any other scholar, it must be recognized that nothing more substantive than these judgments underlies the attempted quantification.

The last part of the book is devoted to budgetary reform. Chapters 13 through 18 are devoted to the experiment that failed, program budgeting. The author presents a summary review of earlier material on the purposes of and experiences with program budgeting. Wildavsky's views on the matter are well-known: programming is itself a political act; and program budgeting ". . . demands abilities to perform cognitive operations which are beyond present human (or machine) capacities" (p. 364). Wildavsky describes a minor reform that succeeded, the Public Expenditure Survey Committee in Great Britain. The final chapter presents two reforms of the author's own invention— continuous budgeting for the poor and uncertain, which seems to be only existing practice formalized and with a new face, and for the United States he proposes an institutionalization of incrementalism along the lines of the Congressional Budget and Impoundment Act of 1974 but without the bureaucratic structure embodied therein.

That much of this material has previously appeared is both a strength and a weakness of the book. It is convenient to have such an overview of the subject available. At the same time, had Wildavsky not been writing a survey, his organization could have been much improved.

So far as the theory of budgetary processes goes, this reviewer is hesitant to attach that term to a set of descriptions of budgeting in a few countries accompanied by ad hoc generalizations. In the final analysis, however, it must be said that this study is neither better nor worse than previous research in an area which would be otherwise untouched.

Thomas S. McCaleb
University of Kansas

THE CITY BOSS IN AMERICA:
AN INTERPRETIVE READER.
Ed. by ALEXANDER B. CALLOW, JR.
New York: Oxford University Press, 1976.
Pp. xi, 335. $6.00, paper.

The running quarrel between machine politicians and public-spirited reformers that raged over much of the past century will doubtless continue to interest students—at least undergraduates—more than any parade of occupational mobility statistics. That the subject is hardly as simple or clear as it first appears only increases the opportunity to bring life to the teaching of urban history and provides a dramatic context for the study of public policy issues.

Callow's book is the fourth anthology in as many years to deal with the urban boss, but it is the first full-length collection designed to cover "the entire history of the boss" from Tweed to the present. The volume contains twenty-seven selections in 327 pages, organized in six sections with interpretive commentaries. The sections deal with the rise of the boss, the operations of the political machine, the connections between bossism and foreign immigration, the varieties of political corruption associated with the machine, bosses, and reformers, and the condition and prospects of modern machine politics.

Callow has assembled a by-now-familiar group: George Washington Plunkitt, Robert K. Merton, Lincoln Steffens, Zane L. Miller, Oscar Handlin, Elmer E. Cornwell, Jr., Melvin Holli, and Callow himself. Added to this assembly are less frequently encountered pieces by

Martin Meyerson and Edward Banfield, Frank Kent (an early twentieth-century journalist), Pat Moynihan, and J. David Greenstone and
Paul E. Peterson, among others. Three excerpts from Edward N.
Costikyan's *Behind Closed Doors* serve to link past and present
through the eyes of a perceptive participant-observer (Carmine De-
Sapio's successor in Tammany Hall in the early 1960s). The last
chapter—with reprints from Fred I. Greenstein, Frank J. Sorauf,
Blanche Blank, David Halberstam, Theodore Lowi, and Costikyan—
provides a reasonably good framework for students to understand
modern city politics against the backdrop of historical origins. The
study of Knocko Minihan's wake, from Edwin O'Connor's *The Last
Hurrah*, is both illustrative and entertaining, and it is a wonder that
it has escaped widespread anthologizing thus far.

At the least, Callow has brought the boss up to date, in a way that
reveals the necessary adjustments of urban political leaders to new
realities as well as the major changes in urban life which made the
adjustments necessary. His commentaries are informative and suggestive, and are laced with anecdotes and vivid descriptions of individual bosses. The discussions of the role of the boss and the
functioning of the machine offer nothing new, but cover the major
points and appropriately emphasize the pragmatic nature of the boss
and the widespread social and political conditions that called him into
being. Callow sees the immigrant as central to the evolution of the big-
city machine; and while one might argue that it was the boss's capacity
to forge links with other groups that led to his citywide and even state-
wide power, the immigrant and the boss are obviously inseparable in
the largest northern and midwestern cities after 1880. It was indeed
a "superb irony," as Callow writes, that the reformers, contemptuous
of the ignorant foreign masses, drove millions of these new recruits
into the phalanx of the machine.

Another irony, even more painful in the post-Watergate era, is that
the old machine has been largely replaced, in the name of reform, by
new organizations that make Boss Plunkitt seem a naive civic booster
in comparison. The ascendancy of second- and third-generation immigrants into the middle class, and the success of reformers in exchanging
civil service for patronage and the bureaucrat for the ward heeler,

have fractured and altered the old machine; but they have definitely not cleansed our political process or rendered it more responsive or compassionate.

Earlier anthologies were largely concerned with stripping the boss-reformer dichotomy of its legitimacy and moralistic overtones, and with demonstrating the real contributions of the boss in meeting the needs of people abandoned by established political institutions in an often brutal urban environment. Callow goes beyond this emphasis by reconsidering the nature and implications of political corruption and the meaning of "reform." The central problem with graft, he suggests, is not its kind or degree, "but rather its impact upon the democratic process." Boss Plunkitt's speculation seems tame when set beside the systematic bilking of the public by utility companies, real estate developers, and large corporations. But graft breeds distrust, which leads to cynicism and a failure of confidence in democratic government. This is a point that those of us who tend to wax nostalgic about the old boss need to keep in mind.

The boss helped to hold the city together, to provide a measure of order and surcease in a chaotic time, and in this he was probably a true representative of his constituent's desires and demands. But he was not a leader in the true sense—pointing the way beyond immediate concerns. Callow argues persuasively that even "reform bosses" were, in their way, often as committed to vested interests and the prevailing order of things as the average ward heeler or big businessman. "Indeed," he writes, "it can be argued that if the boss had instituted a thorough-going program of social reform, he would have changed the very conditions that made his machine possible and, in effect, reformed himself out of existence."

The emergence, dominance, and change of the urban political machine is, in many ways, a mirror of United States urban history over the past century. The boss was, in Callow's words, "an integral part of the urbanization process and a reflection of the growing pains of the American city. As such, he is for the past and present eminently relevant." But the boss was part of a larger urban political process that included a wide range of political types and strategies—and it was this process which, in the final analysis, failed to bring forth radical change and to renew the principles and practice of democracy. If "the boss and the reformer are inseparable," as Callow claims, then perhaps this volume focuses too much on the former and too little on the latter, and results among other things in a neglect of the "reform boss"—the Pingrees and Johnsons who attempted change while getting out the vote with the best of them.

In any event, students will find this book interesting and readable, and probably a better guide to the assessment of city politics in their own generation than the anthologies which preceded it.

Blaine A. Brownell
University of Alabama in Birmingham

THE NEW URBAN HISTORY.
Ed. by LEO F. SCHNORE.
Princeton: Princeton University Press, 1975. Pp. ix, 284. $20.00.

It is never an easy task to review a collection of articles. No matter how well focused the collection is, each author addresses the topic from a different view and with greater or lesser skill. Since this volume is part of the Mathematical Social Science Board's series, *Quantitative Studies in History*, I am tempted to offer a statistical description of the text. One could easily say that the mean value of the papers was very high and that the variance around the mean was low. Roughly translated: I found all the papers to be competent and informative and while there were no failures, neither were there any path-breaking discoveries. There was some variation, however, and it is to the variation that I will address my remarks.

There are two dimensions along which the methodologies used in these studies might be arrayed. The first is the degree to which data of a quantitative nature are marshaled in support of the analysis. The second is the extent to which symbolic logic is used to explicate the analysis. Perhaps not surprisingly these two variables exhibited almost perfect negative correlation. Those papers which presented complex, theoretical models offered little evidence to support their analysis and those papers which dove into the data often offered little theoretical motivation for the importance of the data that were presented. Some of the papers fell between these two extremes.

The opening chapter by Allan R. Pred, "Large-city Interdependence and the Pre-electronic Diffusion of Innovations in the United States" and the closing chapter by Joseph A. Swanson and Jeffrey G. Williamson, "Firm Location and Optimal City Size in American History," are the most boldly theoretical of the papers. Pred, drawing on geographic models, and Swanson and Williamson, using economic analysis, are primarily interested in presenting a framework in which further research could occur. Unfortunately the extensive use of jargon will present serious impediments to the dissemination of their results. The very people that might undertake the historical research which they are suggesting may be unable to follow their arguments. While my own bias is toward the kind of analysis presented in these two papers, in a collection of this sort I am not sure they serve much purpose. If nothing else, perhaps they alert the novice to the existence of more complex models.

The middle chapters are devoted to what might be termed social history of the city. Not having well-developed models to draw on, these writers tend to fall closer to the data-oriented pole. Indicative of this is Kathleen Neils Conzen's use of factor analysis in her description of settlement patterns in early Milwaukee. Completely dependent on specific data, factor analysis is unlikely to reveal patterns that are of general interest or conclusions that might be transferred to other cities. Furthermore Professor Conzen's failure to discuss the statistical significance of her results was disappointing. Since her data were based on a sample, some mention should have been made of sample size, confidence intervals, etc. The lack of a behavioral model is also apparent in Zane L. Miller's study of the black experience in southern cities. Miller tells us that "the idea that the city somehow had a demoralizing effect on Blacks is not supported by the census statistics" (p. 193). To infer from aggregate census data the attitudes of blacks toward their urban experience would require a very elaborate model. The nature of that model is left implicit in the analysis.

Similarly Gregory H. Singleton's "Fundamentalism and Urbani-

zation: A Quantitative Critique of Impressionistic Interpretations"
searches for an explanation of values and culture in behavioral patterns. Again, this approach implies a complex model that is not developed in the text. Moreover, serious problems of collinearity among
the variables undermine Singleton's analysis—a fact that he himself
recognizes. Are his results a function of the economic status of these
people or their religious beliefs? We have no way of separating the
dependent variable from the independent variables. Perhaps by writing
out a few equations, the author could have indicated more precisely
which model he was using, even if the exact form of the equations
could not have been specified.

The other four papers in this volume combine theory and data.
Robert Higgs and Claudia Dale Goldin both apply economic analysis
to traditional questions of urban history. Goldin's study of urban
slavery is primarily a reformulation of the question of whether or not
slavery could have existed in the city. By employing the economist's
definitions of supply and demand, a precision is gained that earlier
historians have not achieved. Her results do not alter the historical
record as much as they lead to a better understanding of the process
that was occurring. Higgs offers an economic formulation of the innovative process in terms of production theory. At this stage, however,
his model is not well enough developed to convince us that the concentration of innovations in urban areas is a result of the factors he
lists.

The papers of Martyn J. Bowden and Kenneth T. Jackson explore
the evolution of the urban spatial structure. Bowden is concerned with
the development of central business districts and the emergence of
specialized areas within these districts. Using the language of the geog-
rapher, he describes a historical process of spatial differentiation which
will be of interest to all students of the city. Jackson, focusing on the
structure of the residential area rather than the business district, employs five commonly used indicators of suburbanization to trace the
process of population deconcentration. He concludes that citizens had
been leaving the city for most of the nineteenth century and that the
suburbanization today is only a magnification of a long-established

trend. Jackson has pointed to an important phenomenon but has not provided a general framework for its interpretation. The analysis could be considerably strengthened by use of some of the central-place models which planners and economists have developed. The five definitions which he uses are in fact just different views of a single, more complex model.

I would be remiss in my duties if I did not mention Eric Lampard's "Agnostic Forward." It overviews the development and promise of quantitative history in general and more particularly of the new urban history. His appreciation for the limits and possibilities of quantitative techniques is perhaps unsurpassed. At a time when some are attempting to reheat the old battles between quantifiers and traditionalists it is reassuring to know that at least some have moved beyond that stage. Lampard is able to evaluate the progress in urban history on its own merits without singing its praises by degrading the work of others.

Clearly urban history has moved to a new plateau of sophistication. These articles do not represent the work of adventurous amateurs attempting to expand the limits of historical methodology. On the contrary, the authors for the most part have received extensive training in these techniques and are therefore at ease with the manipulation of quantitative data or theoretical models. Their expertise has raised the level of research to a point unimaginable only a few years ago. On the basis of this book I would judge that New Urban History is an area in which the prospects for the future are good indeed.

While this collection makes a contribution to our understanding of the process of urbanization, it also raises a challenge to the historical profession. Of the twenty-five people that attended the conference from which these papers emerged, only twelve were historians. Clearly the path charted by these articles is the one that urban history should and will take. Yet one has to wonder who will produce the historians qualified to traverse such a demanding course. The question is not whether history will develop in this direction, but what will be the role of those trained in history departments in that development? If historians continue to view the acquisition of these research skills as of little importance or as something that can be done by the student on the side, then the profession will have to surrender the field to those who have been willing to make the investment necessary to obtain a sufficient mathematical background. I think that surrender would be unfortunate for the profession and for the study of our past.

Alan D. Anderson
Princeton University

CONTRIBUTORS

Edward G. Armstrong is an assistant professor of sociology at the College of Humanistic Studies, Murray State University in Murray, Kentucky.

Donald E. Bain, Jr., is an assistant professor of history at St. John Fisher College in Rochester, New York.

James C. Cobb is an assistant professor of history at the University of Maryland.

Robert Forster is a professor of history at The Johns Hopkins University.

William Harris is a graduate student in history at The Johns Hopkins University.

Nicholas Henry is the director of the Center for Public Affairs at Arizona State University.

Michael Lewis is an associate professor of sociology at the University of Massachusetts.

Irvin Lichtenstein is at Fels Institute, School of Public and Urban Policy, University of Pennsylvania.

Robert Maffin is the executive director of the National Association of Housing and Redevelopment Officials in Washington, D. C.

Gina Oboler received her M.A. in anthropology from Temple University and is currently working on her Ph.D. in Africa.

Leon Oboler is a graduate student in the Department of Communications at Temple University.

Ronald G. Parris is an associate professor of sociology at Vanderbilt University.

Gerald A. Starr is an assistant professor of political science at Georgia College in Milledgeville.

George Sternlieb is the director of the Center for Urban Policy Research at Rutgers—The State University of New Jersey.

Joel Williamson is a professor of history at The University of North Carolina at Chapel Hill.

Wayne W. Zachary is a graduate student in anthropology at Temple University.

Arthur Ziegler, Jr., is president of the Pittsburgh History and Landmarks Foundation in Pittsburgh, Pennsylvania.

INDEX

Times Roman, the type chosen for this series, was designed by Stanley Morison for the London *Times*. Its masculine simplicity, directness of design, and excellent color makes it exceptionally useful for a work of this kind. The basic design objective of maximum legibility in minimum space has resulted in the larger letter structure that makes each point size the equivalent of a size larger in most other types. Perpetua was selected for display.

VOLUME I of *South Atlantic Urban Studies* was manually composed on the Linotype and printed letterpress at Heritage Printers, Inc., Charlotte, North Carolina. It was bound by The Delmar Company, also of Charlotte. The paper on which the book is printed was supplied by the S. D. Warren Company and is watermarked with the University of South Carolina Press colophon. This paper was developed for an effective life of at least three hundred years. The book was designed by Larry Hirst.

UNIVERSITY OF SOUTH CAROLINA PRESS
COLUMBIA